Critical Thinking

An Introduction

Alec Fisher

CAMBRIDGE
UNIVERSITY PRESS

Published by the Press Syndicate of the UNIVERSITY OF CAMBRIDGE
The Pitt Building, Trumpington Street, Cambridge, United Kingdom

CAMBRIDGE UNIVERSITY PRESS
The Edinburgh Building, Cambridge CB2 2RU, UK
40 West 20th Street, New York, NY 10011–4211, USA
477 Williamstown Road, Port Melbourne, VIC 3207, Australia
Ruiz de Alarcón 13, 28014 Madrid, Spain
Dock House, The Waterfront, Cape Town 8001, South Africa

http://www.cambridge.org

First published 2001

Printed in the United Kingdom at the University Press, Cambridge

Typefaces Meridien and Frutiger *System* QuarkXpress®

A catalogue record for this book is available from the British Library

ISBN 0 521 00984 7   paperback

Typeset by Dorwyn Ltd, Rowlands Castle, Hants

The cover illustration is the *Disquieting Muses*, 1925 (oil on canvas), by Giorgio de Chirico
(1888–1978), Private Collection/Peter Willi/Bridgeman Art Library © DACS 2001

Contents

Preface   v
1   What is critical thinking and how to improve it   1
2   Identifying reasons and conclusions: the language
    of reasoning   15
3   Understanding reasoning: different patterns of reasoning   33
4   Understanding reasoning: assumptions, context and a
    thinking map   47
5   Clarifying and interpreting expressions and ideas   61
6   The acceptability of reasons: including their credibility   79
7   Judging the credibility of sources skilfully   93
8   Evaluating inferences: deductive validity and other
    grounds   107
9   Evaluating inferences: assumptions and other relevant
    arguments   124
10 Reasoning about causal explanations   138
11 Decision making: options, consequences, values and risks   154
Questions appendix   170
Answers to questions   201
Glossary   235
Bibliography   243
Index   245

To my grand daughters, Leonora and May

Preface

This book aims to teach *critical thinking* skills: the ability to interpret, analyse and evalute ideas and arguments. It is based on a widely shared conception of critical thinking and it covers many of the basic skills or competencies displayed by good critical thinkers. It aims to develop those skills by teaching them *explicitly* and *directly*, rather than *indirectly*, as many teachers claim to do in the course of teaching their subject – history, physics or whatever. It also aims to teach these skills so that they can be transferred to other studies and to everyday life. Critical thinking is now widely seen as a basic competency, akin to reading and writing, which needs to be taught. That is what this book aims to do.

After an initial chapter, which explains what critical thinking is and how to teach it, the early chapters focus on analysing reasoning. However, students usually want to move on to the task of evaluating arguments and presenting their own! Since students enjoy the process of arguing, I usually encourage them to do this from the very beginning, and I also get them to note their responses. Later, as they learn more about evaluating and presenting arguments, they can then look back at what they did earlier and see how much better they can do it. In this connection I have often required students to keep a 'Critical Thinking Notebook' in which they answer questions as they are set, to help them evaluate their progress. To make this self-evaluation students need to compare their answers with those provided and have their work graded and the grading explained to them. This helps them internalise what they are learning.

Studying critical thinking involves trying to change the ways in which most of us think. To do this we need extensive practice and feedback. That is why the book has many stimulus passages on subjects of topical interest and over 220 questions for the student to answer. Answers are provided to more than three quarters of these to help students check their progress. The 'thinking maps' are sets of questions students should ask themselves when trying to think skilfully in various ways. Of course, critical thinkers not only exhibit the skills we have mentioned, but also value reasonableness. It is to be hoped that working through this material will also encourage what Socrates called the 'examined life'.

The book is suitable for a wide range of students including those studying for the OCR (Oxford, Cambridge and RSA) Advanced Subsidiary GCE in Critical Thinking, the Advanced Extension Award in Critical Thinking in the UK and the Cambridge International Examinations AS qualification in Thinking Skills. Many of the ideas and examples arose in the course of developing and teaching critical thinking to young people and adults. The material is presented in such a way that it can be worked through on a self-study basis, but those who do this should try to discuss their ideas and arguments with other people. This usually turns out to be instructive and fun for both parties!

Teachers who use this book for their students may find the following suggestions helpful. Although some things need to be explained by the teacher, I find that discussion in small groups can be very successful (four per group is a good number). Students love arguing with each other and, given good examples (stimulus passages), this can be both enjoyable and instructive. Applying 'thinking maps' to your own thinking can be difficult at first so it can be useful to put students in pairs for this purpose – one doing the exercise whilst the other helps them focus on answering the questions in the thinking map. There are several good sources for finding further stimulus material of interest to students: look in any 'quality' newspaper at the 'letters to the editor', the editorials or at 'analysis' articles. It can also be very helpful to draw on materials which students are encountering in other courses.

I have enjoyed writing this book. Many people have helped and encouraged me and it is a pleasure to thank them here. My students at the University of East Anglia were both responsive and critical and helped me shape my ideas in the early stages. My colleagues at UEA were also supportive, especially Nick Everitt and Andreas Dorschel from whom I have learned much. I have also learned much from other researchers in the field of critical thinking, especially, in the present context, Robert Ennis, Robert Swartz and Michael Scriven; this is acknowledged in particular places in the text, but there is a general debt too, which I am pleased to acknowledge here. OCR kindly gave permission for me to use much of the material which was developed for the AS examination in Critical Thinking. Cambridge University Press have also been helpful throughout, especially Keith Rose, Noel Kavanagh and Anne Rix. My thanks also to Dinah Thompson who read the whole text, helped me with examples and gave valuable comments. Finally, affectionate thanks to my wife Sarah and my children, Dan, Max and Susannah, on whom I have sometimes practised my ideas!

What is critical thinking and how to improve it

In recent years 'critical thinking' has become something of a 'buzz word' in educational circles. For many reasons, educators have become very interested in teaching 'thinking skills' of various kinds in contrast with teaching information and content. Of course, you can do both, but in the past the emphasis in most people's teaching has been on teaching content – history, physics, geography or whatever – and, though many teachers would claim to teach their students 'how to think', most would say that they do this *indirectly* or *implicitly* in the course of teaching the content which belongs to their special subject. Increasingly, educators have come to doubt the effectiveness of teaching 'thinking skills' in this way, because most students simply do not pick up the thinking skills in question. The result is that many teachers have become interested in teaching these skills *directly*. This is what this text aims to do. It teaches a range of *transferable* thinking skills, but it does so *explicitly* and *directly*. The skills in question are critical thinking skills (sometimes called critico-creative thinking skills – for reasons explained below), and they will be taught in a way that expressly aims to facilitate their transfer to other subjects and other contexts. If you learn, for example, how to structure an argument, judge the credibility of a source or make a decision, by the methods we shall explain in a few contexts, it will not be difficult to see how to do these things in many other contexts too; this is the sense in which the skills we teach in this text are 'transferable'.

It can be dangerous for an educational idea to become fashionable, because it gets pulled in many directions and can lose its focus, so we begin by explaining the idea of 'critical thinking' as it has developed over the last 100 years.

Question 1.1

Please write down what *you* (the reader) think the phrase 'critical thinking' means. You will have heard different uses of the phrase in various contexts, so pull together what makes sense to you from those uses. Even if you have very little idea, do the best you can. At this stage there are no right or wrong answers. Your answer is for you alone – so that you can compare it with what we are about to tell you.

1.1 Some classic definitions from the critical thinking tradition

1.1.1 John Dewey and 'reflective thinking'

In fact, people have been thinking about 'critical thinking' and have been researching how to teach it for about a hundred years. In a way, Socrates began this approach to learning over 2,000 years ago, but John Dewey, the American philosopher, psychologist and educator, is widely regarded as the 'father' of the modern critical thinking tradition. He called it 'reflective thinking' and defined it as:

> Active, persistent, and careful consideration of a belief or supposed form of knowledge in the light of the grounds which support it and the further conclusions to which it tends. (Dewey, 1909, p. 9)

Let us spend a moment unpacking this definition. By defining critical thinking as an 'active' process, Dewey is contrasting it with the kind of thinking in which you just receive ideas and information from someone else – what you might reasonably call a 'passive' process. For Dewey, and for everyone who has worked in this tradition subsequently, critical thinking is *essentially* an 'active' process – one in which you think things through for yourself, raise questions yourself, find relevant information yourself, etc. rather than learning in a largely passive way from someone else.

In defining critical thinking as 'persistent' and 'careful' Dewey is contrasting it with the kind of unreflective thinking we all engage in sometimes, for example when we 'jump' to a conclusion or make a 'snap' decision without thinking about it. Sometimes, of course, we have to do this because we need to decide quickly or the issue is not important enough to warrant careful thought, but often we do it when we ought to stop and think – when we ought to 'persist' a bit.

However, the most important thing about Dewey's definition is in what he says about the 'grounds which support' a belief and the 'further conclusions to which it tends'. To express this in more familiar language, he is saying that what matters are the **reasons** we have for believing something and the **implications** of our beliefs. It is no exaggeration to say that critical thinking attaches huge importance to reasoning, to giving reasons and to evaluating reasoning as well as possible. There is more to it than that, but skilful reasoning is a key element.

Question 1.2

Look at passage 57 in the Questions appendix and, applying Dewey's definition, say whether any critical thinking is being exhibited; try to give reasons for your answer.

1.1.2 Edward Glaser, building on Dewey's ideas

We will return to the central role of reasons and reasoning shortly, but let us look briefly at another definition which belongs to the critical thinking tradition. This one is due to Edward Glaser, co-author of what has become the world's most widely used test of critical thinking, the *Watson–Glaser Critical Thinking Appraisal*. Glaser defined critical thinking as:

> (1) an attitude of being disposed to consider in a thoughtful way the problems and subjects that come within the range of one's experience; (2) knowledge of the methods of logical enquiry and reasoning; and (3) some skill in applying those methods. Critical thinking calls for a persistent effort to examine any belief or supposed form of knowledge in the light of the evidence that supports it and the further conclusions to which it tends. (Glaser, 1941, p. 5)

It is immediately obvious that this definition owes a lot to Dewey's original definition. Glaser refers to 'evidence' in place of 'grounds' but otherwise the second sentence is much the same. The first sentence speaks about an 'attitude' or disposition to be thoughtful about problems and recognises that you can apply what he calls 'the methods of logical enquiry and reasoning' with more or less 'skill'. The tradition has picked up on both these elements, recognising that critical thinking is partly a matter of having certain thinking skills (we will say which shortly), but is not just a matter of having these skills, it is also a matter of being disposed to use them (someone might be very skilled at, say, turning somersaults, but might not be disposed to do so). We will return to these points shortly, but let us now look at a third definition from this tradition.

1.1.3 Robert Ennis – a widely used definition

One of the most famous contributors to the development of the critical thinking tradition is Robert Ennis; his definition, which has gained wide currency in the field, is:

> Critical thinking is reasonable, reflective thinking that is focused on deciding what to believe or do. (Cf. Norris and Ennis, 1989)

Notice the emphasis on being 'reasonable' and 'reflective', which picks up on earlier definitions, but notice also that Ennis speaks of 'deciding what to . . . do', which was not explicitly mentioned earlier; so decision making is part of critical thinking in Ennis's conception. Unlike Dewey's definition, this definition needs no further explanation because the words are familiar to us. We shall see later that there may be questions about how good a definition it is, but it is reasonably clear what Ennis means.

Question 1.3

Did you have all those elements in *your* definition of critical thinking? If so, that is excellent! If you didn't, revise your definition of critical thinking to take account of the tradition as I have just explained it and write down your new definition of critical thinking – as you understand it – preferably using your own words.

1.1.4 Richard Paul and 'thinking about your thinking'

In this section and in section 1.4 below we review two final definitions of critical thinking which have been developed by scholars working in this field and which are important for different reasons. The first is due to Richard Paul who gave a definition of critical thinking which looks rather different from the other definitions given above. It is:

> Critical thinking is that mode of thinking – about any subject, content or problem – in which the thinker improves the quality of his or her thinking by skilfully taking charge of the structures

inherent in thinking and imposing intellectual standards upon them. (Paul, Fisher and Nosich,1993, p. 4)

This definition is interesting because it draws attention to a feature of critical thinking on which teachers and researchers in the field seem to be largely agreed, that the only realistic way to develop one's critical thinking ability is through 'thinking about one's thinking' (often called 'metacognition'), and consciously aiming to improve it by reference to some model of good thinking in that domain. Let us explain this idea with an analogy.

An analogy from basket ball

I lived in California with my family for a year in 1992–3 and my eleven year old daughter wanted to learn how to play basket ball. The basket ball coach at the local high school was just starting a team for eleven year old girls, so my daughter went along. At the first session he divided the girls into two teams, explained that the idea of the game was to pass the ball to your team members until someone from your team could get into a good position to shoot at the basket and that the winner was the one who scored most baskets, then he set them to play against each other. Of course, there are many more rules, but he didn't burden the girls with these to begin with; these could come later. Naturally, this initial game was fairly chaotic, with all the girls chasing the ball at once and few baskets being scored, but it was great fun!

After a while, the coach stopped them and said, 'Well done! But if you are going to be really good basket ball players, you must be able to shoot well, so now we will practise shooting.' He then showed them some of the funny (and ineffective) ways they had been shooting, before showing them how to shoot more skilfully; he drew attention to how he held the ball, where he looked, how he stood and so on. In short he was providing them with a model for shooting well. Having shown them a good model he then set them to practising doing it in the same way, asking them to be self-conscious about how they held the ball, where they looked, how they stood, etc., and saying they should try to do it as much like him as possible. After they had practised shooting for a little while, he said, 'Good. Let's play basket ball again, but this time when you get a chance to shoot, try to do it in the way that we have just practised.' Again the girls played basket ball, but this time they tried to shoot more skilfully. Some could do so and some found it difficult, but, after all, this was only the beginning.

After a while the coach stopped them and said, 'Well done, we'll practise that more another time, but there is something else you need to learn. If you are going to be good basket ball players you need to pass the ball well, so now let's practise that.' Again he showed them some of the funny ways of passing poorly before demonstrating how to pass it fast and straight, with or without a bounce. Again, having shown them a good model, he set them practising this in pairs. After a while, he stopped them and said, 'Great. Now we'll play basket ball again, but this time, when you get a chance to pass, try to do it in the way you have just practised – and if you get a chance to shoot, don't forget what we just practised there too.' Again the girls played, but this time they often passed better (not always of course, because they were just beginning) and they sometimes shot at the basket better than they had at first.

After a while the coach stopped them and said, 'Well done, but now there is something else you need to learn to be good players. Instead of all racing round the court together you need to be good at marking (or "guarding") your opponents. So we'll practise this.' Again, he showed them what had been happening because players from opposing teams were able to keep clear of each other and then he showed them how to prevent someone from passing a ball to another member of their team. Then he set them in threes to practise this.

Question 1.4

What do you think the coach said after they had practised this for a while?

I hope the analogy is reasonably clear by now. Learning to improve your thinking is very similar. Just as we can all run around the basket ball court playing an informal game of basket ball, so we can think about all sorts of issues. But thinking about issues involves all sorts of skills – and most of us could improve these. Just as the basket ball coach identified some fundamental skills for basket ball, so those who have worked in the 'teaching thinking' tradition have identified some fundamental skills for good thinking. Just as the basket ball coach showed ineffective ways of, for example, shooting, then gave a good model, which students then practised before trying to use that skill in real situations, so those working in the teaching thinking tradition have identified ineffective ways of, say, making decisions and have then identified good ways of doing this which can be practised and then used in appropriate situations – whenever needed. That is the way we shall proceed in this book. Like the basket ball coach we shall identify some fundamental skills which are essential to good critical thinking; we shall then show some characteristic weaknesses we are all inclined to display when doing these kinds of thinking; after that we shall show a good model of thinking in that way (say, decision making); then you will practise this kind of thinking; and finally you will be faced with whole tasks (analogous to a whole basket ball game) in which you will need to deploy the relevant skills at the appropriate points. The result should be that we can produce better thought out, more reasonable, beliefs and actions than most of us do in the absence of such practice.

Question 1.5

Discuss this analogy with fellow students (or with friends or family if you are reading this book on a self-study basis) then answer the following questions:

1.5.1   Explain in your own words what are the three stages of learning outlined.

1.5.2   Does the analogy seem to you to provide a good model for teaching a new skill?

1.2 Skills which underlie critical thinking: some basic competencies

I imagine that one question you will ask is, 'What are the "thinking skills" which underlie critical thinking and which are analogous to the skills which underlie basket ball?'. Almost everyone who has worked in the critical thinking tradition has produced a list of thinking skills which they see as basic to critical thinking. For example, Edward Glaser listed the abilities:

> (a) to recognise problems, (b) to find workable means for meeting those problems, (c) to gather and marshal pertinent information, (d) to recognise unstated assumptions and values, (e) to comprehend and use language with accuracy, clarity and discrimination, (f) to interpret data, (g) to appraise evidence and evaluate statements, (h) to recognise the existence of logical relationships between propositions, (i) to draw warranted conclusions and generalisations, (j) to put to test the generalisations and conclusions at which one arrives, (k) to reconstruct one's patterns of beliefs on the basis of wider experience; and (l) to render accurate judgements about specific things and qualities in everyday life. (Glaser, 1941, p. 6)

Glaser was much influenced by Dewey, who saw scientific thinking as a model of 'reflective thinking', and this list is probably best understood as relating especially to scientific and similar thinking. It does, however, contain many elements which belong to modern lists. For modern lists see the Appendix in Norris and Ennis (1989) and see Fisher and Scriven (1997, chapter 3).

In this book we shall deal with **some** of the fundamental critical thinking skills, in particular how to:

> identify the elements in a reasoned case, especially reasons and conclusions;
> identify and evaluate assumptions;
> clarify and interpret expressions and ideas;
> judge the acceptability, especially the credibility, of claims;
> evaluate arguments of different kinds;
> analyse, evaluate and produce explanations;
> analyse, evaluate and make decisions;
> draw inferences;
> produce arguments.

Of course, there are other thinking skills you might wish to develop but these are a good place to start.

1.3 Some instructive examples

Let us ask some further questions to see whether you have a reasonable grasp of what has been said so far.

Question 1.6

Do the following activities involve critical thinking as you understand it?

1.6.1 You are reading a novel for pleasure.

1.6.2 You are solving a routine mathematical problem in a standard, well-learned systematic way, which requires you to reason your way through to a conclusion. Think of an example and discuss your answer with reference to that.

1.6.3 A professional basket ball player is playing in an important match.

1.6.4 You have just completed your GCSE exams and you are now trying to decide which A-level subjects to do.

1.6.5 You attempted to install some new software on your computer but it is not working properly, so now you are trying to follow the instructions for 'trouble shooting'.

Question 1.7

Imagine someone, let us call him Andy, standing beside a used car trying to decide whether to buy it. Andy does not have much money and he does not know much about cars, but he has just left college and has just been offered a new job which requires him to have a reliable car. A salesperson has told Andy all the advantages of the car in question and has offered a 'bargain' price.

(Case 1): Let us suppose that Andy has come to like and trust the salesperson in the course of talking about the car (though they have never met before and Andy knows nothing of the company for which she works) and he likes the 'look' of the car so he decides to buy it.

(Case 2): Let us suppose instead that Andy comes to like the salesperson, but treats what she says with caution, gets an expert mechanic to check the vehicle over, checks prices of comparable vehicles in a used car price guide and gets a knowledgeable friend to advise on negotiating a price.

The question now has three parts:

1.7.1 Look at Dewey's definition above and decide whether Andy displays 'reflective thinking' according to that definition in either case. Is he 'active', 'persistent', 'careful', etc.

1.7.2 Referring to Glaser's list of skills, does Andy:
recognise what the problem is?
find workable means for dealing with the problem?
gather and marshal pertinent information?
recognise unstated assumptions and values (etc.)?

1.7.3 Would you say that Andy had acted reasonably in either case?

Question 1.8

In this case two friends, Bertha and Cheryl, are watching an American TV news report on the 1991 Gulf War. The reporter, who is American, is commenting on the pin-point accuracy of modern US weapons and says that the film shows heat-seeking missiles going down the chimneys of buildings to blow them up and ground-based US Patriot missiles intercepting and blowing up incoming Iraqi Scud missiles. Bertha and Cheryl watch and listen with fascination (as many of us did during the Gulf War); Bertha remarks on how amazing it is that weapons can be so accurate and expresses her relief that America has them. Cheryl, who is majoring in media studies, is not quite so sure; she points out that the sequence showing the heat-seeking missile going down the chimney was supplied by the US air force, since it was taken by the plane which fired it, and that we are not told how many such missiles miss their target completely. She also points out that the sequence showing Patriot missiles exploding Scud's in mid-air was hard for anyone but a military expert to interpret: 'Is the flash a Patriot hitting a Scud, or a Patriot exploding too soon, and how many Scud's are missed altogether? Only the military really know – and perhaps even they don't at the time. But either way, the reporter is clearly relying on the interpretation of the flashes given by military people, and they have a propaganda job to do.' Bertha, who is studying computing and usually says she is 'not really interested in politics', is irritated by Cheryl's scepticism and does not really want to hear about it. However, Cheryl says she has studied similar 'news' reports from other wars, which is why she has her doubts. Bertha says Cheryl's teachers are all liberals and communists. Cheryl says this is rubbish, that some of her teachers are very 'Establishment' figures, sometimes acting as Government advisers, and that her course is one of the most respected in the US.

Again the question has three parts:

1.8.1   Look at Dewey's definition and decide to what extent Bertha and Cheryl display 'reflective thinking'. Again, are they 'active', 'persistent', etc.

1.8.2   Referring to our list of skills, do Bertha and Cheryl:
identify and evaluate assumptions?
judge the acceptability, especially the credibility of claims?
analyse, evaluate and produce explanations?
draw inferences?
produce arguments?

1.8.3   Would you say that Bertha or Cheryl was displaying critical thinking skills? Give your reasons.

1.4 A final definition of critical thinking

One last definition is worth reviewing. Michael Scriven has recently argued that critical thinking is 'an academic competency akin to reading and writing' and is of similarly fundamental importance. He defines it thus:

> Critical thinking is skilled and active interpretation and evaluation of observations and communications, information and argumentation. (Fisher and Scriven, 1997, p. 21)

It is worth unpacking Scriven's definition a little. He defines critical thinking as a 'skilled' activity for reasons similar to those mentioned above. He points out that thinking does not count as critical merely because it is *intended* to be, any more than thinking counts as *scientific* simply because it aims to be. To be critical, thinking has to meet certain standards – of clarity, relevance, reasonableness, etc. – and one may be *more* or *less* skilled at this. He defines critical thinking as an 'active' process, partly because it involves *questioning* and partly because of the role played by *metacognition* – thinking about your own thinking. He includes 'interpretation' (of texts, speech, film, graphics, actions and even body language) because 'like explanation, interpretation typically involves constructing and selecting the best of several alternatives [and it] is a crucial preliminary to drawing conclusions about complex claims'. He includes 'evaluation' because 'this is the process of determining the merit, quality, worth, or value of something' and much critical thinking is concerned with evaluating the truth, probability or reliability of claims.

It is unusual to include explicit reference to 'observations' in a definition of critical thinking, but, as our Gulf War example showed, what one sees or hears, for example, often requires interpretation and evaluation and this may well require the use of critical thinking skills. Scriven takes the term 'information' to refer to factual claims, and the term 'communications' to go beyond information to include questions, commands, other linguistic utterances, signals, etc. Finally 'argumentation' consists of language presenting reasons for conclusions. Perhaps the most striking feature of this definition is the way it recognises that 'observations' can be matters for critical thinking.

This is the last extension of the notion of critical thinking we shall draw to your attention. We have run through this survey of definitions to give you a sense of the development of thinking in this area, to show that it is a changing idea but one which has a core which remains constant, and to show you what a rich idea it is. It should be instructive to contrast what you have read in the previous few pages with the initial definition you gave yourself. In the chapters which follow, we shall give you extensive practice in developing some of the basic skills which belong to the core of critical thinking, but we hope that you will see this work in the rich context we have just described.

1.5 Dispositions and values of the critical thinker

It is clear that someone can have a skill which they choose not to use or not to use much: the example we gave earlier was of someone who *can* turn somersaults but who chooses not to. In the case of critical thinking, it is clear that someone could have the relevant skills but might not bother or choose to use them in appropriate situations; for example, they might show they had the skill by raising the right credibility questions in an examination, but they might not apply this skill in their other work or in everyday situations. Indeed, many people who have worked in the critical thinking tradition have thought there was something intrinsically wrong with such an attitude to good thinking. If we look back at Glaser's definition, we see that he actually includes an 'attitude of being disposed' to consider problems thoughtfully as part of his very definition of critical thinking.

Glaser and others have argued that it makes no sense to have these skills, or to develop them and at the same time to fail to act on them whenever it is appropriate. They argue that if, for example, you are skilled at judging the credibility of evidence, you will see that this produces more reasonable beliefs than if you are rather more gullible – and that you cannot fail to see that this is better – that you will be led astray less often and that this is to your advantage. Thus, they argue, you cannot fail to see that this skill is worth using whenever significant questions of credibility arise; it is valuable and it will pay you to adopt the habit of using it, to be disposed to use it. It is hard to understand someone who develops these thinking skills and then does not bother to use them quite generally. They are undoubtedly valuable skills and, if you can get yourself into the habit of using them, they can greatly increase your understanding in many contexts. The moral is, do not just use them in the critical thinking class, but apply them in your other studies too and in everyday life. You may be surprised to discover how useful they are. To conclude these remarks on a personal note, I have been teaching critical thinking in a university context for some years and, as we proceed through the course, many of my students come to me and say how useful they find these skills in their other courses, then they nearly always add, 'These skills are so useful, I cannot understand why we were not taught them at school.'

There is no doubt that these are valuable skills and that they will help you in many ways if you get into the habit of using them whenever it is appropriate, so do not just acquire the skills, but value them – and use them; in short become a critical *thinker*.

Question 1.9

Which thinking skills, if any, should be applied in the following situations?

1.9.1   Getting information from the Internet?

1.9.2 Finding a telephone number in the telephone directory?

1.9.3 Deciding whether to accept a job offer?

1.9.4 Following a recipe for making a cake?

1.6 'Critico-creative thinking'

As we said earlier, critical thinking is sometimes referred to as 'critico-creative' thinking. There are two related reasons for this. The first is that the term 'critical thinking' is sometimes thought to sound rather 'negative', as though one's only interest is in adversely criticising other people's arguments and ideas. This would be a serious mistake since (and this is the second reason) to be good at evaluating arguments and ideas one often has to be very imaginative and creative about other possibilities, alternative considerations, different options and so on. To be a good judge of issues it is not enough to see faults in what other people say, you need to base your judgement on the best arguments you can devise (in the time available) and this often requires that you think of relevant considerations other than those presented, look at issues from different points of view, imagine alternative scenarios and perhaps find other relevant information – in short, you will need to be quite creative.

For both these reasons some writers have wanted to speak of 'critico-creative' thinking to emphasise the positive, imaginative aspects of critical thinking. Unfortunately the result is a rather unwieldy expression – which has not caught on – so we shall use the term 'critical thinking' which is now so widely used, whilst understanding it in this positive, imaginative sense. Thus we shall use it in the same sense that one speaks, for example, of a theatre 'critic' – as someone whose comments and judgements may be either positive or negative. In short, critical thinking is a kind of evaluative thinking – which involves both criticism and creative thinking – and which is particularly concerned with the quality of reasoning or argument which is presented in support of a belief or a course of action.

1.7 Summary of this introduction

The critical thinking tradition is a long one and is still developing. However, it is not too difficult to summarise the ideas contained in the tradition which we have just explained.

It is clear that critical thinking is contrasted with *unreflective* thinking – the kind of thinking which occurs when someone jumps to a conclusion, or accepts some evidence, claim or decision at face value, without really thinking about it. It is a *skilful* activity, which may be done more or less well, and good critical thinking will meet various intellectual standards, like those of clarity, relevance, adequacy, coherence and so on. Critical thinking clearly requires the interpretation and evaluation of observations, communications and other sources of information. It also requires skill in thinking about assumptions, in asking pertinent questions, in drawing out implications – that is to say, in reasoning and arguing issues through. Furthermore, the critical thinker believes that there are many situations in which the best way to decide what to believe or do is to employ this kind of reasoned and reflective thinking and thus tends to use these methods whenever they are appropriate.

Does this attitude imply that there is just one correct way to think about any given problem? No. But it does imply that most of us could do it better than we do (that is, more skilfully/ reasonably/ rationally), if we asked the right questions.

This tradition is all about improving our own thinking by considering how we think in various contexts now, seeing a better model and trying to move our own practice towards that better model. It does not imply that there is just one correct way of thinking – which we should try to emulate – but that there are better ways of thinking than we often exhibit and that our poor thinking can be at least partially remedied by suitable practice. What follows in this book are the explanations and exercises which aim to do precisely this.

Further reading

Ennis (1996, chapter 1, and skim chapter 14); Passmore (1967).

Identifying reasons and conclusions: the language of reasoning

We often encounter situations in which someone is trying to persuade us of a point of view by presenting us with reasons for accepting it. This is often called 'arguing a case' or 'presenting an argument'. Sometimes, it is easy to see what reasoning is being presented, but sometimes it isn't. Similarly, when we are presenting a case ourselves, sometimes it is easy for others to grasp what we are saying and sometimes it isn't. In this chapter, we explain:

> (I) how to identify what reasoning is being presented when someone is arguing a case, and
> (II) how to present reasoning clearly ourselves.

These are obviously basic critical thinking skills we need to practise if we are to be good at critical thinking in real situations. Clearly, you cannot hope to evaluate a case, which is presented in support of some belief or decision, unless you are reasonably clear what the case is! So, although the questions in this chapter are limited in their scope, think of them on the analogy with practising shooting in basket ball; once you have the critical thinking skills you have learned, you can deploy them in many real situations which involve reasoning, argument or dispute.

2.1 Deciding when reasoning is present

Notice first that we use language for many purposes besides trying to persuade others of a point of view. For example, we report events, we describe things, we tell stories, we tell jokes, we make promises – and much more. It is not always easy to tell if reasoning is being presented, but, in general, our familiarity with the language which is used in these different contexts enables us to tell what is going on, so let us begin by using our intuitions on a few examples to see if we can tell which contain reasoning and which do not.

Question 2.1

Which of the following passages contains reasoning to a conclusion?

2.1.1   James burst out of customs, diamonds and expensive watches falling from his bag as he ran. As he reached the taxi stand customers were sitting in all of the waiting taxis. James ran towards the nearest taxi and leaped into it as it was beginning to move. He pointed a gun at the driver and said just 'downtown'. The taxi turned towards the motorway. (Morton, 1988)

2.1.2   Recent research suggests that our understanding of how clouds interact with sunlight might be wrong: new measurements suggest that clouds absorb four times as much energy as previously thought. Since existing models of how the climate functions are based on the original measurements, if the new measurements are shown to be accurate, models of how the climate works will need to be completely overhauled. Climate models are used in our attempts to measure global warming so, if these climate models are shown to be inaccurate, we will have to completely revise our understanding of global warming.

2.1.3   The nineteenth-century English theologian and biologist Gosse (1810–88) had a problem. He was a devout Christian who accepted the Creation story as set out in Genesis in the Bible but he was also a practising scientist who was well aware that the geological and fossil studies by Lyell and others seemed to show that the Earth was very old, perhaps millions of years old. How could he resolve this conflict? By the simple hypothesis that the Earth was created by God in 4004 BC complete with the fossil record which made it *look* as though it was much older. Of course no amount of evidence could establish or refute his claim.

2.1.4   Many substantial environmental problems cannot be solved by individual or local action, for example, the pollution caused by automobile exhaust gases is a world-wide problem, so such problems can only be addressed by international action.

2.1.5   Phrenology was first propounded by the Austrian anatomist,

Francis Joseph Gall, around 1800. Gall and his followers claimed that you could read someone's character/personality from the bumps on their skull because particular character traits were localised in different parts of the brain and the larger the size of a given region the stronger the trait.

2.1.6   'Teachers teach to the test.' This old slogan is very true, so if examinations just require factual knowledge, this is what will be taught and rote memorisation will be all. However, if the process and quality of thinking is assessed, this is what will be taught. The only way to deliver 'thinking schools' is to assess thinking skills and dispositions directly.

2.1.7   In the Monty Python 'Argument' sketch, a man enters an office and says to the receptionist: 'Good morning. I'd like to have an argument please.' She directs the man to Mr Barnhart in room 12. When he opens the door to room 12 the following dialogue takes place:

Barnhart (angrily):	Whaddayouwant?
Man:	Well, well, I was told outside that . . .
Barnhart (shouting):	Don't give me that, you snotty-faced heap of parrot droppings!
Man:	What?
Barnhart:	Shut your festering gob, you tit! Your type makes me puke! You vacuous stuffy nosed malodorous pervert!!!
Man:	Yes, but I came here for an argument!!

Sometimes our language clearly shows that we are just describing some state of affairs; sometimes it clearly shows we are reasoning to a conclusion and sometimes it aims to ridicule, insult or offend! When you read a newspaper much of it will be reporting events, but the leading articles and letters to the editor will often contain reasoning in support of a conclusion. Novels rarely contain much reasoning. Textbooks often seek both to impart information and to give reasons for believing what they say. Parliamentary debates often contain reasoning but also often contain abuse!

2.2 Some simple examples of reasoning

Let us begin with a very simple example. Imagine a student, say Hans, who has just completed a critical thinking course and has failed the test which was set at the end of the course. Imagine that he sends the following note to the teacher:

Example 1

That test was unfair. I studied for days, reading the material four times, underlining important details and then studying them. After doing all this I should have got a good grade. That test was unfair.

Question 2.2

This question has four parts:

2.2.1   What is the 'conclusion' of Hans's argument? What is he trying to persuade his teacher to accept?

2.2.2   What reasons does he give in support of his conclusion?

2.2.3   Does he make any implicit assumptions? Does he assume anything without actually saying it?

2.2.4   Finally, you might also like to say whether you think it is a good or a bad argument, though that is really going further than just trying to identify what the argument is.

It is important that you write your own answers to these questions before you continue reading.

It is clear that Hans is arguing that 'the test was unfair'. That is his 'conclusion'. That is what he is trying to persuade the teacher to accept. Notice that the 'conclusion' of a piece of reasoning does not have to come at the end, but can come at the beginning of a piece of reasoning; in this case it comes in both places – perhaps for rhetorical reasons – to emphasise what his complaint is about. Notice also, that you might think Hans's 'conclusion' is that the teacher should look again at the test or at Hans's answer's, that Hans's answers should be regraded by the teacher or by some other teacher competent in this field. The clear implication of what Hans says is that something should be done to rectify a wrong – and this goes beyond what he actually says – so you might say that this is his conclusion. Sometimes people do not express, or do not fully express, their conclusions.

Moving on to what Hans's reasons are for his conclusions. He says, 'I studied for days, reading the material four times, underlining important details and then studying them. After doing all this I should have got a good grade', and it is easy to see that these are his reasons for thinking the test was unfair. You can put these reasons in your own words if you wish, but this is a very simple example which does not really raise problems of interpretation, so Hans's words are quite adequate. (English teachers often ask students to put things 'in their own words' and it is surprising how often this produces something quite different from what was said originally!)

Is he assuming anything which needs to be mentioned (something he does not actually say)? This can be a hard question to answer. It is natural to say that he is assuming that the work he did should have been sufficient for a good grade, though he actually *says* that ('After doing all this I should have got a good grade'), so it does not count as an *implicit* assumption. (We will say much more about assumptions shortly if that remark puzzles you – see the glossary and section 4.1.)

Of course, the really interesting question, about this or any other piece of reasoning, is, 'How good is it?'. Does the reasoning justify its conclusion or lend it reasonable support (given the context)? To repeat what I said earlier, you cannot hope to answer this question well unless you are reasonably clear what the original reasoning was. You may also have to take the context into account; for example, if students had been led to think that Hans's mode of studying was sufficient to do well in the critical thinking test (either by the teacher or by general practice in their school or college), then Hans's complaint is much more forceful than if the teacher had made it clear that critical thinking requires people to practise critical thinking skills and think things through for themselves. In this case, it is hard to imagine that a student on a critical thinking course would get the message that it would be sufficient to study critical thinking in the way Hans described (as opposed to practising the relevant skills), so (assuming he was expected to exhibit critical thinking skills) this looks like a poor piece of reasoning to me; indeed Hans deserved to fail!

What lessons did you learn from this simple, initial example?

(a) In this simple example it is quite easy to see which reasons are presented for which conclusions. All that is required is an understanding of our normal use of English.

(b) You know what the words 'conclusion' and 'reasons' mean in a simple context like this. We use these words in their ordinary, everyday sense. Perhaps there is a question about 'assumptions' but we will come to that shortly.

(c) Conclusions do not necessarily come at the end of an argument. They may come at the beginning – or indeed anywhere else. And they may be unstated – they may be 'implied' by what is said.

(d) To judge whether an argument is a good one is surprisingly complex – even in a simple case such as this you need to understand what is said, what is assumed and what the context is.

Here is another, more interesting example. This one is adapted from a letter in an American newspaper which was published a few years ago.

Example 2

We should bring most of our troops home from Europe. The threat from Russia has gone now that the Evil Empire has collapsed; the Europeans can defend themselves now that the threat to their security is less and they are so rich; and we must reduce our federal deficit fast if our economy is not to collapse.

Question 2.3

Again there are four questions to consider:

2.3.1   What is the conclusion of this argument? What is the author trying to persuade us of?
2.3.2   What reasons are given in support of the conclusion?
2.3.3   Is anything assumed (that is, implicit but not actually stated in the text)?
2.3.4   Again, you might like to comment briefly on whether the argument is a good one.

Again, it is important that you write your own answers to these questions before you continue.

It is clear that the conclusion in this piece is 'We should bring the troops home from Europe.' It is also clear that the other three sentences give the author's reasons. Whether anything is assumed is harder to say; in fact it turns out that assumptions are often difficult to be sure about. In this case it seems reasonable to say that the author assumes that bringing the troops home will help to reduce the federal deficit. Perhaps he assumes some other things too. We will come back to this later (in section 4.1).

Whether the argument is any good depends on its reasons, its assumptions, on the support these give to the conclusion and perhaps on the reader's perspective. Some people might challenge the claim that the threat from Russia has gone, pointing out, for example, that Russia is unstable, still has many nuclear weapons and huge land forces. Others might argue that Europe is not rich enough to defend itself, but to judge the truth of this might need careful investigation by military experts and economists. Similarly, economists might be able to say whether bringing the troops home from Europe would help reduce the federal deficit, but this too looks like a matter for expert judgement. To complicate things further, some people might argue that it is in America's interest to maintain a large force in Europe, or that it is in Europe's interest to be largely free of American forces etc., and one can imagine an argument like this being hard to evaluate because of the difficulty in weighing the truth of the various claims made and because of other relevant considerations. For our purposes however, it is reasonably easy to see what the argument is (though we are unsure about its assumptions) and this is what we are really attending to at the moment.

What lessons do we learn from this example?

(a) Again, understanding English is enough to enable us to spot the reasons and conclusion without too much difficulty.
(b) Assumptions are a problem again.
(c) Evaluating this argument seems to require a good deal of expert knowledge.

Now let us look at another, more difficult example.

Example 3
We need to make rail travel more attractive to travellers. There are so many cars on the road that the environment and human safety are under threat. Rail travel should be made cheaper. Everyone wants the roads to be less crowded, but they still want the convenience of being able to travel by road themselves. People will not abandon the car in favour of the train without some new incentive.

Question 2.4

In this case we want to concentrate on the first three questions which arguments pose:

2.4.1   What is the conclusion of this argument? What is the author trying to persuade us of?
2.4.2   What reasons are given in support of the conclusion?
2.4.3   Is anything assumed (that is, implicit but not actually stated)?

Again it is important that you write your own answers to these questions before you continue.

This argument comes verbatim from the *Independent* newspaper. It is included here because it is exactly how people write and express themselves – and yet it is quite difficult to say what the argument is. My experience is that people find question 2.4 fairly hard and often puzzle about it. We will use this example to introduce what is sometimes called the 'therefore' test. The idea is very simple but very powerful. Before we do this let us explain a little about 'the language of reasoning'.

2.3 'The language of reasoning': part I

Suppose someone says to you, 'Have you heard the one about (say, the Englishman, Irishman and Scotsman)?'. What are they about to do? This is the sort of language which English speakers characteristically use to introduce telling a joke. In a similar way, there are certain words and phrases which people characteristically use to indicate that they are arguing a case – that they are presenting reasons for a conclusion. The obvious word which people use in this context is 'therefore'. For example, Hans might have said:

> I studied for days, reading the material four times, underlining important details and then studying them. After doing all this I should have got a good grade. **Therefore** that test was unfair.

Of course there are many other words in English which are used in much the same way as 'therefore'; these include:

> so . . ., hence . . ., thus . . ., consequently . . ., which proves/establishes that . . ., justifies the belief/view that . . ., I conclude that . . ., from which we can infer that . . ., it follows that . . ., demonstrates that . . ., . . . must . . .

and many other phrases. These are all used to show that the claim indicated by the dots is a conclusion for which reasons have been presented. In saying this we are not claiming that the use of such phrases **always** signals the occurrence of a conclusion to an argument, just that it often does and that, taken in conjunction with the context, such language often gives you a vital clue about the structure of the reasoning. For this reason, these phrases are commonly called '**conclusion indicators**' – they indicate the presence of a conclusion, for which reasons have been presented.

We not only have words in English which characteristically indicate the presence of a conclusion, we also have words which we commonly use to indicate the presence of reasons. Not surprisingly, these are usually called '**reason indicators**' and they include such words as:

> because . . ., since . . ., for . . ., follows from the fact that . . ., the reasons are . . ., firstly . . . secondly . . . (and so on)

and many other such phrases (where the dots show where the reason is given). When we wish to refer to both 'conclusion indicators' and 'reason indicators' we commonly speak of '**argument indicators**'; these are linguistic clues which help us grasp whether reasoning is present and what argument the author intends. For an example of a piece of reasoning which clearly contains argument indicators consider the following passage:

> Planting genetically modified crops will enable farmers to use more powerful weed-killers (which would have killed the crops if used previously), **so** there will be a substantial reduction in the number and density of weed seeds on farmland. **Thus**, it is likely that the many farmland birds which depend on these seeds to survive during the winter will decline still further.

Question 2.5

In the following examples identify which words and phrases are 'argument indicators'. Also say which sentences they indicate are reasons for which conclusions:

2.5.1 During the football game he committed a serious foul, so he deserved to be sent off.

2.5.2 Women's brains are on average smaller than men's, therefore women are less intelligent than men.

2.5.3 The butler was in the pantry. In that case he couldn't have shot the master, who was in his study. Hence the butler couldn't have done it!

2.5.4 The sovereignty of Parliament is open to abuse by any Government as power in Britain is too centralised.

2.5.5 The Green Movement is mistaken in thinking we should recycle materials like paper and glass because paper comes from trees, an easily renewable resource, and glass is made from sand, which is plentiful and cheap. Furthermore, in some American cities recycling schemes have been abandoned because they are too expensive.

2.5.6   Questions appendix, passage 4.

2.5.7   Questions appendix, passage 17.

2.5.8   Questions appendix, passage 27.

For a more complicated example of a piece of reasoning which clearly contains argument indicators consider the following passage:

> Most parents want their children to have successful careers. **Since** education is essential to success, it is the duty of parents to give children the best possible education. **Because** it is also in the country's economic interest to have a highly educated population, the Government should help parents to provide for their children's education. **Therefore** all parents should receive financial help towards the cost of their children's education, **so** the low paid should receive tax credits and those who are better off should receive tax relief.

With such argument indicators in place it is relatively easy to see the structure of the reasoning, to see what the author is trying to persuade us of and what reasons he or she gives, but it is not quite as easy as the exercises you have just done.

Question 2.6

Say which of the words marked in bold in the above passage are reason indicators and which are conclusion indicators and then say which sentences they indicate are reasons and which are conclusions. Finally say what reasons you think are presented by the author in support of which conclusions.

Again it is important that you answer question 2.6 before you continue.

It is clear that **since** and **because** are reason indicators and that **therefore** and **so** are conclusion indicators. It is also reasonably clear that the reason indicated by **since** is 'education is essential to success' (perhaps another too?). Similarly, the reason indicated by **because** is 'it is also in the country's economic interest to have a highly educated population' (and another?). The occurrence of **therefore** signals the conclusion 'all parents should receive financial help towards the cost of their children's education' and this leads to the further conclusion **so** 'the low paid should receive tax credits and those who are better off should receive tax relief'. For a full answer about which reasons are presented for which conclusions see the **Answers to questions** appendix, 2.6.

We shall return to this example later, but before doing so let us look back at example 3 above and see how 'the language of reasoning' might help us better to understand this piece.

2.4 The 'therefore' test

Just as there is a characteristic way of introducing a joke ('Have you heard the one about . . .?') which people *often don't use*, so people often fail to use argument indicator words in reasoning and persuasive speaking and writing. Sometimes it is quite clear that someone is arguing a case – is trying to persuade us of a point of view – but it is not so clear what their argument is. This is the case with example 3, in section 2.2 above. Sometimes, of course, you can ask the person what they meant, but if that is not possible what should you do? One way which is surprisingly helpful and powerful, to deal with this lack of clarity, is to imagine the piece rewritten, perhaps with the order of the sentences changed, but crucially with words like 'therefore', 'so' and 'because' inserted, in order to show explicitly which claims are reasons and conclusions.

To do this in the case of example 3 proceed as follows: imagine pairs of sentences with 'therefore' inserted and ask whether the result 'makes sense' to you. For example, does it make sense to read the author as having meant, 'We need to make rail travel more attractive to travellers **therefore** there are so many cars on the road that the environment and human safety are under threat'? The answer is clearly 'No'. Trying some other sentences, does it make sense to say, 'People will not abandon the car in favour of the train without some new incentive **therefore** we need to make rail travel more attractive to travellers'? This time the answer is surely, 'Yes'. If you repeat this process with various combinations of sentences, some arrangements get ruled out as not making sense and others fall into place. In this particular example, the rewriting which most people agree makes most sense is:

> There are so many cars on the road that the environment and human safety are under threat [**and**] everyone wants the roads to be less crowded, but they still want the convenience of being able to travel by road themselves [**and**] people will not abandon the car in favour of the train without some new incentive. **Therefore** we need to make rail travel more attractive to travellers. **Therefore** rail travel should be made cheaper.

In saying that this interpretation of the original makes most sense we are not saying this must have been what the author meant; rather we are saying that this interpretation makes sense to us and gives us a basis on which to proceed – a basis on which to evaluate what has been said. In general, critical thinkers argue that one should be charitable to others when considering their arguments (since one's objective is to find out the truth of things and make wise judgements rather than to score points off others) and this is what we are doing here. Perhaps the author of the original was muddled, or was unclear what he or she really meant, but in interpreting them we try to make sense of what they said, in the way I have just explained, rather than just picking holes in their remarks.

In some ways, it may sound strange to say that the author of the original might have been unclear 'what he or she really meant' but this is not at all uncommon. When I have taught my students how to rewrite short passages like example 3, so as to reveal the structure of the arguments contained within them, then, if time permits, I sometimes ask them to look at a recent argumentative essay they have written for some other teacher and to rewrite its essential argument inserting 'therefore', 'so' 'because' and other appropriate argument indicators to show the structure of their reasoning. Most of them respond to this exercise with the same comment, namely, 'That was a hard exercise because I found it very difficult to fathom what I meant or what I was arguing in the original essay!'

To summarise, the 'therefore' test asks whether it *makes sense* to insert the word 'therefore' between two sentences and can be very useful in deciding when and what reasoning is being presented.

Question 2.7

Let us try this on a few relatively straightforward but instructive examples. For each of the following passages, reconstruct them by inserting argument indicator words so that an argument which makes sense results (and remember, you may need to re-order the sentences).

2.7.1   Questions appendix, passage 4.
2.7.2   Questions appendix, passage 5.
2.7.3   Questions appendix, passage 14.
2.7.4   Questions appendix, passage 15.
2.7.5   Questions appendix, passage 21.

2.5 'The language of reasoning': part II

Once you have realised that words such as 'therefore', 'so' and 'because' have this special role in signalling what we mean to say when we are arguing a case, it is immediately obvious that there are many other words which can also play an important role in reasoning. Let us look at some of these:

1 Sometimes, in expressing a claim, we use language such as the following: 'my intuition/faith/ opinion/view/thesis is . . .', 'I am certain that/I can't prove it but I believe that . . .', 'the facts are/appear to be . . .', 'I observe(d)/saw that . . .', and we use language such as this to indicate how sure we are of our view (how strongly we are committed to it) and perhaps its source (say observation or intuition) among other things.

2 Sometimes we recognise that we are making assumptions and we may signal the fact by saying: 'I am assuming that . . .', '. . . implies/presupposes that . . .'.

3 Sometimes we use quite general terms to show that we are giving reasons for a conclusion, words such as 'because . . .', 'the reasons are . . .' and 'if . . . then . . .' (see section 3.6), but sometimes we like to indicate the nature of the reasons and the sort of support they give, as with words such as, 'the evidence is/implies . . .', 'by analogy . . .' (or 'similarly . . .'), 'for example . . .', 'my experience is . . .', 'the authority on this says . . .' (or 'experts believe . . .').

4 When our reasoning is about a causal explanation we sometimes signal this by saying '. . . explains why . . .', 'that is why . . .', 'the causes are . . .'.

5 When we are making a recommendation or are deciding something we may signal this by saying: 'I recommend . . .', 'we should . . .', 'despite the risks the best option is . . .'.

6 When we are clarifying or interpreting something we may use such expressions as: 'to clarify . . .', 'what I mean is . . .', 'for example . . .', 'by contrast . . .', 'let us define . . .'.

7 When we are inferring something we sometimes signal this with phrases such as: 'I infer/deduce/conclude that . . .' '. . . implies/suggests/leads me to think . . .'.

8 There are many ways of evaluating a claim and the language we use may be from any of the following dimensions: '. . . true/plausible/false . . .', '. . . fair/biassed..', '. . . concise/oversimplified . . .', '. . . credible/unbelievable . . .', '. . . misrepresents the position/represents the position fairly . . .', '. . . is subjective/objective . . .', '. . . is vague/imprecise/ambiguous . . .', '. . . is (un)acceptable . . .'.

9 If we are evaluating the support offered for a view we commonly use language such as the following: '... proves/justifies/supports/is consistent with/conflicts with/contradicts/refutes ...', '... is a fallacy/mistake ...', '... is relevant/incidental/irrelevant ...', '... provides weak/telling/strong support/criticism ...'.
(For a related list of 'key' words in these contexts, see Fisher and Scriven, 1997, pp. 104ff.)

Note also that there are some semi-technical notions which can be useful in argument (words such as: consistent, contradiction, converse, counter-example, valid, entail/imply, hypothetical, necessary and sufficient conditions); we shall discuss these as the occasion arises.

Question 2.8

The following passages contain language from our previous lists or language performing similar functions. Where such language occurs say what it is and what it indicates.

2.8.1   Questions appendix, passage 10.
2.8.2   Questions appendix, passage 18.
2.8.3   As a Darwinian, something strikes me when I look at religion. Religion shows a pattern of heredity which I think is similar to genetic heredity ... Out of all the sects in the world, we notice an uncanny coincidence: the overwhelming majority [of believers] just happen to choose the one their parents belonged to. ... : when it comes to choosing from the smorgasbord of available religions, their potential virtues seem to count for nothing compared to the matter of heredity. This is an unmistakeable fact; nobody could seriously deny it. (From passage 57 in the Questions appendix)
2.8.4   It is often said ... that although there is no positive evidence for the existence of a God, nor is there evidence against His existence. So it is best to keep an open mind and be agnostic.
  At first sight that seems an unassailable position ... But on second thoughts it seems a cop-out, because the same could be said of Father Christmas and tooth fairies. There may be fairies at the bottom of the garden. There is no evidence of it, but you can't *prove* that there aren't any, so shouldn't we be agnostic with respect to fairies?
  The trouble with the agnostic argument is that it can be applied to anything. There is an infinite number of hypothetical beliefs we could hold which we can't positively disprove. On the whole, people don't believe in most of them, such as fairies, unicorns, dragons,

Father Christmas, and so on. But on the whole they do believe in a creator God, together with whatever particular baggage goes with the religion of their parents. (From passage 57 in the Questions appendix)

Of course, often when people are engaging in what is clearly intended to be persuasive writing or speaking they leave out words such as the ones we have just discussed. The absence of such words in such a context can be as revealing as their presence. Sometimes such words are omitted for rhetorical reasons but sometimes they are omitted because the author is unclear about exactly what he or she is saying (remember how difficult my students found it to rewrite their argumentative essays using argument indicators because they found it hard to fathom quite what they had meant). Whatever the reason, just as it helped us make sense of our example (3) about making rail travel cheaper, to rearrange the sentences and insert argument indicator words, so it can be very helpful to 'write in' the words from the lists we have just discussed which help to 'make sense' of someone's writing or speaking.

2.6 How to express arguments clearly yourself

At the beginning of this chapter we said that one of our objectives was to show you how to express arguments clearly yourself. A key part of this skill is being able to use the language of reasoning appropriately. The explanations which have been given and the questions you have already answered should have helped you considerably in understanding and using this language, but here are some more questions to give you a little more practice. Write your answers carefully since you will return to some of them later (at the end of chapter 4, though don't look there yet!).

Question 2.9

There are four questions to consider:

2.9.1   Choose a conclusion you would like to argue for (it can be anything) and then present some persuasive reasoning; *make it very clear what your reasoning is.*

2.9.2   Look at the leading articles in one of today's broadsheet newspapers and decide which are arguing a case and which are doing something else.

2.9.3   If when tackling question 2.9.2 you found an argument, write it out briefly so that it is very clear what is being argued.

2.9.4   Referring back to question 2.9.1, write out the best argument you can think of against your conclusion. Again, make it crystal clear what your argument is by using the language of reasoning we have discussed above.

2.7 Back to identifying an author's meaning: the 'structure' of reasoning

Even with relatively simple pieces of reasoning, such as those we have already encountered, there may be problems in identifying quite what the author meant or what makes sense. Needless to say, this is even more true of more complex reasoning, but inserting 'argument indicator' words and the other words we have discussed can be a great help. However, this is not all that is needed, because there is another aspect to reasoning we have not yet discussed much and that is its 'structure'. Let us explain the basic idea with two examples:

(I) Burning vast quantities of fossil fuels is causing global warming, which is hurting us all, **so** it is vital to negotiate reductions in the production of the gases which are doing the damage. **Thus** we need an international argreement under which countries reduce the production of such gases in proportion to the extent to which they are creating the problem. **Therefore** the United States must not be allowed to 'buy' permissions to produce these gases from other countries.

(II) Dissecting creatures in the biology classroom teaches students that animal life is expendable and unimportant. *Also* a recent study showed that certain companies who supply these creatures are careless of the suffering and pain inflicted on them. *Furthermore,* there are good alternatives available now in computer simulations, which teach the lessons taught by dissection just as well. **So for all these reasons** we should no longer use dissection of animals to teach students in the biology classroom.

In example (I) the reasoning goes like this:

(A) **so** (B) **thus** (C) **therefore** (D)

The first claim (A) is presented as a reason for accepting the second one (B), whilst conclusion (B) is also presented as a reason for accepting (C), which in turn is given as a reason for accepting (D), so we have what we might call a 'chain' of reasoning, where successive conclusions are also reasons for the next conclusion.

In example (II), on the other hand (where we put *also* and *furthermore* in italics to help the reader), the structure of the reasoning is this:

(A) *also* (B) *furthermore* (C), **so for all these reasons** (D)

In this case we are given three *separate* reasons for accepting (D). (A) is not given as a reason for (B), nor is (B) given as a reason for (C); all three reasons are presented so to speak 'side by side' as supporting the conclusion (D). In fact each of them separately gives you *some* reason for the conclusion, and taken *together* they give quite a weighty case (though, of course, there may be other reasons which tell *against* the conclusion (D)). For the moment we are not concerned with the strength or weakness of these arguments, we are just concerned to note that they have a very different 'structure': one gives a sequence or 'chain' of reasons for a conclusion and the other gives several reasons 'side by side' to support its conclusion. This is such an important difference that we shall need to spend the next chapter explaining the different structures or 'patterns' which reasoning can display.

2.8 Summary

In this chapter we first gave you some practice in recognising the differences between reasoning, quarrelling, debating, explaining, reporting and story telling. We then introduced some basic questions you need to ask if you are confronted with a piece of reasoning and want to understand it. To help you answer these questions, we discussed the language of reasoning – the language which is characteristically used when people are reasoning – and explained the special role of argument indicator words (such as *therefore, because, so, if . . . then, must* and so on). We also explained the 'therefore' test and how it, too, can help you identify an author's meaning. We also noticed that conclusions do not necessarily come at the end of an argument; they may come at the beginning – or indeed anywhere else. Furthermore, they may even be unstated – they may be 'implied' by what is said.

After making these points, we introduced a more extended 'language of reasoning' (including *evidence, opinion, inference, support, proof, refute, fallacy* and so on) and gave you some practice in using it, including when presenting arguments of your own.

Understanding an author also includes grasping what reasons are being presented in support of which conclusions, so we briefly introduced some ideas about the 'structure' of reasoning, in preparation for going into this at much greater length in the next chapter.

Whatever ideas we have explained we have then given you practice in applying them. For the most part answering the questions only requires that you understand our normal, everyday use of various English words, such as 'conclusion' and 'reason'. Inevitably, some words present problems, such as 'assumption', but we willl deal with these in due course.

As we noted early in the chapter, it can be quite complex to judge whether an argument is a good one – which should persuade you – or not. Certainly you need to understand what is said, what is assumed and what the context is. You may also need some expert knowledge, some imagination and perhaps some research. But, whatever else is necessary, it is clear that no one can evaluate arguments until they are clear what the arguments are, and that is mainly what we have been dealing with in this chapter – and will be doing in the next three!

Further reading

Ennis (1996, chapter 2), Fisher (1988, chapter 2).

3

Understanding reasoning: different patterns of reasoning

3.1 The simplest case

Here is an example of a piece of reasoning which has a very simple structure:

> The damage which has been caused to the ozone layer is an international problem **so** the problem can only be solved through international agreement.

It is clear that just *one* reason is presented in support of *one* conclusion, so we could write its structure like this:

> \<Reason\> **so** [conclusion]

where \<Reason\> stands for 'the damage which has been done to the ozone layer is an international problem' and [conclusion] stands for 'the problem can only be solved through international agreement'.

3.2 Giving 'side-by-side' reasons

Now, here is a piece of reasoning which is slightly more complex:

> It **must** be very rare for religious people to base their faith on rational consideration of alternative world views. Nearly all religious believers adopt the religion of the people among whom they live, whether Christian, Hindu, Moslem or whatever. And

what is more, there is very little serious evidence to support their beliefs about the supernatural.

It is natural to construe this as presenting *two* reasons for the author's conclusion. The second and third sentences each give a reason for the conclusion and the author presents them as standing 'side by side' in support of the conclusion (neither reason is presented as supporting the other reason). So we might represent the structure of this argument as:

<Reason1> **and** <reason2> **so** [conclusion]

At the end of the previous chapter we discussed an example in which, arguably, *three* 'side-by-side' reasons were given for the conclusion 'we should no longer use dissection of animals to teach students in the biology classroom'. Here is a last example of this kind of argument which, arguably, gives *four* reasons for its conclusion:

> The Truman Doctrine was a turning point in American history for at least four reasons. First, it marked the point at which Truman used the American fear of communism both at home and abroad to convince Americans they must embark upon a cold war foreign policy. Second . . . Congress was giving the president great powers to wage this cold war as he saw fit. Third, for the first time in the postwar era, Americans massively intervened in another nation's civil war. Finally, and perhaps most important, Truman used the doctrine to justify a gigantic aid programme to prevent a collapse of the European and American economies. (Walter LaFeber, *America, Russia and the Cold War, 1945–1996*, McGraw-Hill, pp. 56–7)

The natural way to see the structure of LaFeber's reasoning is as four 'side-by-side' reasons presented for his conclusion, which we could represent as:

<Reason1> **and** <reason2> **and** <reason3> **and** <reason4> **so** [conclusion]

where each <reason . . .> is one LaFeber gives and the [conclusion] is, 'The Truman doctrine was a turning point in American history.' Of course, LaFeber actually *says* there are 'at least four reasons'. Authors are rarely as helpful as that! However, even without his remark, it would still surely be natural to see the argument as having this structure.

This pattern of reasoning, where someone gives a number of reasons 'side by side' in support of some conclusion, is very common. If you want to decide whether such an argument is a good one, whether the reasoning really does support the conclusion, you have to decide whether the reasons are correct, true or otherwise acceptable (they might be value judgements, or definitions) and whether they justify the conclusion. I shall explain how to do this later (especially in chapters 6–9 inclusive), but first let me explain a contrasting pattern of reasoning.

3.3 A 'chain' of reasoning

Look at the following example:

> Planting genetically modified crops will enable farmers to use more powerful weed-killers (which would have killed the crops if used previously), **so** there will be a substantial reduction in the number and density of weed seeds on farmland. **Thus**, it is likely that the many farmland birds which depend on these seeds to survive during the winter will decline still further.

In this example, we clearly have the structure:

> <Reason1> **so** [conclusion 1] **therefore** [conclusion 2]

where conclusion 1 is also the reason for conclusion 2. This 'chain' or 'serial' structure is clearly quite different from the case we just discussed, of giving 'side-by-side' reasons. Evaluating such a chain is different too, so it is important to be clear about the different structures reasoning can exhibit. We saw at the end of the previous chapter an example of a chain of reasoning which contained four steps:

> Burning vast quantities of fossil fuels is causing global warming, which is hurting us all, **so** it is vital to negotiate reductions in the production of the gases which are doing the damage. **Thus** we need an international agreement under which countries reduce the production of such gases in proportion to the extent to which they are creating the problem. **Therefore** the United States must not be allowed to 'buy' permissions to produce these gases from other countries.

Clearly, such chains could be longer. This pattern of reasoning is quite common in mathematical and some scientific contexts, where the chains can be quite long.

Question 3.1

Decide which of the following is 'side-by-side' reasoning and which has a 'chain' structure:

3.1.1   Questions appendix, passage 3.
3.1.2   Questions appendix, passage 11.
3.1.3   Questions appendix, passage 17.
3.1.4   Questions appendix, passage 30.
3.1.5   Many of the dangers to our health resulting from the food we eat arise from the way it is produced, that is, the modern intensive farming practices involved. Thus a national food safety agency that fails to address the question of food production will be unlikely to protect us effectively from damaging our health through the food we eat. So we need a much broader approach to the issue than the traditional British approach where local health officials only intervene at the level of food retailing, for instance inspecting premises where food is prepared or sold.

Question 3.2

Most of our previous examples make the structure of their reasoning very clear by the use of explicit argument indicators, but writers often write in ways which are less explicit. Use the 'therefore test' to decide which of the following is 'chain' reasoning and which is giving 'side-by-side' reasons for its conclusion:

3.2.1   Questions appendix, passage 21.
3.2.2   Questions appendix, passage 28.
3.2.3   Questions appendix, passage 36.
3.2.4   Questions appendix, passage 38.

3.4 Reasons which *have to be taken together: 'joint'* *reasons*

Commonly, when an author presents two or more reasons side by side in support of a conclusion, she sees each of the reasons as giving *some* support to the conclusion *on its own* – even without the other reasons. Let us return to an example we have already seen:

> Dissecting creatures in the biology classroom teaches students that animal life is expendable and unimportant. *Also* a recent study showed that certain companies who supply these creatures

are careless of the suffering and pain inflicted on them. *Furthermore,* there are good alternatives available now in computer simulations, which teach the lessons taught by dissection just as well. **So for all these reasons** we should no longer use dissection of animals to teach students in the biology classroom.

Even if this author could be persuaded that tight controls had transformed or eliminated the companies which had been 'careless of the pain and suffering inflicted on [animals]' she would still believe that the other two reasons support her conclusion. No doubt she thinks that all the reasons together present a stronger case (if they are true), but even if one reason is shown to be mistaken or false, the other reasons still support her conclusion.

Sometimes with 'side-by-side' reasoning this is not the case. Look at the following example:

> If you do all the exercises in this book conscientiously that is sufficient for you to do well in this course. You are doing all the exercises conscientiously. **So** you will do well in this course.

In this case, the first and second sentences give two 'side-by-side' reasons for the conclusion that 'you will do well in this course'. However, notice that the first reason *on its own* gives no support to the conclusion. Consider the argument:

> If you do all the exercises conscientiously that is sufficient for you to do well in this course. **So** you will do well in this course.

It is clear that the reason does not support the conclusion unless we also know that 'you are doing all the exercises conscientiously'.

Similarly with the argument:

> You are doing all the exercises conscientiously. **So** you will do well in this course.

Unless we also know that doing the exercises conscientiously 'is sufficient for you to do well', this reason lends no support to the conclusion either (it might also be necessary to be quite clever to do well in the course and not to suffer badly from examination nerves!).

Reasons like these, which *have to be taken together* to give support to their conclusion are commonly called *joint* reasons. Sometimes, when a person presents several reasons for a conclusion side by side, these are each intended to lend some support to the conclusion independently of the others, and sometimes this is not the case – they are meant to work together, jointly, to give their support. Sometimes it is clear which is intended, but in many cases it is hard to decide. If it is hard to decide, then interpret the argument in whichever way gives the strongest case.

Question 3.3

Which of the following side-by-side reasoning is joint reasoning?

3.3.1   If the civil population cannot be defended in the event of nuclear war, we do not need a civil defence policy. But we do need a civil defence policy if deterrence is to be a convincing strategy. Therefore deterrence is not a convincing strategy.

3.3.2   There are in fact good reasons why one would not expect blood cholesterol to vary with diet. First, the liver manufactures three or four times as much cholesterol as is normally ingested. Secondly, the body itself regulates the amount of cholesterol in the blood: its level is normally kept constant regardless of what is eaten, though some unfortunate people have too high a setting and are likely to die young through heart attacks.

3.3.3   If the world's climate was getting warmer, we would find that some of the ice at both the North and the South Pole was melting at an unusually high rate. If the ice was melting, we would see its effect in the raising of the level of the sea. There is evidence that this level is increasing, so the world's climate must be getting warmer.

3.5 More complex patterns of reasoning

Generally speaking, when someone is arguing a case, they will do so using several of these simpler patterns in combination with each other. Let us look at another example to illustrate this:

> Most prospective parents would prefer to have sons. So if people can choose the sex of their child, it is likely that there will eventually be more males than females in the population. This could produce serious social problems, therefore we should prohibit the use of techniques which enable people to choose the sex of their children.

It is reasonably clear that the structure of this argument is:

R1<Most prospective parents would prefer to have sons>. **So** C1[if people can choose the sex of their child, it is likely that there will eventually be more males than females in the population] **and** R2<This could produce serious social problems>, **therefore** C2[we should prohibit the use of techniques which enable people to choose the sex of their children].

For the moment, we are not trying to evaluate this reasoning. We are just trying to be clear what the author is saying (since only then can we evaluate it properly).

Here is a more complex example:

Much of the genetic diversity in humans has evolved to protect us against the huge variety of pathogens that prey on us, from viruses and bacteria to protozoa, worms and other parasites. This inevitably means that some of us are more susceptible than others to a particular disease. But ... that genetic diversity can also protect this susceptible group. If the people who are likely to catch a particular disease are in a minority, then each of them will be surrounded by others who are more resistant to the disorder. This makes life difficult for the pathogen causing the disease, because the few susceptible hosts will be thinly scattered throughout the resistant population. So, many susceptible people might never come in contact with the disease. (*New Scientist*, 23 March 1996, p. 41)

There are several lines of argument here. But it is plausible to 'mark it up' as follows:

R1<Much of the genetic diversity in humans has evolved to protect us against the huge variety of pathogens that prey on us, from viruses and bacteria to protozoa, worms and other parasites>. **This inevitably means that** C1[some of us are more susceptible than others to a particular disease]. **But** ... C3[that genetic diversity can also protect this susceptible group] **because** R2<If the people who are likely to catch a particular disease are in a minority, then each of them will be surrounded by others who are more resistant to the disorder. ... **So**, C2[many susceptible people might never come in contact with the disease].

where the dots ... are mainly a repetition of the line of reasoning we have marked up as 'R2 so C2 so C3'. This is not the only way to see the structure of this argument, but it seems quite natural and once picked out it enables you to see what needs to be evaluated if you are to decide whether the reasoning is persuasive.

Question 3.4

Decide what the structure of the reasoning is in each of the following passages (the 'therefore test' may help you):

3.4.1   Questions appendix, passage 18.
3.4.2   Questions appendix, passage 19.
3.4.3   Questions appendix, passage 24.
3.4.4   Questions appendix, passage 39.

3.6 Aside: hypotheticals and other complex sentences

Just as some arguments have a more complex structure than others, so some reasons and conclusions have more complex structures than others. To take a simple example, suppose the police have been investigating the theft of money from a school safe and have evidence leading them to the conclusion that:

> 'Either the headmaster stole the money or the secretary did.'
> (either H or S)

A sentence like this, of the form 'either A or B', is sometimes called a *disjunction*, and the important thing to remember when analysing an argument into its reasons and conclusions is that disjunctions should not be broken up. At this stage, the conclusion reached by the police is the whole disjunction (they are not claiming that the headmaster stole the money, nor are they saying the secretary did; they are saying one of them did). Of course, if the secretary is able to produce cast-iron evidence that she could not have stolen the money, this, together with the reason 'either H or S', gives us a further argument with the conclusion that 'the headmaster stole the money' (and in this case one reason is a disjunction).

As another example, consider the following medical claim:

> You have noisy breathing and loss of weight, so you've either got a thyroid problem or lung cancer or maybe something else.

In this case it is clear that the conclusion is a disjunction, which should not be broken up until further tests enable the doctors to decide.

For a famous but quite difficult argument involving disjunctions see the Questions appendix, passage 56 [Pascal's Wager], which has the form A or B, if A then C, if B then C, therefore C.

Disjunctions do not normally create difficulties when we are analysing arguments into their reasons and conclusions, however some other sentences often do. For example, one of the commonest expressions to be found in argumentative contexts, as you may have already noticed, is 'if . . . then . . .' or words with an equivalent meaning, and these frequently give people trouble. Consider the claim:

> **If** global warming is happening on a significant scale, **then** the area of polar ice will show a steady decline over the long term.

This might look as though the author is presenting a reason for a conclusion, but she is not. She is claiming that there is a link, a connection between global warming and the size of the polar ice cap, but she is not saying that 'global warming is happening on a significant scale'. She is just reasoning about the connections between different phenomena.

When analysing arguments, the important thing to notice is that hypotheticals should not be broken up as though they present a reason and a conclusion; the whole hypothetical is functioning as a reason or as a conclusion. There is a considerable difference between saying:

> (a) **If** the accused is lying about where he was on the night of the murder **then** he's probably guilty.

and saying:

> (b) The accused is lying about where he was on the night of the murder **so** he is probably guilty.

The latter (b) is giving a reason for a conclusion, whereas (a) is just saying *if* the one thing *then* the other.

We were careful not to break up hypotheticals in earlier examples ('if people can choose the sex of their child, it is likely that there will eventually be more males than females in the population' and 'if the people who are likely to catch a particular disease are in a minority, then each of them will be surrounded by others who are more resistant to the disorder'). Mostly it is quite natural to do this, but sometimes people get confused; hence our insistence that hypotheticals should not be broken up when identifying reasons and conclusions.

Question 3.5

What is the structure of the following reasoning (be careful not to break up hypotheticals)?

3.5.1   Radioactive elements disintegrate and eventually turn into lead. If matter has always existed there should be no radioactive elements left. The presence of uranium and other radioactive elements is scientific proof that matter has not always existed.

3.5.2   If the civil population cannot be defended in the event of nuclear war, we do not need a civil defence policy. But we do need a civil defence policy if 'deterrence' is to be a convincing strategy. Therefore deterrence is not a convincing strategy.

3.5.3   Questions appendix, passage 7.

3.5.4   If homeopathic pills are too dilute to have any effect, they can't really help the many people who use them. Since tests have shown they really do work in many cases, they can't be too weak.

3.7 Arguments versus explanations

Sometimes people offer explanations in language which is very similar to the language in which we present reasoning. Imagine that you are talking to a friend who says, 'Jane was angry with him *because* he had crashed her car.' It is natural to understand this as an explanation rather than an argument; your friend is explaining *why* Jane was angry, she is not trying to *persuade* you that she was angry as she would be if that were her *conclusion* (it would have been different if the friend had said, 'Jane had every right to be angry with him because he had crashed her car'). Occurrences of 'because' (and other phrases such as 'that's why') sometimes signal that a reason is being given for a conclusion but sometimes signal that the author is giving a causal explanation. In some cases it is very clear what the author intends and in others it is quite unclear. Here are some examples to illustrate this:

(a) We should restrict the production of 'greenhouse' gases **because** they are damaging the ozone layer.

(b) Napoleon died **because** he was poisoned with arsenic.

(c) The dinosaurs died out **because** a huge meteor crashed into the Earth.

(d) The scope for out-of-school play activities has been greatly diminished over recent years **because** parents want to protect their children from harm, whether from traffic or from molesting strangers.

(e) Our street lights are too dim. **That's why** we have more accidents and more crime than we should.

It is reasonably clear that in example (a) the author is trying to persuade us of a conclusion; she is saying that the damage done to the ozone layer *is a reason* for limiting the production of 'greenhouse' gases. In example (b), it is surely clear that the author is giving us a *causal explanation*; she is not giving us a reason for believing that Napoleon died, but is telling us what *caused* his death. In example (c), again it is surely clear that the author is not trying to persuade us that the dinosaurs died out, but is giving a *causal explanation*, explaining what caused them to die out. In examples (d) and (e) it is not quite so clear; you could construe them as presenting reasons for a conclusion or as presenting explanations – it might depend on the context – or it might not matter or it might just be unclear.

Given that the use of words such as 'because' (and 'that's why') sometimes signal the presence of a reason and sometimes signal a causal explanation, how should we tell which it is in any given case? Here is a practical test which will often help you to decide (in a sentence of the form 'A because B', call A the 'consequence'):

> **Test**: *If the author seems to assume that the consequence is true then you probably have a causal explanation; on the other hand, if the author is trying to prove the consequence, then it is probably an argument.* (Cf. Ennis, 1996, p. 31)

If you apply this test to our examples (a)–(e) above it seems clear that (a) is an argument, (b) and (c) are causal explanations and (d) and (e) remain unclear! (Knowing more about the context of their use might enable us to decide.)

The point here is that sometimes what people say or write can look like an argument when in fact it is an explanation. It is important not to confuse the two because they have to be evaluated in different ways. In an argument, the author is trying to persuade his or her audience that the conclusion is true, whereas in an explanation the sentence, which might look like a conclusion (what we called the *consequence*), is assumed to be true already and the author is trying to explain how it happened, or to account for it (see chapter 10 on how to evaluate explanations).

Of course an explanation might function as a reason in an argument. Here is an example:

> Several accidents have occurred at this road junction because it is very hard for drivers to see other cars coming round the bend as they pull out to cross the main road on which the traffic is travelling quite fast. The only realistic answer is to install traffic lights to control the flow of traffic.

Question 3.6

Decide which of the following quoted remarks is an argument and which is an explanation:

3.6.1   A councillor speaks at a council meeting and says, 'Because our street lights are too dim, we have more accidents and more crime than we should. Furthermore they are so low that they are easily and often damaged by vandals. That is why we should get new, bright high-level sodium lights.'

3.6.2   The police have found the body of a woman lying near a footpath; after a post-mortem the pathologist reports, 'She died because she had a heart attack and no one found her soon enough to help.'

3.6.3   A newspaper reports, 'Thailand and India have had to fight costly legal battles to protect Thailand's jasmine rice and India's basmati rice because a company in Texas, called Rice Tec, was granted patents in the United States on varieties of rice it claimed to have developed, which closely resembled the Thai and Indian versions.'

3.6.4   A Government spokesperson says, 'Though investigations are continuing, the trawler which sank suddenly in relatively calm seas last week probably went down because a submarine fouled its nets and dragged it down.'

3.6.5   A financial journalist writes, 'The Bank will almost certainly reduce interest rates at the next opportunity because the economy is slowing down fast, many companies are in great difficulties and demand has fallen off dramatically.'

3.6.6   A seismologist says, 'There are huge "plates" on the surface of the Earth which press and move against one another. Because there is friction between these plates, they fail to move for many years until the pressure becomes huge and then they move suddenly, an event we experience as an earthquake. That is why San Francisco had a huge earthquake in 1906 and also why they expect another one at any time now.'

3.8 Drawing more than one conclusion

Sometimes an author's reasoning leads him or her to what might look like two (or perhaps more) conclusions; consider the following example:

> Random drug-testing of prisoners was introduced in 1995 in order to solve the many problems associated with prisoners taking drugs. Since cannabis can be detected in the body up to a month after having been smoked, prisoners are tempted to switch to heroin, which stays in the system for only 48 hours. As a result, since drug-testing was introduced, cannabis use has declined by a fifth, whereas heroin use has doubled. Heroin is not only a much more damaging drug than cannabis, but it is also extremely addictive. There is evidence that heroin addiction encourages prisoners to intimidate others in order to pay for the drug.

One can easily imagine drawing various conclusions from this passage, for example one might conclude that 'the results of random drug testing have been unforeseen and unintended' and/or 'random drug testing has not solved the drug problem in prisons'. It might also seem natural to draw a further conclusion, namely, 'if we want to combat drug taking in prisons we need new strategies'. Sometimes it is natural to put such conclusions together as one conclusion, but sometimes it may be helpful to clear thinking to separate them out, especially if one seems justified and one does not; for example, someone might conclude from the above passage that 'random drug testing has not solved the drug problem in prisons' and 'prison officers must be colluding with prisoners'.

Question 3.7

What alternative conclusions might be drawn from the following:

3.7.1   Questions appendix, passage 9.
3.7.2   Questions appendix, passage 35.

3.9 Summary

Arguments have a structure. Reasons can support (or aim to support) their conclusions in different ways. In this chapter we introduced some simple notation for displaying the structure of arguments and then used this to help explain the basic difference between side-by-side reasoning and a chain of reasoning.

Sometimes an author presents two or more reasons side by side in support of a conclusion and sees each of the reasons as giving *some* support to the conclusion *on its own* even without the other reasons. However, sometimes when two or more reasons are presented side by side they *have to be taken together* to give any support to their conclusion; this case is called *joint* reasoning and we explained how it contrasts with other cases of side-by-side reasoning.

These basic patterns of reasoning can be combined to make much more complex patterns and we looked at some of these. In this connection we also noted that when identifying reasons and conclusions it is important not to break up hypotheticals and some other logically complex sentences.

It is very easy to confuse arguments and causal explanations, because the language which is used is so similar and can be systematically misleading, but we gave a practical test for distinguishing these which is often very helpful; the test was:

> *If the author seems to assume that the consequence is true then you probably have a causal explanation; however, if the author is trying to prove the consequence, then it is probably an argument.*

Finally we noted that an argument may lead to several conclusions, so one must be aware of this possibility when considering the structure of a piece of reasoning, bearing in mind that conclusions can be anywhere in an argument.

Further reading

Fisher (1988, chapter 2); Ennis (1996, chapter 2).

4

Understanding reasoning: assumptions, context and a thinking map

4.1 Assumptions

When someone presents an argument, explanation or a similar kind of reasoning, it is very common for them to leave things unsaid which they nonetheless believe to be true (or otherwise acceptable) **and** relevant to the issue, perhaps even vital to the issue. Almost all *real* arguments (arguments which people either do use or have used with a view to convincing others of a point of view) leave things unsaid – which are in a certain sense *assumed*.

To give a very simple example, imagine a skater sitting at the edge of a frozen lake putting on her skates, when a passer-by tells her, 'The ice is thawing and another skater had to be rescued when it broke and he fell through earlier today, so it's not advisable to skate there now.' In this case the speaker's argument assumes the skater does not want to fall through the ice. (If she does want to fall through, now might be a good time to go skating!) We commonly call a belief like this an *assumption* when it is clearly 'taken for granted' by a speaker or writer but is *not stated or made explicit* by them. To give a quite different example, someone who is arguing in favour of believing in miracles may fail to mention that he believes in the existence of an omnipotent Christian God, but it may be obvious that he is assuming this from other things he says or from the context (say, if he is a Roman Catholic priest).

In general, when we use the word 'assumption', this is the sense in which we shall mean it; it is a belief which is clearly accepted or 'taken for granted' by a speaker or writer but is *not stated or made explicit* by them.

However, notice that in ordinary language we sometimes call a claim which is made *explicitly* by a speaker or writer an 'assumption'. To return to our skating example, the skater might respond to the speaker's warning by saying, 'You are assuming the ice is still thawing, but I checked earlier and in fact the temperature has been falling for some hours.' This is a case in which the intending skater calls the *explicit* claim of the passer-by an 'assumption'. Sometimes we call an explicit claim an assumption because: (i) we wish to note that the speaker or writer *has given no reasons for us to accept it* and sometimes we do it because (ii) *we wish to challenge the claim*. In our skating example, the skater does it because she thinks the passer-by is wrong and she gives her reason for thinking so. Returning to our example about miracles, if someone based their case for believing in miracles on (among other things) the explicit claim that there is an omnipotent Christian God, one might say: (i) 'but this is only an assumption; why should I accept it?', or (ii) 'but this is only an assumption; I don't believe it at all'. To return to an earlier example (section 2.2, example (1) p. 18) where Hans complained about the unfair critical thinking test, it would be natural to say to him, 'You are assuming that what you did was sufficient; but you are mistaken.' However, he actually says, 'After doing all this I should have got a good grade', so this is a case where we call his belief an assumption because we want to challenge it, not because it was implicit rather than explicit.

In general we are keen to use language in the way it is ordinarily used (we do not want to give terms a restricted usage, or a technical sense, if we can avoid it), thus we shall use the word 'assumption' in the ways it is commonly used, but in this section we shall mostly be interested in the case where assumptions are apparently accepted by the speaker or writer but are not explicitly stated – and are **implicit**.

Let us look at a few examples where it is natural to say that something is assumed (in the sense of being implicit):

Example 1

The civil population cannot be defended in the event of nuclear war. Therefore we do not need a civil defence policy.

Isn't it natural to say that this assumes (A), 'if the civil population cannot be defended in the event of nuclear war then we do not need a civil defence policy'? Students sometimes say of example (1) that it is not a very compelling argument because there might be other reasons for having a civil defence policy, for example to give the civil population a sense of security (even though it was a false sense of security!). Some say this in response to the original argument, (1), but others find this easier to see once they have identified (A) as the assumption of the argument.

Here is an example of reasoning which clearly makes some substantial assumptions:

Example 2

Some people have solved their own unemployment problem by great ingenuity in searching for a job or by willingness to work for less, so all the unemployed could do this.

Is this assuming that, 'if *some* people have solved their own unemployment problem by great ingenuity in searching for a job or by willingness to work for less, then *all the unemployed* could do this', or is it assuming something like, 'if some people have done X then everyone could'? The latter (very general) assumption would clearly be false (if some people have jumped over six feet high it does not follow that everyone could), but the former assumption requires considerable expertise in (presumably) labour economics to know whether it is true or false.

Consider the following example:

> Because our street lights are too dim, we have more accidents and more crime than we should. Furthermore they are so low that they are easily and often damaged by vandals. That is why we should get new, bright high-level sodium lights.

The explicit reasoning here is clear, but what is assumed? Most real arguments do not include a reason which says, 'If the reasons are acceptable the conclusion is too', but writers in this field commonly say such arguments assume this. I shall not discuss this here (but see section 9.1), but it seems reasonable to say that several other things might be assumed too, for example that the explanation offered for the problem is probably correct, that there are no better alternative ways of dealing with it, that the cost of the new high-level sodium lights is not prohibitive, that there are no other significant disadvantages to high-level sodium lights and perhaps more. Of course the author might not have even thought of these things, but for the argument to carry much weight, they have to be assumed to be true as well as the reasons which are explicitly given.

Consider example 2 from section 2.2 (the letter from an American newspaper of some years ago):

> We should bring most of our troops home from Europe. The threat from Russia has gone now that the Evil Empire has collapsed; the Europeans can defend themselves now that the threat to their security is less and they are so rich; and we must reduce our federal deficit fast if our economy is not to collapse.

It is surely natural to say that this argument assumes something like: (I) 'we do not want our economy to collapse' and (II) 'if we bring most of our troops home from Europe this will reduce our federal deficit fast'. Assumption (I) presents no problems but if assumption (II) is false this greatly weakens the argument and this shows part of the importance of eliciting assumptions. Incidentally, I usually find when discussing this example that students call some of the explicit claims assumptions too – but these are assumptions in the sense that either no reasons are given or they are questionable.

Sometimes in arguing a case speakers simply make *implicit* assumptions and say nothing about doing so; however, as we mentioned in section 2.5, people sometimes draw attention to assumptions they or others are making, using phrases such as, 'I am (Jones is) assuming . . .'. Sometimes such phrases will be referring to implicit assumptions and sometimes to explicit ones (for which no reasons have been given or which are questionable) but the context will enable you to tell which is the case. In the present context, what interests us most are *implicit* assumptions.

Question 4.1

Identify at least one *implicit* assumption in the following passages:

4.1.1   Questions appendix, passage 3.
4.1.2   Questions appendix, passage 6.
4.1.3   Questions appendix, passage 30.
4.1.4   Questions appendix, passage 32.
4.1.5   Questions appendix, passage 33.

4.2 Context

Arguments, explanations and so on, are always presented in some context and the context contains all sorts of assumptions, presumptions, background beliefs, facts relevant to interpreting what is meant, rules of conduct, etc. If we return to our skating example above, it is easy to imagine a context in which: (i) the person giving the warning assumes the skater does not know about the accident earlier in the day and is not aware of any danger but would want to know or (ii) the intending skater is a weather expert from the local university who happens to be monitoring the current freezing conditions, who assumes her instruments are working correctly, that she can interpret them correctly and so on. In general the context includes the people involved, with their purposes, beliefs, emotions and interests, and also includes the physical, social and historical context.

Let us look at a few examples to illustrate why the context of an argument matters and what we can elicit from it. Look first at example 1 from 2.2 in which the student Hans had failed a critical thinking test which was set at the end of a course in critical thinking; he wrote as follows:

> That test was unfair. I studied for days, reading the material four times, underlining important details and then studying them. After doing all this I should have got a good grade. That test was unfair.

It is easy to grasp his line of argument, but the interesting question is, 'Is it reasonable (and what should be done about it)?'. I have been surprised by reactions to this question because my presumption is that any worthwhile critical thinking test would demand more than Hans describes and that his argument is worthless, but in some places where I have discussed this example, some teachers have said, 'If Hans had been told that studying like that would be sufficient and/or that kind of study was a normal expectation in his college, then Hans's argument would be quite reasonable.' It is hard to imagine defending that view after a *critical thinking* course, but it is true that, if Hans studied in such a context, his argument might carry more weight than I have suggested and his teacher or institution might have to react more seriously to his complaint.

To take a different example, consider the following argument set in two different contexts:

> Despite the appalling mortality rate from polio in the past, some parents choose not to have their children vaccinated against it, because they think there is now only a low risk that their children will become infected with the disease. Moreover, some believe that there is a more than negligible risk that the vaccine will have harmful side effects. In their eyes, a decision to avoid vaccination may appear entirely rational. But what they do not

realise is that if a substantial percentage of a population is not vaccinated against polio, there will be regular outbreaks of the disease every few years as the number of non-immune people increases. (Questions appendix, passage 35)

This comes from a British context, where polio was a serious killer but is not now, where increasing numbers of people are wary of having their children vaccinated because of perceived risks and where general attitudes towards individual health, public health and individual freedom provide a context (of assumptions, interests, points of view, etc.) which influences how you construe this argument and evaluate it. This would be rather different if you imagine the argument in the context of a country which still has a significant polio risk, where vaccination programmes are widely recognised to have delivered great advances in health and where individual freedom in such matters is seen as far less important than public health programmes.

Sometimes the context of claims and arguments can greatly influence how much credibility and weight you give them (see chapters 6 and 7 on credibility); for example, 'Jones is lying about X' said in court during a trial carries much more weight than when said informally over a pint with friends. Consider the following, weightier, example:

> The forensic experts who were sent to Kosovo in 1999 after NATO's bombing campaign have been coming to some surprising conclusions. They were sent to unearth the evidence of genocide by the Serbs which had precipitated NATO's action. During the war the US Defence Secretary said that up to 100,000 Albanians had been killed by the Yugoslav military. The British Minister of State at the Foreign Office said 10,000 had been killed. President Clinton said tens of thousands had been killed on President Milosovic's orders. The UN told experts from 15 countries to expect 44,000 deaths. However, Emilio Perez Pujol, head of a Spanish team which went home in disgust last month after finding just 187 bodies, said there may be far fewer dead than previous estimates; several sites publicised by NATO as possible mass graves turned out to be empty. Stratfor, an analytical group examining data from Kosovo, suggests that the final toll might be as low as a few hundred. (Abbreviated from a leading article in *The Times*, 2 November 1999)

If you remember anything about this war it will probably be that the Governments who launched the war did so ostensibly because of genocide by the Serbs. But this article strongly suggests that there was no such genocide. How could Government and military intelligence before the war have been so wrong? Or did they have some quite different motive from the one they publicly declared? Either way, the implication is that when you read reports like those which preceded the Kosovo campaign you should be very wary. There are many other examples of inaccurate Government and military information relating to conflict situations (for example American Government information about the success of their Patriot missiles against Saddam Hussein's Scud missiles in the Gulf War has subsequently been shown to be wildly inaccurate; NATO estimates of Soviet weapons stocks were shown subsequently to have been wildly inaccurate for many years), but a leading article like this, appearing in a newspaper like *The Times* has to be given considerable credence.

The context of claims can help interpret their meaning, for example if someone refers to the 'left wing' in a political discussion this may be a very vague thing to say, but in the context of, say, a discussion about French political parties, it has a much more specific meaning (mainly the Socialist and Communist parties) or in the context of the British Labour Party it means particular people, such as Tony Benn, and particular groups or organisations, such as Tribune. Thus, in general, though vague terms have some meaning, they often have much more meaning in a particular context (cf. chapter 5, page 62).

Historical context can be very important in interpreting and evaluating an argument. For example, in 1798, Thomas Malthus famously argued that population growth inevitably meant that it was impossible to have a society 'all the members of which should live in ease, happiness and comparative leisure and feel no anxiety about providing the means of subsistence for themselves and families'. To understand and evaluate this famous argument you need to take account of its historical context. Following the French Revolution there was much discussion about whether it was possible to establish a society based on social and economic equality. Malthus argued against that possibility, and he did this in the context of a society which was very unequal, which was very influenced by the thinking of Charles Darwin (on natural selection and evolution) and where the French Revolution had set many people thinking about the possibility of revolutionary change in unequal societies (for a fuller discussion of this argument see Fisher, 1988, chapter 3).

To summarise, the context of an argument can influence its interpretation and evaluation, largely because of the assumptions, presumptions and other background information which context can supply. A particular speaker might have a particular point of view, for example that of a Roman Catholic priest. Arguments can carry quite different weights in the contexts of different countries, where underlying assumptions, experiences and values are different. And arguments can deserve different interpretations and evaluations in different historical contexts.

Question 4.2

Consider the following passages and draw on what additional information you can to say what underlying assumptions are likely in the context of each:

4.2.1   Many cold and flu remedies and appetite suppressants which can be bought over the counter contain phenylpropanolamine (PPA), a drug which has been licensed for use for more than a decade. After years of legal and scientific wrangling over its safety, scientific advisers to the American Federal Drugs Administration (FDA) voted unanimously in November 2000 that it should no longer be considered safe, after it was the subject of a study by scientists at Yale University. In America, PPA is said to have been responsible for between 200 and 500 strokes a year in people aged under 50. The first warning signs came in the 1980s when medical journals cited several dozen puzzling cases of young women who suddenly had strokes within days of taking appetite suppressants. However, the drug industry successfully argued that more research was needed to determine whether PPA was to blame, so the Consumer Healthcare Products Association funded a five year study by Yale University. The study found that young women were at increased risk of a stroke within three days of taking an appetite suppressant containing PPA or within three days of taking their first PPA dose ever. Scientists who spoke on behalf of the drug industry said the Yale study was flawed. (Adapted from a report in *The Times*, 7 November 2000)

4.2.2   In the very short term, the Government should take upon itself the responsibility of lifting the ludicrous speed restrictions which have disrupted railway timetables, paralysed the country and vastly increased the danger of travel-related death in Britain by forcing millions of extra vehicles on the roads. Railtrack is obviously not going to do this, nor should it. It is a private company with no responsibility for the general welfare and convenience of the nation or for minimising road traffic deaths. Railtrack's prime concern is, quite reasonably, to avoid lawsuits and blame in the event that another rail accident occurs after speed restrictions are lifted.

If the government wants travel patterns to return to normal, ministers must accept that they may be blamed if there are subsequent accidents – and rely on the good sense of the British public when they explain that lifting speed restrictions was nevertheless a rational course that minimised the overall loss of life. (Excerpt from Anatole Kalentsky, *The Times*, 30 November 2000)

4.2.3   The following very famous argument was first published by Thomas Malthus in 1798 in his *Essay on the Principle of Population* (for further discussion of it see Fisher, 1988, chapter 3):

'Population, when unchecked, increases in geometrical ratio. Subsistence increases only in arithmetical ratio. A slight acquaintance with numbers will show the immensity of the first power in comparison with the second.

By that law of nature which makes food necessary to the life of man, the effects of these two unequal powers must be kept equal. This implies a strong and constantly operating check on population from the difficulty of subsistence. This difficulty must fall somewhere and must necessarily be severely felt by a large portion of mankind. . . .

[This] appears, therefore, to be decisive against the possible existence of a society, all the members of which should live in ease, happiness, and comparative leisure, and feel no anxiety about providing the means of subsistence for themselves and their families'.

Question 4.3

The following reasoning comes from a British newspaper in 1998. How differently do you think readers would respond to it in England and in the American Mid-West (assuming the same piece was published in a newspaper there)?

We need to make rail travel more attractive to travellers. There are so many cars on the roads that the environment and human safety are under threat. Rail travel should be made cheaper. Everyone wants the roads to be less crowded, but they still want the convenience of being able to travel by road themselves. People will not abandon the car in favour of the train without some new incentive.

4.3 A thinking map for understanding and evaluating reasoning

We have looked at a large number of pieces of reasoning and explained some ideas about how best to understand and evaluate them. As we explained in chapter 1, our plan is to proceed rather like the basket ball coach (see section 1.1.4), except that we are doing so in the context of critical thinking. Thus we have been looking at small pieces of reasoning, thinking about how to handle them, drawing attention to some of the mistakes we commonly make in responding to reasoning and in reasoning things through for ourselves, then pointing to better ways of doing these things and giving you practice in adopting these ways. In the absence of such guidance most people tend to react rather superficially to reasoning, by immediately challenging any claim they disagree with, or simply responding from their own point of view without

'Thinking Map'

SKILFUL ANALYSIS AND EVALUATION OF ARGUMENTS

Analysis

1 What are/is the main **Conclusion(s)** (may be stated or unstated; may be recommendations, explanations, and so on, conclusion indicator words and 'therefore' test may help.)?
2 What are the **Reasons** (data, evidence) and their **Structure**?
3 What is **Assumed** (that is, implicit or taken for granted, perhaps in the **Context**)?
4 Clarify the **Meaning** (by the terms, claims or arguments) which need it.

Evaluation

5 Are the reasons **Acceptable** (including explicit reasons and unstated assumptions – this may involve evaluating factual claims, definitions and value judgements and judging the **Credibility** of a source)?
6 (a) Does the reasoning **Support** its conclusion(s) (is the support strong, for example 'beyond reasonable doubt', or weak?)
   (b) Are there **Other Relevant Considerations/Arguments** which strengthen or weaken the case? (You may already know these or may have to construct them.)
7 What is your **Overall Evaluation** (in the light of 1 through 6)?

considering the arguments presented and so on. As we have said before, the key to better critical thinking is asking the right questions, so we now introduce a basic model or 'thinking map' for handling reasoning more skilfully than most of us do in the absence of such guidance. The 'thinking map' is a list of key questions you should ask when weighing up an argument – whether someone else's or your own.

You will see that the questions are divided into two sets, the first called **Analysis** and the second called **Evaluation**. You cannot respond reasonably to an argument unless you first understand it, so the 'analysis' questions guide you in understanding what is being said and argued. The 'evaluation' questions then guide you in deciding whether you should be persuaded by the argument or not.

However, it is clear that the process of evaluating an argument might lead you to spot assumptions, or a need for clarification which you did not notice at the initial analysis stage. For this reason, although it helps you to be clear-headed to separate these tasks, you may need to jump back and forth as you go through the process.

It is clear that so far we have only really given detailed attention to the first three of these questions, but we have introduced the whole 'thinking map' here to provide a context for what we are doing, so that you can see how what we have done so far fits in with our general approach and where it is leading.

It is clear from our earlier chapters that behind these questions lies a lot of detail. It is easy to ask the question, 'What are the **Reasons** (data, evidence) and their **Structure**?', but it has taken us some two chapters to explain in detail how to identify reasons and how to identify the structure of reasoning. It will, therefore, not come as a surprise to learn that there is also a lot of detail to be explained about how to clarify ideas and how to evaluate arguments, but we shall come to these in the next few chapters.

For the moment, there are some things to notice about this thinking map. First, notice that the first question is, 'What is/are the main **Conclusion(s)**?'. Although in general the thinking map questions do not have to be asked in the order in which they are presented above, it is worth saying that it is nearly always a good idea to ask this question first; it helps enormously to organise your thinking about a piece of reasoning if you know what the author is trying to persuade you of – what he or she is trying to convince you of. My students have often told me how trying to get this clear *first* has changed their way of thinking and greatly improved their ability to focus on the issue in hand. Sometimes it is quite easy to spot the conclusion but sometimes it is quite difficult, but, either way, it is instructive to do so. Digging out the reasons and assumptions is then usually easier than it would otherwise have been. Of course, if assumptions or reasons strike you first, by all means make or note those, but do not then forget the importance of identifying the conclusion(s).

A second thing to notice is the question, 'Are there **Other Relevant Considerations/Arguments** – which strengthen or weaken the case?'. As we have said elsewhere, there is a very 'creative' side to critical thinking, which some have wanted to emphasise by calling it critico-creative thinking, and which requires us to consider any other relevant ideas we know or can think up which will help us to arrive at a good judgement for the case in hand. It is hard to overestimate the importance of this question in the context of arriving at reasonable beliefs; we need to make our beliefs fit together as much as possible if we are to be justified in having confidence in them. So, when considering any issue where our judgement matters we should bring to bear all the relevant ideas we can. This implies that someone who knows a lot about related issues, and who can be imaginative about the possibilities, is more likely to come to a sound, well-justified judgement than someone who knows little and is unimaginative. (Of course, anyone can *practise* the skills we are teaching on material they know little about; it is just that they will not think of some relevant knowledge or possibilities which experts will.)

One last thing to notice is that this thinking map will be supplemented later by other thinking maps, for example we shall provide them for deciding how to clarify ideas, how to judge acceptability of a claim, how to judge the credibility of sources and so on. In case this seems rather overwhelming, let me hasten to add that you do not need to use them all at once or in any given case. The thinking map we have just presented provides a kind of framework into which the others can be slotted if you need them. Sometimes, for example, nothing needs to be clarified and no questions of credibility will arise, but still our initial framework will be useful in organising your thoughts on the subject.

One final remark which probably hardly needs repeating by now: you should employ this thinking map not only when you are considering other people's reasoning but also when you are constructing your own – it can be surprisingly instructive. If you have a good case, it should be possible to organise it so that your readers or listeners will have a clear understanding of what you are trying to establish, and how you are doing it; it will usually help to use the language of reasoning to make your intentions clear and to make your conclusion and your reasoning clear. Of course, if you have a weak case, obfuscation may serve your purpose better!

Question 4.4

For each of the following passages, use the thinking map to help you analyse the argument (noting any important assumptions) and then write a brief evaluative response:

4.4.1   Questions appendix, passage 33.

4.4.2   Questions appendix, passage 34.

4.4.3   Questions appendix, passage 39.

4.4.4   These big art exhibitions, which collect paintings from all over the world, are bad for the paintings. However they are transported, there is a danger of accidents and resultant damage or destruction and it can't be good to subject paintings to the changes of pressure and humidity that even carefully controlled travel is likely to bring.

Question 4.5

Look back at your answers to either question 2.9.1 or question 2.9.4 and use the thinking map to identify its strengths and weaknesses, then re-write it to remedy the defects if there were any.

4.4 Summary

Almost all real arguments leave much unsaid – much that is hidden but is 'implicitly assumed'. We use the word 'assumption' in several ways, which are explained, but here we are mainly concerned with those which are not explicitly stated – the implicit ones.

The context of an argument can supply a good deal of background information. This can help us understand it, including what it (or the author) implicitly assumed or meant.

The implication of what we have been saying so far is that there are more effective ways of thinking issues through than most of us normally use. With the analogy of the basket ball coach in mind, we presented a model for 'skilful analysis and evaluation of arguments' in the form of a thinking map, a set of key questions we should ask when confronted by reasoning which aims to convince us of a point of view.

Our contention is that if we follow the model provided by the thinking map, we shall be far better placed to weigh reasoning skilfully. If we are responding to someone else's reasoning, we should not just jump in with some opposing comment, but should try to be clear first what they are arguing for (what their conclusion is), what their reasoning is, what they are assuming, etc., and then proceed systematically to weigh the case they have made. If, rather than responding to someone else's reasoning, we are trying to construct a well-reasoned case ourselves, we need to ask ourselves much the same questions.

As we have explained in this chapter, doing all this involves detailed attention to implicit assumptions and context, as well as the explicit reasoning. It may also require that we clarify some ideas, so we shall explain how to do this in the next chapter.

Further reading

Ennis (1996, chapter 7).

5

Clarifying and interpreting expressions and ideas

Suppose you read a newspaper article in which a nutritionist advocates eating 'organic foods'; is it clear (or clear enough) what she means – or how could you find out? Suppose you hear someone arguing about the merits of 'Baroque architecture'; could you explain what a Baroque building is? If not, what would enable you to understand what that phrase means? Imagine that you are a juror in a criminal case and you are instructed to decide whether the case has been 'proved beyond a reasonable doubt'; is it clear what that phrase means, and if not, how could you clarify it so that you know what test to apply? Suppose a child, who is doing her mathematics homework, asks you what a 'polygon' is; how would you explain? Suppose you are reading an article about the developing conflicts over water supplies in various parts of the world and which refers to water as a 'natural resource like oil and coal'; is it clear what this claim means – or what it might entail?

The process of reasoning often encounters a need for clarification. Terms may be used, or claims may be made, whose meaning is unclear, vague, imprecise or ambiguous. As we have said, in order to evaluate an argument skilfully we must first understand it; this means not only being reasonably clear what reasons, conclusions and assumptions are being presented, but also being reasonably clear what all of these mean. Often, in simple examples (like many we have seen earlier), this raises no problems at all, but in more complex ones it is surprising how often questions about meaning and interpretation arise. It is probably a safe guide to say that, once you feel you do not immediately understand what is being said, you are into questions of meaning and interpretation.

Of course, a measure of unclarity is not always a bad thing. Suppose someone makes the claim that, 'Jones is tall'. Tallness is obviously a fairly vague concept, but, if we take the claim in context, so that we know whether it refers to an adult basket ball player, a six year old child or a racehorse, then it may well be precise enough for the purpose in hand. As Scriven says:

> a vague term (1) has some meaning, (2) often has a good deal more meaning when we have a context from which we can make further inferences, (3) can be given an abstract definition by referring it to another abstract term ('average height'), and (4) can be given a somewhat more precise meaning if we restrict that meaning to uses of the term in particular contexts. (Scriven, 1976, p. 108)

Bearing this example in mind, it is easy to see that it would be inappropriate, and often tedious, to demand clarification in many situations, because the context will make the meaning clear enough for the purpose of communication. Judging when enough is enough is a central part of the skill of clarification. However, there are many situations in which clarification is needed and in this chapter we explain how to deal with such situations – how to clarify expressions and claims about which we are not immediately clear. We shall explain some procedures which will help you to clarify what writers and speakers mean by what they say, including yourself of course. What is needed will depend on the **audience** and on the **purpose** of the clarification. Furthermore, there are different **methods** of clarifying meanings and we shall spend much of the chapter explaining these.

Question 5.1

There are three parts to this question:

5.1.1   Suppose you read a newspaper article in which a nutritionist advocates eating 'organic foods'. Explain what this phrase means, in enough detail for fellow students to understand, or explain how you would find out?

5.1.2   If you do not know what 'Baroque architecture' is, what would enable you to understand the idea?

5.1.3   Describe evidence which would 'prove beyond a reasonable doubt' that X murdered Y.

5.1 What is the problem? (Is it vagueness, ambiguity, a need for examples, or what?)

When you encounter a situation in which you are not clear what someone means, the first thing to do is to be as clear as you can about the nature of the problem and the purpose of providing clarification. Looking again at the examples with which we began this chapter, they pose rather different problems.

If you do not know what the phrase 'organic food' means, how can you find out? Perhaps the context will help; it might suggest that 'organic foods' are those produced without using chemical pesticides and artificial fertilisers and this might be sufficient for your purpose. If the context does not help or if you want more detail, how can you get it? It is unlikely that the dictionary will help you, though it might. You could ask someone whom you believe to have the relevant expertise, perhaps a biology teacher or a keen gardener. But, this is a term which has been introduced into the language relatively recently; it means different things to different people and its usage is developing all the time. As new problems emerge its meaning changes so, for example, the meaning just suggested leaves open the question whether genetically modified crops are 'organic' if grown without chemical pesticides and artificial fertilisers. This is a case where the term has some meaning but is **vague** to some degree; this might not matter, but if you need more detail it might well be that the only way to find out more would be to ask the author what she meant.

If you know what 'Baroque architecture' is, how would you explain it to a friend? If you do not know what it is, again the context might tell you enough, or you could look in a dictionary or ask someone you would expect to know (like an historian or architect). The *Shorter Oxford English Dictionary* will tell you it is 'characterized by an exuberant and ornate style prevalent in the seventeenth and early eighteenth centuries'. This certainly rules out many modern buildings which are undecorated boxes, but you would probably still feel you had little idea how to identify Baroque buildings. Almost certainly the best way to understand the meaning of this expression is to see some pictures of good **examples** of Baroque buildings – perhaps with some descriptions of their distinctive features. This would still leave the idea open in some respects but you could recognise some clear examples which might be sufficient for your purposes.

The phrase 'proved beyond a reasonable doubt' does not contain any words which are problematic but if, as a juror in a criminal case, you want to know what it means, your problem is to know what **standard** or **criterion** to apply, what counts as a *'reasonable* doubt'. Since this phrase has a well-established usage in the law, you might expect that this is well documented in law books and could be explained to you by the judge, so it would be natural to ask him (the expert in this case) how you should interpret the phrase, and his guidance should be sufficient for your purpose.

Question 5.2

What is the problem in the remaining examples from the first paragraph of this chapter:

5.2.1   Explaining what a polygon is to a child?
5.2.2   Grasping what is meant by calling water a 'natural resource like coal and oil'?

5.2 Who is the audience? (What background knowledge and beliefs can they be assumed to have?)

Returning to the examples we have just been discussing, it is clear that what clarification is needed will depend on the audience. For example, if the person who asks what 'organic foods' are has no idea what the phrase means, it might be sufficient in the context to say 'produced without chemical pesticides and artificial fertilisers'; but, if the audience consists of the people who make contracts with farmers for the food which supermarkets sell and who want to be sure they can safely label some of their products as 'organic', they may need much more detail. Yet again, 'organic foods' might be the subject of a university seminar for specialists in food production, and you can imagine that for such an audience it might be necessary to give still more detail about the ideas which lie behind the demands for organic foods in order to help them decide whether genetically modified foods produced without chemical pesticides and artificial fertilisers could reasonably be said to count as organic.

If someone asks what 'Baroque architecture' is because they have absolutely no idea, it might be sufficient for their purpose to say 'characterized by an exuberant and ornate style prevalent in the seventeenth and early eighteenth centuries'; but, if someone already knows that much and wants to be able to recognise clear examples of such buildings, they will probably need to be shown some good examples or pictures of some. Again, if someone is writing a book on Baroque architecture for an audience of university specialists, they will need to go into still more detail, distinguishing Baroque from 'Classical' and 'Rococo' and so on.

Question 5.3

There are two parts to this question:

5.3.1 Describe three audiences for whom the phrase 'proved beyond a reasonable doubt' might need to be explained and indicate how much detail each might need.

5.3.2 Do the same for the phrase 'critical thinking'.

5.3 Given the audience, what will provide sufficient clarification for present purposes?

There are many different ways of clarifying ideas, depending on the need, so we now explain some of these with suitable examples. Sometimes you will want to get clear what someone else means, in which case these methods will help, but sometimes other people will want to clarify what **you** mean, so you need to bear these methods in mind when writing or talking yourself, so that your ideas are presented reasonably clearly to your audience. We divide our explanations into two sections: possible sources and ways of clarifying expressions:

5.3.1 Possible sources of clarification

(a) A dictionary definition (reporting normal usage)

Imagine that you are reading something and you encounter a word the meaning of which you do not understand. The context might enable you to make a good guess, but, if you want to check, an obvious course of action will often be to look in a dictionary. That is what dictionaries are for – to tell you how a word is normally used and perhaps give some specialist uses too. For example, if you are reading some Charlotte Bronte and you encounter the sentence, 'Eleemosynary relief never yet tranquillized the working classes', it is unlikely that you will know what 'eleemosynary' means. The context might give you a clue and this might be sufficient, but, if not, the obvious course is to look in a dictionary. My *New Shorter Oxford English Dictionary* says, 'Of, pertaining to, or of the nature of, alms or almsgiving; charitable'. This might give you enough *in the context*. Of course, some vagueness will remain (for example, is a charitable organisation like OXFAM 'eleemosynary'?), but that might not matter.

Dictionaries can be useful when you need to clarify terms but they have a very particular role in the process of clarifying ideas. In short they tell you the way in which words are normally, generally, standardly used by native speakers of a language. They **report** common usage and they do so for a general audience, an audience of those who do not know the meaning of a word and need to have it briefly explained in terms of other, more familiar words from the same language (cf. Ennis, 1996, pp. 321ff. on 'reported definitions').

Question 5.4

Use a dictionary to answer the following. Suppose you read a court report in a reputable newspaper which says that the 'circumstantial evidence' strongly suggests that Jones stole the valuable paintings found in his house. Explain what 'circumstantial evidence' is and say what sort of circumstantial evidence might suggest Jones was guilty in this case.

(b) A definition/explanation from an authority in the field (reporting specialised usage)

Sometimes, when you are reading relatively specialised material, you will encounter a need for clarification and a dictionary will not be enough because the language is being used in a technical, specialised or strict sense which you need to know. A good dictionary might point you in the right direction, but you will often have to consult some standard text, work of reference or authority in the field to get an explanation of its special usage. For example, you might be reading something which requires you to know the technical meaning of 'standard deviation', 'mean' and 'median' in statistics, or 'tort', 'hearsay evidence' and 'circumstantial evidence' in the law, or 'real wages', 'economic growth', 'price–earnings ratio' in economics, or 'force', 'molecule', 'virus' in science.

To check the meanings of such technical words you can either look in textbooks or works of reference in that field (encyclopaedias, general or specialised, might be a good source too). Alternatively you can ask someone you would expect to know, like a statistician, a lawyer, economist or scientist in our examples (or the teacher who asked you to read the Bronte novel in our earlier example). Provided the person you consult has the relevant expertise – and is thus a **reliable source** – this will be a good way of proceeding too and one advantage of consulting such an authority is that she can tailor her explanation to her audience (as in our example above about explaining the meaning of 'polygon' to a child).

Question 5.5

There are two parts to this question:

5.5.1   Explain to friends who are not studying critical thinking what it means to say that the conclusion of some argument 'necessarily follows' or 'does not necessarily follow' from the reasons given.

5.5.2   Suppose a class-mate who knows little about politics asks you how to define 'democracy'; using any suitable source provide a suitable explanation.

(c) Deciding on a meaning; stipulating a meaning

In the two previous sections we have been asking how some expressions are generally used by native speakers of the language or how they are used by some special group – like mathematicians, economists or lawyers. The use of ordinary language among native speakers usually just develops and changes without anyone making any special decisions. Specialised usage of the kind we discussed under (b) may develop in a similar way, but more commonly will have involved decisions by specialists to use a phrase in way which captures some idea which is important to their field. Sometimes *we* are faced with the need to make such decisions. For example, earlier in this book we wanted to speak of the words which indicate that arguing or reasoning is taking place, so we introduced the phrase 'argument indicators' and *gave* it a quite specific meaning. Similarly, in writing about critical thinking, I wanted to escape from using hackneyed old logicians' examples (such as 'All men are mortal, Socrates is a man, therefore Socrates is mortal'), so I introduced the phase 'real arguments' and explained that I would use it to mean 'arguments which are or have been used to convince others of a point of view' intending these to be the focus of my writing (see Fisher, 1988, p. 15). What happens in a case like this is that we do not want to report a usage already established but we want to *declare* one, *stipulate* one, or *decide* on one to capture some idea which is important to us.

    Lawyers need to distinguish between different kinds of evidence, so, as we have seen, they have introduced special terms like 'circumstantial evidence', 'hearsay evidence', etc. and have *given* them special meanings. Economists have done something similar with 'money wages' and 'real wages'. Lawyers, economists and many others, find new ideas they want to capture and are then faced with the need to *give* new meanings to words or phrases, to stipulate, declare or decide a meaning which serves their purpose. To justify such a decision you have to show that it serves your intended purpose. Of course, making such a decision may still leave open some important questions as the following example illustrates.

The UK's Race Relations Act (1968) prohibits discrimination 'on the ground of colour, race or ethnic or national origin' in, among other things, selling or letting a house. Thus, if you refuse to let your house to someone simply because they have a black skin or because they have German ancestors, you break this law. But what happens if a Housing Authority rules that you are only eligible for a council house in its area if you are a British citizen. This case actually arose when Ealing Borough Council made such a rule in the early 1970s. Their rule excluded a Mr Zesko, who was a Polish national (though he had lived in Britain for a long time) and they found themselves in conflict with the Race Relations Board in a case which eventually went to the House of Lords. The question is whether discriminating 'on the grounds of national origin' includes discriminating on the grounds of a person's legal nationality. This is not easy to decide; in fact there are plausible grounds for either interpretation. In the event, both sides argued their case and the various judges involved differed in their interpretations of the law and gave reasons for their opposing interpretations. Clearly checking in a dictionary or legal text will not help much here; in this case what is needed is a decision. A decision which *gives meaning* to terms which were in a sense vague (cf. MacCormick, 1978, pp. 66f. and 78f.).

The implication of this section and what we said about different audiences is that, if you are writing in an academic context (school or college papers), you will often need to review how the use of an expression has developed over time as successive thinkers have encountered new problems and have given a new or revised meaning to the expression.

Question 5.6

5.6.1 Suppose a local law, passed seventy years ago, prohibits 'vehicles in the park'. This is clearly intended to exclude cars, lorries and the like, but how would you decide whether it was intended to exclude the electrically powered vehicles now used by some disabled and elderly people (assuming the matter had not yet been decided anywhere)?

5.6.2   Suppose you wanted to investigate what proportion of the UK population was living in poverty; how would you define poverty for your purposes?

5.6.3   How would you resolve the following problem?

According to evolutionary theory, a 'successful' individual must somehow ensure that the next generation contains creatures more like itself than like others of the species. Worker bumblebees are 'successful' in that each generation of bumblebees contains a significant proportion of workers, which exist to feed other members of their community. Worker bees thus pose a special problem for evolutionary theorists because the worker is the only sterile member of the bumblebee community. (Cf. Law Schools Admission Test June 1985 B 3)

5.3.2 Ways of clarifying terms and ideas

We shall explain five ways of clarifying expressions: (a) by giving another expression which has much the same meaning, (b) doing (a) in very precise terms by giving another expression which has precisely the same meaning, (c) by giving examples (and non-examples), (d) by drawing contrasts, (e) by describing the history of an expression.

(a) Giving a 'synonymous' expression – or paraphrase

'Synonymous' (which has Greek origins) means 'has the same meaning'. So, one way to explain the meaning of an expression is to give some other expression which 'has the same meaning' but which the audience might be expected to understand – usually because the audience is familiar with the words which provide the explanation. This is sometimes called giving a paraphrase. In fact, the explanation I have just given of the word 'synonymous' clarifies the term precisely by providing a synonymous expression, or paraphrase, which is easily understood by most people! Dictionaries commonly explain meanings by giving synonymous expressions (or paraphrases) and technical words are commonly defined in the same way; for example, we saw this with 'circumstantial evidence' and 'democracy'.

(b) Giving necessary and sufficient conditions (or an 'if and only if' definition)

Sometimes we explain the meaning of an expression by giving a synonymous expression or paraphrase which means **much** the same, without necessarily meaning **exactly** the same. However, sometimes we are explaining the meaning of an expression which is very exact so we want our explanation to be very exact. Here are some examples where the intention is that the meanings of the italicised words should be exactly explained by the words following 'is':

A *triangle* is a plane geometrical figure with three straight sides.
Momentum is mass times velocity.
A *bachelor* is human, male, and unmarried but of marriageable age.

There is a tradition which has been important in philosophy and some other fields (it derives from Plato) that this kind of definition is an ideal to which we should aspire for many ordinary words. Thus, for example, philosophers have tried to define knowledge very precisely, like this:

'A knows that P' if and only if (i) 'P is true.'
(ii) 'A believes that P.'
(iii) 'A is justified in believing P.'

where A is a person and P is a claim that could be true or false.

Sometimes it is right to try to give very exact explanations of the meanings of words because they are being used very precisely, as is often the case in mathematics and science. However, everyday words tend to be used rather more loosely so it can be a mistake to try to explain their meaning too precisely. Of course, this depends on your purpose. If you simply wish to explain everyday usage, you need to preserve its looseness, but, if you want to make that usage more precise for a particular purpose, that may be right too. For example, ordinary usage of the word 'argument' is fairly loose, but we gave the word a more precise meaning to enable us to focus on the kinds of 'arguments' in which we are interested.

In the case of the philosopher's definition of knowledge this has proved problematic, because this explanation of the meaning of 'knowledge' is meant to capture ordinary usage of the word but other philosophers are able to think of exceptions, cases where we would still want to say 'A knows that P' but where the three conditions are not satisfied (or the other way round, where the conditions are satisfied but we don't want to say 'A knows that P').

In general you will find that it is very rare to be able to explain meaning in terms of 'necessary and sufficient conditions' except in mathematics and science (or where you have deliberately defined a new expression that way). Most ordinary language has a 'vagueness' about its application which prevents us from being able to give 'if and only if' or other exact definitions. The philosopher Ludwig Wittgenstein (for example, *Philosophical Investigations*) demonstrated that this was a very important fact about our use of language, so we must be careful not to try to be more precise than we really can if we are trying to grasp normal usage. We may be able to give some kind of general expression which means much the same and we may be able to give good examples and non-examples, and draw some contrasts, but that may be the limit; native speakers of a language often mention or use quite a variety of characteristics when trying to decide whether something really is an X or not and this may just be the way the language is used (cf. Scriven, 1976, p. 133).

Question 5.7

There are three parts to this question:

5.7.1 Suppose someone explains that by a 'good teacher' they mean 'a teacher who scores well above average on student evaluation forms'. How would you evaluate this definition/explanation?

5.7.2 See if you can think of necessary and sufficient conditions for something to be a 'game' (like football and cricket are games). Every time you settle on an answer see if you can think of an exception – something to which your definition does **not** apply but which **is** a game, or something to which it **does** apply but which is **not** a game.

5.7.3 Do you think the definition of 'bachelor' given above genuinely supplies the necessary and sufficient conditions for being a bachelor. (Cf. Everitt and Fisher, 1995, pp. 14, 15)

(c) Giving clear examples (and non-examples)

It is often very helpful to give really good examples to clarify an idea (and examples to which the idea clearly does **not** apply). As we said earlier, probably the best way to explain what baroque architecture is, is to give good examples; then examples which contrast with that style will help to draw its limits, probably as finely as you require. This is also true elsewhere; for example, it could help jurors to interpret the phrase 'proved beyond a reasonable doubt' to be given examples where this clearly was the case and examples where it was not. So if the question is whether 'X murdered Y' and we know that X's finger prints were on the gun which killed Y, that Y's blood was found on X's clothes immediately after the murder, that reliable witnesses say they saw X shoot Y, that X was very jealous of Y's relationship with X's wife, that X had a history of violence, that X had no alibi for the time of the murder and indeed confessed after police put their evidence to him, it is surely proved beyond a reasonable doubt that X did it. You can easily imagine weaker versions of this case where you would **not** say it was proved beyond a reasonable doubt. Really good examples which help to identify and clarify an idea are sometimes called 'paradigm' examples.

(d) Drawing contrasts (including *per genus et differentiam*)

One of the most useful things to do when considering the meaning of a claim or term is to ask what contrasts are being drawn – what is being ruled out. For example, when we say that Jones is 'tall', we are contrasting Jones with short or average members of the group. When we discussed what 'critical thinking' was in chapter 1, we contrasted it with jumping to conclusions, deciding impulsively, and much more. Before doing any work on 'critical thinking', you probably had only a vague idea about the meaning of the expression. If you wanted to get a clearer view at that stage, you might have reflected on how you had heard people use the term (as we asked you to do in question 1.1) or looked in a dictionary or other suitable reference works, like encyclopaedias or classic works in the critical thinking tradition. If you did the first of these, you might have found it easier initially to say what critical thinking is **not** than to say what it is (which illustrates a point often worth making in connection with clarifying ideas). For example, most people will agree that a person who believed whatever they read in the newspapers, or who made decisions 'on impulse', without weighing the reasons for and against, or who worked routinely on a production line – doing repetitive actions without needing to think about them – would not be engaging in critical thinking. By contrast, the critical thinker would decide which newspaper stories to believe partly by using considerations about the reliability of sources (and would be sceptical of the *National Enquirer's* story that the Titanic recently resurfaced!), and would consider options and weigh the pros and cons before taking a decision that mattered (and might, for example, seek independent, expert advice before buying a used car). Even this much reflection identifies critical thinking as a 'considered' activity, a 'reflective' activity – an activity which is contrasted with unreflective, impulsive and routine ones. Sometimes contrasts are drawn by saying what *kind* of thing you are talking about and what *differentiates* it from other things of that kind; books in this field often call this *per genus et differentiam* in case you are reading around on the subject.

Question 5.8

Providing clarification where necessary, write a brief response to the following argument, either supporting it or criticising it:

> Men generally have difficulty in being sensitive to others. If it is desirable for our society to consist of fully developed human beings, then people who are sensitive should make a special effort to help those who are not. Generally, this means that women should make a special effort to help men to be more sensitive. I say this even though some might feel that it places an unfair burden on women. (Ennis, 1996, exercise 2.57 (2.51))

(e) Explaining the history of an expression

You have already seen an example of this in chapter 1 where I explained the history of the term 'critical thinking'. Of course, if you come to this subject having no idea what critical thinking is, it might help to see what is in a dictionary. My *New Shorter Oxford English Dictionary* (1993) has no entry for 'critical thinking' as such and gives several different definitions of 'critical', the most relevant being, 'given to judging, esp. unfavourably, faultfinding, censorious: skilful at or engaged in criticism, especially of literature or art; providing textual criticism: involving careful judgement or observation; nice, exact, punctual'. This begins to point you in the right direction but it is not very helpful and if you really want to learn what the subject is about you need quite a full explanation. Explaining the historical development of the idea will often help in this kind of case (partly because that development occurred in response to recognising problems in the area). It is easy to think of other ideas where you might need to look at the history of its development to get a sophisticated grasp of what is meant – democracy, punishment, power, mass . . . We spoke earlier about university audiences to whom ideas (like 'organic food', 'Baroque architecture', etc.) might need to be explained; clearly such explanations will often require an extensive look at the history of an idea and will require us to consult classic works on the subject for that information.

5.4 How much detail is needed by this audience in this situation?

This is really a question to remind you to tailor your answer to your particular audience; we do not need to add to what has already been said on this except to give the following exercise.

Question 5.9

The following passages, which are both taken from a widely used legal textbook, explain two contrasts. The first distinguishes 'direct evidence' from 'circumstantial evidence', and the second distinguishes 'original evidence' from 'hearsay evidence'. Rephrase both to explain the differences to a child of twelve, giving your own examples (suitable for a twelve year old).

5.9.1   Direct evidence consists either of the testimony of a witness who perceived the fact to be proved or the production of a document or thing which constitutes the fact to be proved. Circumstantial evidence is the testimony of a witness who perceived not the fact to be proved but another fact from which the existence or non-existence of that fact can be deduced, or the production of a document or thing from which the fact to be proved can be deduced. Suppose the fact at issue is whether A used a certain knife. If T says he saw A use the knife, he is giving direct evidence of a fact at issue; if T says he saw the knife in A's hand he is giving direct evidence of possession but only circumstantial evidence of A's using the knife. If T says he saw the knife among A's belongings he is giving circumstantial evidence of A's possession of the knife and circumstantial evidence of A's using the knife. All witnesses necessarily give direct evidence of whatever it was they perceived. (Phipson and Elliott, 1980, p. 11)

5.9.2   Original evidence is the evidence of a witness who deposes to facts of his own knowledge. If his information is derived from other persons and he himself has no personal knowledge of the facts to which he deposes, then his evidence is said to be hearsay. (Phipson and Elliot, 1980, p. 12)

5.5 Problems requiring clarification in reasoning

Sometimes an expression may be used in the context of reasoning in a way which is misleading so far as its meaning is concerned and this can lead the reasoner(s) astray. Here is a famous example which illustrates one way of misleading people:

> The only proof capable of being given that an object is visible is that people actually see it. The only proof that a sound is audible is that people hear it: and so of the other sources of experience. In like manner, I apprehend, the sole evidence it is possible to produce that anything is desirable, is that – people do actually desire it.

This argument, which comes from John Stuart Mill's book, *On Liberty*, seems powerful until you realise that 'visible' and 'audible' mean *'can be seen'* and *'can be heard'* whereas 'desirable' does not usually mean *'can be desired'* but means 'is good' or 'ought to be desired' or something like that. So the reasoning only looks plausible if you do not notice that.

Here is another, lighter example. Tate and Lyle used to advertise sugar with a character called Mr Cube, saying things like:

> For sporting success you need a balanced diet – and loads of energy. As everyone does, every day of their lives. And one of the cheapest ways of getting the energy you need is with Tate and Lyle's pure British-refined sugar.

Well, is sugar going to give you the *energy* that makes you feel full of *energy* – full of go? As one witty commentator, Magnus Pyke, commented:

> The scientific meaning of energy is quite complicated. A brick lying on the top of a cliff is full of *energy* because if someone pushes it over the edge it is capable of braining someone down below. And Roly Poly pudding is full of *energy* in the chemical sense, but if you eat it, it does not give you vigour.

So this was an advertisement trading on one word meaning at least two different things, but this was obscured by the language (this is sometimes called the *fallacy of equivocation*).

Ambiguity of these kinds can lead to errors in reasoning. So much so that some have been given special names (like the 'fallacy of equivocation') but we shall give them no further attention here, except to say that they occur and one needs to keep as clear a head as possible about what is meant when thinking things through.

Question 5.10

Are Mary and Peter disagreeing in the following?

Mary: 'I've been learning about equality before the law. I had no idea it was so important in our political system.'

Peter: 'Human beings vary enormously in intelligence, strength, wealth and many other qualities, so all this talk of equality is a nonsense.'

5.6 The purpose of this chapter

It is quite common in argumentative contexts for there to be some lack of clarity about what is meant. In explaining the ideas of this chapter we do not mean to suggest that you should see lack of clarity every-where or that you should meet every claim or argument with the question 'What do you mean?'. Sometimes the effect of this kind of chapter is to incline students to do precisely that, but there is often no problem about what is meant and people understand each other per-fectly well for the purpose in hand. However, you do need to be alive to the importance of vagueness, ambiguity, etc. so that you can spot it when it matters and then automatically ask the right questions. In this chapter we have explained several different ways of clarifying expressions for different purposes and we hope that it will become fairly automatic for you to use these methods when they are called for, but not otherwise! Note that when clarification is needed the expla-nation which is given is often imprecise in some respects but is adequate for the purpose of communication; not everything can be defined or explained!

Thus, if you are considering buying a mobile phone and one company tries to persuade you to buy their product by advertising their tariff as being 'up to 25 per cent cheaper' than their rivals, is it clear what the company is claiming – what their advertisement means – and should you be persuaded by their advertisement or should you automatically ask, 'Wait, what does that mean?'. Of course, it might be straightfor-ward; it might be easy to see that an average user will save 25 per cent compared with the charges of some widely used company, but it might be an empty claim.

The exercises were designed to give you practice in recognising when ideas need to be clarified and practice in some different ways of doing this. You may have realised that you already know quite a lot about clarifying meanings, though you never thought about it systematically before; in any event the hope is that this practice will have had an impact on the way you think in future so that it will be fairly automatic for you to clarify what you say and write and so that your audience has a good chance of understanding you. In short be as clear as you can and need to be given your audience.

5.7 To summarise

Hopefully the thinking map is sufficient to summarise this chapter.

CLARIFYING IDEAS SKILFULLY

1 What is the **problem**? (Is it vagueness, ambiguity, a need for examples or what?)
2 Who is the **audience**? (What background knowledge and beliefs can they be assumed to have?)
3 Given the audience, what will provide sufficient clarification for present purposes?
4 Possible **sources** of clarification:
   (a) a **dictionary definition** (reporting normal usage),
   (b) a definition/explanation from an **authority** in the field (reporting specialised usage),
   (c) deciding on a meaning; **stipulating** a meaning.
5 Ways of clarifying terms and ideas:
   (a) giving a **'synonymous'** expression – or paraphrase,
   (b) giving **necessary and sufficient conditions** (or an 'if and only if' definition),
   (c) giving **clear examples** (and non-examples),
   (d) drawing **contrasts** (including *per genus et differentiam*),
   (e) explaining the **history** of an expression.
6 How much detail is needed by this audience in this situation?

Question 5.11

5.11.1 Read Questions appendix, passage 23 and decide what 'fair' means in that context.
5.11.2 Steven J. Gould, the famous Harvard biologist writes in a piece called 'The Median isn't the Message', how he was diagnosed in July 1982 as suffering from abdominal mesothelioma, a rare and serious cancer, usually associated with exposure to asbestos. After surgery he decided to check the literature on this illness, and it was very clear. 'Mesothelioma is incurable, with a median mortality of only 8 months after discovery.' After sitting stunned for some time, he began to think and asked himself, 'What does "median mortality of 8 months" signify'. What did Gould want to know?

5.11.3 Consider the following reasoning:

Whenever there is a plan to divert part of the flow of some river to supply other areas with water, this rightly raises objections from those who will 'lose' the water. It is absurd to expect the 'losers' to stand idly by while a sizeable proportion of their water flows away so that others may benefit in some distant place. Fresh water is a natural resource in the same sense that crude oil and iron ore are natural resources. Does Saudi Arabia give away its crude oil? Does Russia give away its iron ore? Why should those who are threatened with losing part of their water supply be expected to view their natural resources any differently? If development in other areas is limited by lack of water, it should stay that way. (Adapted from the Law School Admission Test, December 1985, D 18)

Is water like oil and iron ore? What are the implications of your answer?

5.11.4 What do you think it means to say that someone *loves* someone else?

5.11.5 How would you respond to Dawkins' description of religious faith as 'belief in spite of, even perhaps because of, the lack of evidence'. Questions appendix, passage 57.

5.11.6 What are the 'costs' spoken of in the following report:

According to Parliament's Trade and Industry Select Committee (which is dominated by Labour MPs) the Government and companies are in danger of seriously underestimating the cost of joining the Euro (for example, the cost of converting computer systems and vending machines, training staff and providing information to the public). The Chairman of the committee said the cost could easily be £35 billion. MPs noted that the accountants Chantrey Vellacott had estimated the cost at about £32 billion. However, the chairman of Anderson consulting said that its survey of companies in Britain and elsewhere in the European Union suggested that business costs would be relatively small at 'no more than 0.5% of turnover'. Others pointed out that companies were regularly upgrading their computer systems so these costs could easily be absorbed and costs to one company were income to another. (Adapted from a report in *The Times*, 17 November 2000)

5.11.7 For a really difficult last question try to answer the case made by John McPeck in Questions appendix, passage 55.

Further reading

Scriven (1976, chapter 5).

6

The acceptability of reasons: including their credibility

In previous chapters we have concentrated on some techniques required to understand what authors mean, especially when they are reasoning. These techniques imply lessons about how to express yourself clearly and we have given some attention to this task too. Now it is time to move on to the process of **evaluating** authors' reasoning. If someone gives reasons which aim to persuade us of a point of view (conclusion, explanation, recommendation, interpretation or whatever) we not only want to *understand* what they are saying but want to be in a position to *evaluate* it – to decide whether it is *good* reasoning, whether we *should be persuaded* by it. To do this skilfully, we have to ask the right questions. The following chapters are mainly devoted to explaining what these questions are in different contexts and to giving you practice in applying them.

6.1 Acceptability questions put in context

What tends to happen when we hear someone else arguing a case? If you check this out (by looking back at the way you and others were inclined to react to arguments you encountered in the first few chapters), you will find that people commonly react in the following ways. If they agree with what the person is getting at (their conclusion) they say, 'Yes, I agree with that' without considering the details of the argument. If they disagree with the conclusion, they say, 'I do not agree with that' and perhaps say something **against** the conclusion, either simply denying it or rejecting one of the claims given as a reason or perhaps introducing some new reason which they take to tell against the conclusion. It is very rare for listeners to take the argument seriously and weigh carefully whether it is a good argument for its conclusion. Of course, such quick reactions are fine in some contexts (for example, informal conversation over a coffee with friends), but if you want to get to the truth about substantial issues, you have to be more systematic. It is this more systematic and more skilful approach to evaluating arguments which we shall study here. So, how should we proceed?

If we are going to evaluate reasoning thoroughly and skilfully, we shall need to ask at least three *quite different* questions about any piece of reasoning, namely questions 5, 6a and 6b from our thinking map in section 4.3 (repeated below). To set the context for our present work, let us look at an example we have already considered, to explain what these questions are and how they work:

> Most prospective parents would prefer to have sons. So if people can choose the sex of their child, it is likely that there will eventually be more males than females in the population. This could produce serious social problems, therefore we should prohibit the use of techniques which enable people to choose the sex of their children.

Question 6.1

Write a brief initial evaluative response to this argument, saying whether you agree with its conclusion or not, and why.

Remember that we already decided that this argument's structure was:

> R1<Most prospective parents would prefer to have sons>. **So** C1[if people can choose the sex of their child, it is likely that there will eventually be more males than females in the population] **and** R2<This could produce serious social problems>, **therefore** C2[we should prohibit the use of techniques which enable people to choose the sex of their children].

Now, if we want to evaluate this systematically, we need to ask the following questions:

5 Are the reasons **Acceptable** (true, etc.)?

6 (a) Does the reasoning **Support** its conclusion(s)?

   (b) Are there **Other Relevant Considerations/Arguments**?

7 What is your **Overall Evaluation**?

Let us run through these questions showing how they work in the case of our example. First we have to decide whether it is true that: 'Most prospective parents would prefer to have sons.' My guess, based on general knowledge, is that this claim is true in many societies, for example in many groups in China and India, but it may well be false in others; to find out, we might need to refer to survey information or to other relevant social reports.

The next question is, 'Does this reasoning support its conclusion?'. Well, **if** it is true that 'Most prospective parents would prefer to have sons', then doesn't it follow that 'if people can choose the sex of their child, it is likely that there will eventually be more males than females in the population'? If people **prefer** boys and **can get** boys, doesn't it seem very likely that more boys than girls will be born? It is surely hard to see much wrong with that inference (as such a move is usually called; see chapter 8).

The next reason is, 'This could produce serious social problems' and the question is whether this claim is acceptable. It is not quite so easy to say how to judge this reason. Much surely depends on the scale of the problem – if there is a small surplus of boys this might create little or no social problems, but if it is large, the story might be different. Also, it might matter where these surpluses occur, some societies coping better than others with the imbalance. Furthermore, if the surplus of boys takes a long time to develop, some societies might find ways of adapting to it. This one is hard to judge, but, on the face of it, one can see that this could produce problems.

The next question is, 'Do the preceding claims support the conclusion that "we should prohibit the use of techniques which enable people to choose the sex of their children" '? Well, if allowing these techniques to be used does produce a surplus of boys which will in turn produce serious social problems maybe we should ban them. There is certainly a case here, perhaps not conclusive but a case to be answered.

But there is another question we should ask, namely, 'Are there other relevant considerations/arguments?'. This is the point in thinking about an issue where we often have to be imaginative, 'think outside the box' or even be quite creative. Well, we will leave this as a question for the moment, since this is not our main concern in this chapter (but see chapter 9 for much more on this).

Question 6.2

Think of as many further considerations/arguments as you can which are relevant to the question of banning the use of these techniques for choosing the sex of children.

To summarise: once you are reasonably clear what an author is saying, what his or her reasons and conclusions are, you are in a position to evaluate the reasoning. This involves asking the three quite different questions we have discussed before you come to your overall judgement.

In this chapter and the next we shall concentrate on the first of these three questions: how should you judge whether claims (which may be explicit or assumed) are acceptable to you – or should be accepted by the intended audience?

6.2 Different kinds of claims

First we need to note that people can make rather different *kinds* of claims when arguing a case. For example, some claims present *facts*, *evidence* or *data*, others express *value judgements*, others state *definitions*, *criteria* or *principles*, others give *causal explanations*, and yet others *recommend* that we should take a certain course of action, to name some important ones considered in this book. For example, here is a factual claim, 'According to official figures, 13 per cent of the UK population lives in poverty.' Here is a value judgement, 'It is shameful that such a rich society as the UK allows so many people to live in poverty.' Here is a famous definition, 'Individuals, families and groups in the population can be said to be in poverty when they lack the resources to obtain the types of diet, participate in the activities and have the living conditions and amenities that are customary, or at least widely encouraged or approved, in the societies to which they belong' (Townsend, *Poverty in the United Kingdom* 1979, p. 31). Here is a causal claim, 'Poverty in the UK has many causes, including unemployment, low pay, low educational achievement and long term illness.' And here is a recommendation, 'The Government should try to eliminate child poverty over the next twenty years.'

Clearly claims which are of such different kinds have to be evaluated in different ways, so it is important for you to be able to recognise what sort of claim is being made.

Question 6.3

Consider the following argument and identify which claims are factual, which are value judgements and which are definitions before reading on:

> Many people claim that violence on TV has no effect on people's behaviour. I am sure this is false because if what was shown on TV did not affect behaviour, TV advertising would not work and we know it does. However, even if it is true that TV violence affects people's behaviour, that is still no reason for censorship because people should be free to watch what they choose. Freedom means being able to do what you want to do.

Clearly, in this passage the author makes the *factual claims* that 'violence on TV affects people's behaviour' and that 'TV advertising works'; she also makes the *value* claim that 'people should be free to watch what they choose'; and she gives a *definition* of 'freedom' as 'being able to do what you want to do'.

Clearly, such different kinds of claims need to be assessed quite differently. On the one hand it is proper to ask for **evidence** that TV violence affects people's behaviour or that TV advertising works, which are both *factual* claims.

Question 6.4

What kinds of evidence would show such claims to be true or false?

On the other hand, defending (or attacking) the claim that 'people should be free to watch what they please' may require us to consider the possible consequences of such a principle (for which we may be able to produce some factual evidence) and may also require reference to other moral, legal and political principles.

Question 6.5

What might these be?

And, finally, a definition of the term 'freedom' is different from a factual claim or a value judgement, and needs to be evaluated either in terms of accuracy (Is this normal usage?) or in terms of its utility (Is it a good definition for the purpose in hand?).

In short, factual claims may require evidence; value claims may require to be judged in terms of their likely consequences and other values; and definitions may need to be judged in the way we explained in chapter 5. Of course, in any given case, claims of all these different kinds might be uncontroversial and might thus require no further justification; however, the point is that if they do require further justification this will need to be appropriate to the claim being made.

Question 6.6

Look at Questions appendix, passage 53 ['Acupuncture'] and see if you can find a factual claim, a value judgement, a causal claim, a recommendation or a definition (you will not find them all). Say very briefly how you would evaluate the ones you find.

6.3 The acceptability of claims

The question of acceptability is often about credibility, to which we shall return shortly. However, value judgements and definitions may be accepted or rejected without credibility being an issue; furthermore, a factual claim might be acceptable simply because it is 'generally accepted', so, again, credibility might not be an issue. Thus we begin with some general questions on acceptability, which then lead into considerations about credibility. (Remember, of course, that whether a claim is acceptable may depend on first clarifying what it means; but we have already dealt with this issue in the previous chapter.)

6.3.1 How certain is it claimed to be?

As we explained earlier (section 2.5):

> Sometimes, in expressing a claim, we use language like the following 'my intuition/faith/opinion/view/thesis is . . .', 'I am certain that/I can't prove it but I believe that . . .', 'the facts are/appear to be . . .', 'I observe(d)/saw that . . .', (etc.)

This and similar language indicates both where our views came from ('I observed it' or 'It is my faith that . . .') and how sure we are of them – or how strongly we are committed to them ('I am certain that . . .' or 'My hunch is that . . .'). Clearly then, if someone says in the course of their argument that they have a 'hunch' that their country's central bank is about to raise interest rates, this may well be acceptable in the context (as a hunch – and no more) whereas if they say they are certain this is going to happen, this may need much more justification to be acceptable. A 'hunch' does not need much defence; a claim to 'certainty' may (unless, for example, it is plain for all to see).

Thus, whether a claim is acceptable may depend on the strength of commitment which the author's language suggests; a given claim may well be acceptable as a 'guess' or a 'possibility' (say, at an early stage in an investigation), but its acceptability will be judged by more severe standards if it is presented as being true or even 'certain'.

6.3.2 Does the context of the claim influence its acceptability

Imagine a detective reasoning with colleagues at an early stage of her investigation, saying, 'I think the butler did it . . .', it may be perfectly legitimate to 'think aloud' in this way on the basis of relatively little evidence in such a situation; it would be clear from the context that this was an 'informed guess' rather than a 'proven fact' and as such it could be perfectly acceptable to all concerned as a basis for their further enquiries. Of course, if the same detective made the same claim at the butler's trial, whether the claim was acceptable would depend on whether it was based on sufficiently convincing evidence.

So whether a claim is acceptable might depend on the context in which it is made.

6.3.3 Does it require expertise/research to decide?

Sometimes reasons which are given for some conclusion require specialist knowledge or expertise to decide whether they are acceptable, and sometimes you will have this knowledge and sometimes not. For example, here is an argument about the effects of smoking cigarettes in Britain:

> In Great Britain about 300,000 people die each year from heart disease, while about 55,000 die from lung cancer. Heavy smoking approximately doubles one's chances of dying from heart disease, and increases the chance of dying of lung cancer by a factor of about ten. Most people will conclude that smoking is more likely to cause lung cancer than heart disease and indeed both in Britain and elsewhere government campaigns against smoking have been largely based on this assumption. But it is false. If one takes into account the greater frequency of heart disease, then for every smoker who brings lung cancer on himself there will be more than two who die of self-induced coronary illness.

Clearly, whether this argument has any weight depends on whether the first two sentences are true and most readers will not have this specialist knowledge. Where such expertise is required, it may be difficult or impossible for you to judge the strength of an argument (though research in a reliable source might enable you to do so).

6.3.4 Is it widely known or believed?

Sometimes a reason which is presented in support of a conclusion is widely known or believed. For example, someone might begin an argument with the claim:

> Since the Earth is roughly spherical . . .

In any normal context, it would be pedantic to raise questions about the acceptability of the claim, so in appraising the argument we should simply accept this reason as true. Of course, there might be specialised, scientific contexts in which it was right to challenge the claim (as being inaccurate or misleading for the purpose in hand) but for normal purposes it cannot seriously be doubted. To take another example, someone might begin an argument by saying:

> It is morally wrong to commit murder so . . .

and this is acceptable in most contexts (outside the debating club or the philosophy classroom!).

6.3.5 How well does it fit with our other beliefs?

Sometimes the reason you are considering 'fits well' with other beliefs you hold and sometimes it does not. For example, someone might begin an argument about global warming with the claim that, 'There is clear evidence that sea levels have risen during the past 50 years', which fits well with everything else you know and believe so you have no real reason to challenge it. However, someone might begin their reasoning about Darwin's theory of evolution by saying, 'I accept what is written in the book of Genesis about God creating the world in seven days', and you might feel there is no scope for further discussion because this view is so remote from your own. In general, some new belief might fit well with other things you believe and might therefore be plausible and easy to believe, or it might not fit well and therefore seem unlikely given your other beliefs.

Question 6.7

In each of the following say what you can about the acceptability of the claims made there.

6.7.1 The first three paragraphs of passage 57 in the Questions appendix.
6.7.2 Questions appendix, passage 53.
6.7.3 The huge Norwegian company called Norsk Hydro wants to grow more fish in the sea by spreading fertiliser over the ocean. The company, which is the world's biggest producer of fertilisers, believes that this will grow more marine algae, which in turn will encourage the expansion of fish stocks. Marine scientists from Sweden and Canada who reviewed the plan at the request of the Norwegian Research Council say it is unlikely to work. They say it ignores basic principles of marine ecology and could do irreversible damage. (Adapted from 'Norway's fish plan "a recipe for disaster" ', *New Scientist*, 13 January 1996, p. 4)

6.3.6 Is it from a credible source?

Sometimes we have good reason to accept or reject a claim because of the source from which we learn it, and this is so important that we shall devote the rest of the chapter and the next to discussing the different considerations which apply. We introduce this question now simply as one of the questions you need to ask when deciding whether a claim – in particular a reason presented in the course of arguing a case – is acceptable or not.

6.4 To summarise, a thinking map for judging acceptability

'Thinking Map'

JUDGING ACCEPTABILITY SKILFULLY

1 How **certain** is it claimed to be?
2 Does the **context** of the claim influence its acceptability?
3 Does it require **expertise/research** to decide?
4 Is it **widely known** or believed?
5 How well does it **fit** with our other beliefs?
6 Is it from a **credible source**?

This last question of the thinking map is very important because most of what we learn is learned from others. We learn from teachers, experts, parents, friends, television, radio, newspapers, magazines, learned journals, textbooks, the Internet and many other sources. The question is, 'Which of these can we believe?', and we will now discuss how to answer this question.

6.5 Judging the credibility of sources skilfully

6.5.1 Some initial examples

Since so much of what we learn is learnt from other people, any activity which aims to improve our critical thinking has to deal with the questions about whom one should believe (and to what extent), on what subjects and in what contexts. We begin with some examples:

Example 1
You are considering buying a second-hand car, but, since you know very little about cars, you have employed an expert mechanic (who is not acquainted with and has no other connection with the present owners) to check the vehicle over; he tells you that the car is in good condition and that it would be a good buy. Should you believe him and why or why not?

Example 2
You are reading an article in a popular magazine which mainly reports stories about extraordinary events, such as sightings of UFOs, visits from 'aliens', statues of saints weeping real tears, etc. The story which catches your eye states that there are human beings living in a remote part of Africa who have several 'horns', each about four inches long growing out of their backs, rather as some dinosaurs did millions of years ago. The article refuses to say where in Africa these people live because it wants to 'protect them from interference by the outside world'. What credence should you attach to this article and why?

Example 3

You are learning to drive with a driving instructor who has taught many of your friends and acquaintances and has a good reputation among them as a driving instructor. You ask her about a particular driving problem and she gives you quite categorical advice, saying 'In this sort of case you must . . .' Again, should you believe her and why or why not?

Example 4

You are watching an evening TV news programme in which a reporter is describing the British Government's new immigration policy, following a news conference on the subject given by a Government spokesman earlier in the day. Should you believe the news report, and why or why not? To what extent do you think the report is, or is not, a reliable source of information on this subject?

In each of these examples, the question is similar. It is, 'Given the source of the "information" and the context, to what extent should I be inclined to believe it? Is it very likely to be true, very unlikely to be true, or somewhere in between? And why do I think that?' And to answer that question, we have to ask a prior question, which is, 'How **credible** are these sources on this subject and in these circumstances?'

Question 6.8

Before you read on write your own notes in response to the questions contained in examples (1)–(4) above, taking special care to say *why* you make the judgement you do.

6.5.2 Discussion of example (1): should you accept the mechanic's advice?

Of course, what we really want to know is whether **the car is in good condition** for its age and whether it is **worth** the price. But, since we are not expert enough to judge these things ourselves, we have to get advice. Now the question is, 'How credible is the mechanic we have asked to advise us?' In Britain there are motoring organisations, like the Automobile Association (AA), who are reputable and who will provide this service for a fee; let us suppose that we have hired such a mechanic to check our vehicle over. Then, in normal circumstances, we can be reasonably confident in accepting his advice. This is essentially because; (i) he has the relevant **expertise** – he has been trained and he knows what to look for, (ii) he does not know the sellers – so there is no **pressure** on him from that source to hide anything from us, he has no **bias** as we might say, and (iii) the organisation for which he works has a good **reputation** in connection with providing this service.

Of course, none of this will absolutely **guarantee** that his report is correct – that what he says is **true** – but reasons (i)–(iii) above give us *good reason* to accept his judgement in the circumstances. If it mattered to us a great deal, we might get someone else with the relevant expertise to check the car too, perhaps a friend or relative (whose judgement we also had good reason to trust) and if their judgement agreed with the AA mechanic's (**corroborating** his judgement) this would give us even greater confidence in our intended purchase. (If they disagree, then we have a problem about whom to believe.)

We cannot be experts about everything and we often need to rely on what other people tell us. Think how often you believe something because you were told it by a teacher, relative or friend, or you saw a report about it on TV or heard it on the radio or you read it in a newspaper, textbook, journal or magazine of some kind. Most of what we learn we learn from other people. That is why it is so important to be clear about whom to believe and in what circumstances.

6.5.3 Discussion of example (2); should you believe the magazine report about 'dinosaur' people?

On the face of it, this story is not at all credible. There are several reasons for saying this: (i) The claims about human beings having 'horns' growing out of their backs is contrary to all (other) evidence about human beings. We know a great deal about human physiology and we know a great deal about the variations among different human beings. The claims about horns growing out of people's backs conflict with everything else we know and are thus inherently implausible; this is a fact about the **nature of the claim** (see section 7.4). (ii) The magazine is not a serious scientific journal (which would be careful about checking its facts) but a popular magazine (which mainly 'reports' extraordinary events, events which are contrary to most things we know). Given what we know about the magazine, it is more likely to have a reputation for telling far-fetched stories than for being able to verify them; this is a matter of its **reputation**. (iii) The article refuses to say where these people live and thus makes it impossible to check the **evidence** for this story, so there is no possibility of **corroboration**. These are surely reasons enough seriously to doubt the truth of this story.

Question 6.9

There are two parts to this question:

6.9.1 Suppose the article carried a 'photograph' of people with 'horns' growing out of their backs. How would that affect its credibility?

6.9.2 In the light of our discussions of examples (1) and (2) see if you want to amend or supplement the answers you gave in response to Question 6.8 for examples (3) and (4).

6.6 Credibility is different from truth, but helps us judge what is true

Notice that although we make judgements about credibility in order to help us decide what is true, credibility and truth are different. To see the difference, suppose that Fred, who has a long criminal record for theft and is well known to be an habitual liar, is found in possession of a stolen TV. When he denies having stolen the TV, should we believe him – does he deserve to be believed? Given his record and, other things being equal, he almost certainly does not deserve to be believed – his **reputation** means that his credibility is very low and we have no good reason to believe him, *though he may be telling the truth on this occasion.*

Conversely, we may have good reason to believe someone who tells us something which is in fact false; for example, suppose that Mary is well known to us as an expert 'twitcher' (bird-spotter) and suppose that she identifies a bird which is flying quickly past us as a flycatcher 'because of that distinctive flight'. Given her **expertise**, we have good reason to believe her – her credibility is high, *though she may in fact be mistaken on this occasion.*

The general point is that we judge someone's credibility on various grounds (and of course without knowing independently whether what they say is true or false) and we do this as a guide to deciding on the truth of what they say, but this is not an infallible guide.

The question then is how we can tell when to accept another person's word (or to what extent we should be willing to rely on their word).

Though this is often difficult to decide, there are some principles which can help us, even though they do not guarantee that we make the right judgement. We *do* often rely on what other people tell us; this is often entirely reasonable (and it is a mistake to think, for example, that all *appeals to authority* are fallacious, as philosophers have sometimes suggested), but it is not always safe. So let us now move to thinking about the principles we should apply in trying to judge the credibility of sources skilfully.

6.7 To summarise

Chapters 2–5 dealt with the process of understanding reasoning. The remaining chapters deal with evaluating arguments. In this chapter we explain how to decide whether reasons which are presented in support of a conclusion are acceptable.

We first distinguish five different kinds of claims – factual claims, value judgements, definitions, causal explanations and recommendations – and point out that their differences mean they have to be evaluated in different ways. We also give you some practice in recognising these differences.

We then explain some tests for deciding whether a claim is acceptable. These are:

1 How **certain** is it claimed to be?
2 Does the **context** of the claim influence its acceptability?
3 Does it require **expertise/research** to decide?
4 Is it **widely known** or believed?
5 How well does it **fit** with our other beliefs?
6 Is it from a **credible source**?

The last question leads us into an initial discussion of credibility, but this is such a large subject most of the discussion is reserved for the next chapter.

Further reading

Ennis (1996, chapters 4 and 5).

7

Judging the credibility of sources skilfully

Since so many of our beliefs are based on what other people tell us, in writing, on TV or by word of mouth, the critical thinker needs to know how to decide who to believe and in what circumstances. The criteria which apply will depend on the case, but relevant considerations will often include:

- the source's **reputation** for reliability (contrast the BBC and the *Sun* newspaper),
- whether the source has a **vested interest** (e.g., someone accused of war crimes who denies any responsibility),
- whether there is **corroboration** of the claim from independent sources (as when it was claimed that 'cold fusion' had been produced),
- whether the source has the relevant **expertise/training** (as when a police officer gives evidence in court),
- the **nature of the claim** itself (as when someone claims to have witnessed a miracle),
- whether the source can provide **credible reasons** for the claim they make (as when someone claims to have encountered 'aliens' from another planet).

We shall divide what we say on this topic into five sections; these will deal with questions about:

(i)   the **person/source** whose credibility we wish to judge,
(ii) the **circumstances/context in which the claim is made** which affect its credibility,

(iii) the **justification the source offers or can offer in support of the claim** which affects its credibility,

(iv) the **nature of the claim** which influence its credibility,

(v) whether there is **corroboration** from other sources.

Thus, for example, a British policeman (the source) might testify in court (the context) that he saw (the justification) the defendant pass a sword through a woman on stage (nature of the claim), and others might testify that they saw it too (corroboration); or a newspaper reporter employed on the US *National Enquirer* (the person) might report in that newspaper (the context) that he had been informed (the justification) that the Titanic had resurfaced (nature of the claim), and that the US Navy had eye-witness reports about this remarkable event (corroboration) (such a report was really published in the *National Enquirer* a few years ago). The division of our comments into these categories is arbitrary to some extent (for example, where should one put the discussion of vested interest?) but it helps to organise one's questioning.

7.1 Questions about the *person/source* whose credibility we wish to judge

7.1.1 Do they have the relevant expertise (experience, knowledge and, perhaps, formal qualifications)?

Suppose you are walking in the mountains with an expert geologist when you find some strange rocks, 'Yes', she says, 'it is not so very unusual to find evidence of volcanic activity in these mountains because that is how they were formed millions of years ago.' In the normal course of events you believe what she says because of her expertise – because she has the experience and knowledge to know what she is talking about. If she then goes on to tell you that the bird you can see gliding in the distance is probably an eagle you may have less reason to believe her unless you also know that she is an expert on birds too (or at least on the birds in that area). In general, if someone has sufficient experience and knowledge in a given domain, then that gives us good reason to believe what they say about such matters. Of course it doesn't guarantee the truth of what they say, but it gives us reason to believe them in normal circumstances.

Robert Ennis describes a case for which he was a member of the jury where a pathologist gave evidence to the court and says the jury accepted her as an expert because 'she was a medical doctor regularly employed by the civil authorities to do autopsies. She testified that she had performed over 200 of them . . .' (Ennis, 1996, p. 58).

> Having background experience and knowledge does not guarantee that a person will be right about something. It only helps to make the person's statement more credible. The person, we then think, is at least in a position to make accurate statements. The criterion can be stated as follows: *The person should have the background training and experience appropriate for making the statement.* (Ennis, 1996, pp. 58, 59)

As our examples show, having the relevant experience and expertise to be a reliable source of information is sometimes a matter of having formal training and qualifications, though often it is not.

Question 7.1

How does **this** question apply to examples (3) and (4) in section 6.5.1? (You would need to consider other questions before reaching an overall judgement.)

7.1.2 Do they have the ability to observe accurately (eyesight, hearing, proximity to event, absence of distractions, appropriate instruments, etc.)?

Let us introduce another example to illustrate this principle.

Example 1

Consider the following case: there is a cross-roads with traffic lights on both roads and there has just been a collision between a red car and a white one (all as shown on the diagram). The driver of the white car accuses the driver of the red car of having jumped the red light; the red car driver denies this. A mother and child were waiting to cross the road as shown on the diagram; the mother says the red car driver did jump the red light and the child says he didn't. A policeman was also watching the junction and he says the red car driver did jump the red light. Now the question is, 'Why should you believe or disbelieve and why?'

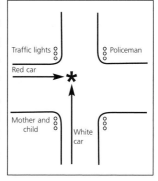

Question 7.2

If you need further information in order to decide whether a witness is credible, then note down the further information which is relevant to deciding the question before you read on.

Clearly, in a case like this we would want to be sure that all the witnesses had good eyesight, were not under the influence of drugs which distort perception (like alcohol), had a clear view of what was happening on the junction, and were attending to it – to the extent that these conditions are **not** fulfilled the credibility of a witness's evidence is reduced. For example, if the mother's attention was partly distracted because the child was having a tantrum, her testimony is less reliable. Again, if one of the drivers was driving under the influence of alcohol, this would reduce their credibility as witnesses.

Notice that in this example as described, only ordinary human eyesight and hearing were employed by those giving evidence. But, suppose the driver of the red car had slurred speech and smelled of alcohol, leading the policeman to suspect that the level of alcohol in his blood was above the legal limit, then appropriate instruments would be used to obtain evidence about the level of alcohol in his blood. This would require the driver either to breath into a breathalyser or to submit to a blood test and any evidence that was given about the level of alcohol in his blood would have to depend on the correct instruments being used in the prescribed way, and the reliability of the evidence would depend crucially on this.

There are many situations in which we base claims not simply on the evidence of our senses but on the readings of instruments. For example, when we buy petrol for our car we normally assume that the gauge correctly reads the quantity of petrol we have pumped into our tank, when we buy vegetables we assume the scales correctly measure the weight, and so on. It is common in the sciences to use instruments to measure all manner of things – speed, energy, distance, wavelength, viscosity, etc. – and these always need to be the right instruments correctly used if the claims based on their use are to be reliable.

Sometimes there is dispute about whether someone has used the appropriate instruments correctly in arriving at a judgement. For example, breathalyser evidence is often contested. It is also quite common in science to dispute what others claim to have witnessed, using various instruments, if their results cannot be corroborated by other groups of scientists (as happened a few years ago when two well-known physicists claimed to have found evidence of 'cold fusion'). A classic case of this occurred when Galileo claimed to see the moons of Jupiter through a telescope in 1610. No one had used a telescope to see such things before and many people were sceptical about what Galileo's 'tube' really showed. We have similar disputes these days when people claim to have photographed UFOs.

Question 7.3

Assuming all the witnesses had good eyesight, were not under the influence of any drugs, had a clear view of what was happening on the junction and were attending to it (except the child, who was having a tantrum), write notes on how the evidence is beginning to stack up and why.

7.1.3 Does their reputation suggest they are reliable?

Closely related to the question of experience and knowledge is a person's (or other source's) *reputation* for being honest, or telling the truth, or being correct. Reverting to an earlier example, someone with a long criminal record who is well known to be an habitual liar does not deserve to be believed when he is found in possession of a stolen TV which he denies stealing. His reputation for dishonesty means that his credibility is very low in a situation like this.

By contrast, the BBC is widely regarded as a reliable source of news and information about world affairs. It has a reputation for accuracy. This reputation has been established over many years of reporting and normally gives us good reason to accept any particular BBC news report. Of course, this reputation does not mean that the BBC is *always* right, but its reputation is based on general agreement that it has *mostly* been right in the past.

In contrast to the BBC, many newspapers have a quite different reputation, a reputation for 'disregarding the truth' or simply for carelessness, and this reduces their credibility in the case of any particular news story, for example, the magazine we considered in example 2 of section 6.5 was unlikely to have a reputation for carefully reporting the truth.

The reputation of academics and teachers is often very important in deciding whether to accept their views in their areas of expertise. For example, a teacher may be renowned for her knowledge of mediaeval history and may have established a reputation for reliability in that domain, and that reputation alone gives us good reason to accept what she says about her special subject (though she might also be very unreliable about some other things, like judging the qualities of people). By contrast, a physicist may have established a reputation for eccentric physical theories which he can not prove and will thus be suspect when speaking on such matters (but might be very reliable about some other things, like judging the merits of different cars).

Question 7.4

Think of a couple of examples of people or 'sources' (like the BBC) you know and identify the areas in which they have a well-justified reputation for reliability and those in which they do not.

7.1.4 Does the source have a vested interest or bias?

Think back to example 1 in section 6.5. Suppose the salesperson tells you that the car is a bargain. How much credence should you attach to her claim? Almost certainly not much because she is very probably paid by commission on the sales she makes, **so she has a financial interest in selling the car rather than in giving strictly truthful information**. You might also imagine a friend urging you not to buy the car, because she hated such cars after having been injured by one in an accident. This would not be a case of vested interest, but would display a bias based on no good reason.

Suppose you are watching a TV report of a civil war which is raging between two ethnic groups in country X. Suppose also that the commander of one side in the conflict has been accused of war crimes by the International Red Cross; during the TV report he denies quite categorically that he ever gave the orders of which he is accused. Presumably one should give less credence to his declaration **because he has much to lose if the charge against him is proved true**.

Sometimes people are paid to say certain things – as when a football star is paid to advertise a particular breakfast cereal, saying that 'it makes you feel good all day'. Sometimes people are at risk when they say certain things – as when a witness in a trial is warned by the Mafia not to say what he knows (maybe they 'make him an offer he can't refuse'). In cases like these, there is often good reason to doubt the truth of what is said, **because the speaker may have something to lose or gain from doing other than telling the plain, unvarnished truth**.

Question 7.5

You are listening to a court case in which Rufus, who collided with another car, is accused of driving at twice the speed limit in the city and with three times the legal limit of alcohol in his blood. Rufus denies the charges but the doctor who attended the accident tells the court that Rufus smelled very strongly of alcohol and blood tests showed alcohol in his blood at three times the legal limit. Who is credible and why?

In general, the credibility of an informant is weakened if they **appear** to have an incentive to do something other than simply tell the truth – if they would gain by doing something else or lose by telling the truth. The salesperson who is trying to sell you the car is almost certainly paid by commission (because most are), so we assume she has an incentive to be less than wholly truthful. Similarly with the other cases – what matters is whether the speakers **appear** to have an incentive to be dishonest, or to be 'economical with the truth', or to 'varnish the truth', etc. (For example, in the case of the witness who has **actually** been 'got at' by the Mafia, if there is no suspicion that he has been threatened, then there is every reason to believe him – unless his credibility can be challenged on other grounds.)

Question 7.6

Think of two examples of your own which illustrate how credibility can be affected by vested interest or bias.

7.2 Questions about the *circumstances/context in which the claim is made* which affect its credibility

The same claim might be made in very different circumstances. For example, someone might say to friends in a bar that he saw A stab B or he might say this on oath in a court of law. If a reputable, refereed medical journal publishes a report that a cure has been found for AIDS, this carries more weight than if a report with similar claims is published in a tabloid newspaper. If a Member of the British Parliament, alleges in Parliament that Jones has acted illegally, he is protected from prosecution by 'Parliamentary Privilege', so this often reduces the credibility of what is said (since the author does not risk legal action). Someone might claim within hours of B's death that he had seen A stab B or he might make this claim many years later; because memory is fallible and for other reasons we tend to attach less credence to claims which are remote in time from the events to which they refer (though this is not always the case).

Look back to example 4 in section 6.5.1:

> You are watching an evening TV news programme in which a reporter is describing the British Government's new immigration

policy, following a news conference on the subject given by a Government spokesman earlier in the day. Should you believe the news report, and why, or why not? To what extent do you think the report is, or is not, a reliable source of information on this subject? Do you need to know more in order to know how much credence to give the report? If so, what?

A news report on a reputable news programme warrants far more credence than a similar story overheard in a bar, just as evidence given in a court of law carries more credence than the same claims made in the course of gossiping to neighbours. In this case, of course, the source of the report is a Government spokesman who will want to portray the policy in the best possible light so that may raise questions about its credibility, but that is another issue.

7.3 Questions about the *justification the source offers or can offer in support of the claim* which affects credibility

Suppose a close friend tells you that she is quite convinced that aliens visit the Earth and land here in space-ships. You ask her why she believes this and she is unable to give any reason; she just says that is what she believes. On the other hand, she might say she has witnessed just that in a clearing in the woods; she might say that she knows it sounds crazy, but she has seen a spaceship land and aliens leave it and walk about. Alternatively, she might say that though she has never seen any such thing, she has read many convincing reports from reputable scientists who claim to have seen this kind of thing and she believes them.

If someone can offer no justification for what they claim, one has little reason to take it seriously or to give it any credence. But if they can give reasons, grounds or evidence, these will often affect the decision as to whether it is reasonable to believe what they say. However, there are several different kinds of evidence/[reasons] people can produce and these need to be assessed differently in deciding credibility.

7.3.1 'I witnessed X' versus 'she told me X'

Someone's justification for her claim (that aliens land on Earth, or whatever) might be that she has 'seen it with her own eyes' or otherwise perceived it with one of her other senses; in this case she claims to have personal, 'direct' or 'first hand' knowledge of what is reported. This is obviously very different from reporting what has been learned from others and raises quite different questions so far as its credibility is concerned.

To take another example, I may report that there has been an explosion in the World Trade Center in New York, on the ground that I saw it reported by CNN; this is obviously quite different from claiming to have witnessed it myself, but if my source is reliable (and CNN is) then my claim gains in credibility because of that.

Of course, sometimes when one's justification is that someone else told you, this may make it unreliable (or unreliable for some purposes). Suppose Jones is accused of shooting his wife and that Mrs Smith may have been an eye-witness, but our only evidence for this is that Mr Smith tells us his wife told him she saw Jones do it. Here Mr Smith's evidence is what the courts call 'hearsay' evidence, not 'direct' evidence that Jones shot his wife, and though it may strongly suggest to the lay person that Jones did it (assuming the Smiths have no dispute with the Jones, etc.), it would not be admitted in a court of law as evidence that Jones shot her. And what this suggests is that there are different standards of proof for different purposes, which of course there are (see section 8.3).

7.3.2 'Primary' versus 'secondary' sources

The distinction we just made in the previous section corresponds quite closely with the distinction made by historians between 'primary' and 'secondary' sources. If we want to know what it was like during the Great Plague in London in 1665, we could either go to the British Museum and search for documents written by people who experienced those events and wrote about them at the time, or we can read a modern historian's account of them. The modern historian makes no pretence to have lived through the experiences she recounts, but her researches will almost certainly involve reading some 'first-hand' accounts of the Plague and some reputable 'secondary' sources, accounts written by historians before her.

7.3.3 'Direct' justification/evidence versus 'circumstantial' evidence

The courts make a distinction between 'direct' evidence and 'circumstantial' evidence. Direct evidence in favour of some claim X whose truth is in question is provided when a witness testifies that he or she witnessed X; circumstantial evidence is contrasted with direct evidence and is evidence of relevant facts from which the claim in question, X, may be inferred. For example, suppose Jones is accused of murdering his wife by shooting her, then if a witness says, 'I saw Jones shoot and kill his wife', this is direct evidence. But, even if no one witnessed Jones shooting his wife, there may be evidence of other relevant facts from which it can be inferred that he did – for example, there may be good evidence that he had a motive (she was having an affair and he was a very jealous man at the best of times) and that he had the opportunity (they were together in their bedroom, where he was known to have kept a gun) and ballistic evidence shows that she was killed by a bullet from his gun, which was found buried in the garden of their house with his finger prints on it. It is sometimes said that circumstantial evidence proves a case by eliminating possibilities. It has been likened to a rope; with one strand it may be unable to carry much weight, but with several it might be quite strong.

Question 7.7

Explain the distinction between direct and circumstantial evidence in the case of the claim that aliens have visited the Earth in a spaceship.

7.3.4 Justifying a claim by direct reference to credibility considerations

It is quite easy to imagine someone justifying her claim to have seen aliens landing in a forest clearing by saying, 'I saw it and I wasn't drunk, visibility was excellent, I have good eyesight and, as anyone will tell you, I have always been sceptical of such claims when others have made them in the past – I am not the gullible type', thus answering some of the credibility questions we might raise and which we have discussed in other sections of this chapter. She might go further, saying, 'What is more, my friend saw it too and scientists who came the next day to photograph the indentations in the soil where the grass had been flattened couldn't explain the marks any other way.' In this case, the person is justifying her claim precisely by invoking the very credibility considerations this chapter is about.

To take another example, it is easy to imagine a scientist reporting some surprising phenomenon and justifying her claim by saying that she used standard equipment, which is well known to be reliable in similar experiments, that observation conditions were good, that the team who did the work has a good record for careful scrutiny of experimental evidence, that her results have subsequently been corroborated in many respects by other scientists trying similar experiments in different places, etc. – in short using credibility considerations to justify her claim.

To give a last example, an expert witness in court might be able to support her judgement in a particular case not only by evidence directly relevant to the claim in question, but also by referring to her training and qualifications, her wide and varied experience, her reputation for reliability, to corroborative evidence, etc. – in short again, to the very credibility considerations we are talking about here.

Question 7.8

How do such considerations apply to the evidence given in the case of the car accident, example 1 in section 7.1.2?

7.4 Questions about the *nature of the claim* which influence its credibility

7.4.1 Is it very unlikely, given other things we know; or is it very plausible and easy to believe?

If a friend tells you that she just had coffee with some mutual friends (in the normal circumstances in which people say such things) this will be easy to believe. But, if she says that she has just had coffee with the Queen of England, this will be harder to believe, because very few people do this. Of course it may still be true, but, in the absence of a much fuller story and some evidence, this is not a very credible claim.

Suppose now that the friend says she has just seen a miracle – she has seen her lover, who had been dead for two days raised up like Lazarus by a priest who prayed over him. How credible would this claim be? David Hume (1711–76) the famous British philosopher had much to say about this kind of claim in his *Enquiries Concerning Human Understanding* (first published 1748, section X). Here is part of his argument:

> When anyone tells me that he saw a dead man restored to life I immediately consider with myself, whether it be more probable, that this person should either deceive or be deceived, or that the fact, which he relates, should really have happened. I weigh the one miracle against the other; and according to the superiority which I discover, I pronounce my decision, and always reject the greater miracle. If the falsehood of his testimony would be more miraculous than the event which he relates; then, and not until then, can he pretend to command my belief or opinion. (David Hume, *Enquiries Concerning Human Understanding*, section X, part

1, para. 91; for more of the argument see Questions appendix, passage 45)

In short, the more unlikely it is that some claim is true, given what else we know, the less its credibility and the more we shall need persuading before we believe it. This was the case with the story about people with 'horns' growing out of their backs.

7.4.2 Is it a basic observation statement or an inferred judgement?

On the face of it there is a distinction between saying, 'I saw a man open the car door using a coat hanger and drive the car away', and saying, 'I saw a man steal the car': in the latter case the speaker is going beyond what she actually saw and is inferring that the man's actions amounted to theft (though he might have lost his keys, etc.).

Question 7.9

Give your own examples of two statements which differ in the way the two statements in our explanation differ.

7.5 Is there *corroboration from other sources?*

In our earlier example 1 (section 7.1.2) of the car accident, two different people, who are quite independent of each other (the mother and the policeman) give the same testimony (that the red car jumped the red light). Let us assume that the evidence of the mother is itself credible on its own account and so is that of the policeman (that is, both had the necessary faculties to witness what happened, both were attending to the scene, neither had a vested interest and so on); in that case the two pieces of evidence corroborate each other. For evidence to be corroborative it must be independent, credible and it must support the claim in question.

Question 7.10

Use the considerations you have studied in this chapter to come to a verdict about whether the red car jumped the red light (example 1). Briefly state your case, citing the credibility considerations which lead you to believe or disbelieve witnesses, making clear any assumptions you make. Obviously, you may draw on your answers to earlier questions.

Of course, all the preceding criteria apply to one's own testimony too, to one's own observations, claims, judgements and conclusions.

7.6 To summarise

The simplest way to summarise the contents of this chapter is to present a thinking map for judging credibility skilfully. In short then, when judging the credibility of sources, the questions you may need to ask are shown in the thinking map.

JUDGING CREDIBILITY SKILFULLY

1 Questions about the **person/source:**
(a) Do they have the relevant expertise (experience, knowledge, and perhaps formal qualifications)?
(b) Do they have the ability to observe accurately (eyesight, hearing, proximity to event, absence of distractions, appropriate instruments, skill in using instruments)?
(c) Does their reputation suggest they are reliable?
(d) Does the source have a vested interest or bias?

2 Questions about the **circumstances/context** in which the claim is made.

3 Questions about the **justification** the source offers or can offer in support of the claim:
(a) Did the source 'witness X' or was he 'told about X'?
(b) Is it based on 'primary' and 'secondary' sources?
(c) Is it based on 'direct' or on 'circumstantial' evidence?
(d) Is it based on direct reference to credibility considerations?

4 Questions about the **nature of the claim** which influence its credibility:
(a) Is it very unlikely, given other things we know; or is it very plausible and easy to believe.
(b) Is it a basic observation statement or an inferred judgement?

5 Is there **corroboration** from other sources?

Here are some concluding exercises, some of which are quite extended. Doing one or two of these some time after you have studied this chapter will help to consolidate the good habits which I hope you will have developed during working on this chapter.

Question 7.11

7.11.1 Refer back to question 1.8 about Bertha and Cheryl and use cred-ibility considerations to decide who is being more reasonable.

7.11.2 See the Questions appendix, passage 11. What is your response to the claims made there?

7.11.3 What is your response to the Questions appendix, passage 41 [Kosovo] in the light of the current chapter?

7.11.4 Answer the question set in Questions appendix, passage 42 [AS level question 1].

7.11.5 Answer the question set in Questions appendix, passage 43 [AS level question 2].

7.11.6 Answer the question set in Questions appendix, passage 44 [AS level question 3].

Further reading

R. Swartz and S. Parks (1993) or (1994) on credibility.

Evaluating inferences: deductive validity and other grounds

We commonly *infer* all sorts of things from other things we know. For example, if you know that Mary is a normal newborn human baby, you might infer that she cannot yet feed herself, walk or talk – and you could be very confident about such inferences. We also make inferences about which we cannot be so confident; for example, if you know that John is an eighteen year old British student you might infer that he is likely to have a mobile phone (because so many do) but of course you can not be sure of this in John's case. Scientists commonly infer beliefs from their observations and experiments and sometimes they are very confident about them and sometimes less so. For example, many experts in the field are very confident that the evidence allows them to infer that birds evolved from dinosaurs (this has to be an *inference* since no one could have watched it happening!). However, the same experts are less sure whether the evidence allows them to infer that the first birds began to fly by leaping off high places, like trees, or by running fast from predators flapping their rudimentary 'wings'; some experts make one inference from the evidence, some the other, and neither is wholly confident of their view. To give a last but famous example, Sherlock Holmes was a great one for making inferences (which he called 'deductions') and for inferring clever insights from the sorts of facts most of us do not even notice; thus, in *The Science of Deduction* Holmes infers from the pawn-brokers' scratched numbers inside a valuable watch that the owner had gone through successive periods of impoverishment and prosperity – the former forcing him to pawn the watch and the latter allowing him to redeem it. Holmes comments on these inferences, 'Where is the mystery in all this?'. Time for us to unravel the 'mystery' in inferences.

8.1 What inferences are

In the examples we just discussed people start from one or more beliefs and 'move' from these to other beliefs which they take to be justified by the first ones. In effect they use arguments of the kind we have been discussing throughout this book. When we argue a case we present reasons – which we take to be true or otherwise acceptable – and we present these as *supporting* our conclusion, interpretation, decision or whatever. To put it differently, we *infer* our conclusion from our reasons. Arguments always consist of both reasons and inferences and 'inferences' are the *moves* we make from reasons to conclusions, the moves in which we say 'R1 (etc.) *therefore* [the conclusion]', or 'given these reasons I conclude that . . .' with varying degrees of confidence. Thus, in the argument:

> some people have solved their own unemployment problem by great ingenuity in searching for a job or by willingness to work for less, so all the unemployed could do this,

the inference is the *move* from 'some people have solved their own unemployment problem . . .' to 'all the unemployed could do this'. Someone who presents this argument, as Margaret Thatcher's Ministers did, believes that the first claim justifies the second (and hence can be inferred from it). Whether it does is another matter – and is the interesting question.

Question 8.1

Identify the **inferences** in the following passages:

8.1.1   Questions appendix, passage 1.
8.1.2   Questions appendix, passage 3.
8.1.3   Questions appendix, passage 10.
8.1.4   Questions appendix, passage 17.
8.1.5   Questions appendix, passage 36.
8.1.6   Questions appendix, passage 39.

8.2 An initial test for good inferences

Once we are clear what inferences are, we want to be able to judge when they are good and when they are not. In the previous two chapters we looked at what can be said about judging the acceptability of reasons, but generally speaking reasons and inferences have to be evaluated *quite differently*. In most cases, it is one thing to judge whether the reasons presented in some argument are true or otherwise acceptable; it is quite another thing to judge whether the inferences based upon those reasons are justified. Let us illustrate the difference with an instructive example:

Example 1

Women's brains are on average smaller than men's, **therefore** women are less intelligent than men.

Question 8.2

Before reading on, say whether this is a good or a bad inference/argument and say **why** that is your view.

When I use this example with students, nearly everyone says it is a bad argument, but it is not quite so easy to say why. People tend to say that they do not know whether the reason is true or false but they are sure the conclusion is false. When pressed, they say something like 'even if the reason is true, there is no connection of the kind suggested between brain size and intelligence, so the reason does not support the conclusion' or 'even if the reason is true, I am sure the conclusion is false, so it cannot be a good argument'. (Perhaps your answer to question 8.2 resembled one of these?) Both these responses are right. The first one points to the fact that we expect to be able to see some reasonably secure *connection* between reason and conclusion if the one is to justify the other – a *link* we can understand and accept in the light of everything else we believe. The second says that if the reason is true but there are reasons (other relevant considerations) for thinking the conclusion could be false it *cannot* be a good inference.

Both these ideas yield *tests* for deciding whether an inference is a good one. Since the second one has been very influential in the history of thinking about inferences, that is the one we shall introduce here. It provides us with a rather fierce test for deciding whether an inference is acceptable but it is a good place to start. The basic idea is that if the reason(s) do not *compel* you to accept the conclusion – *if you can think of some way in which the reasons could be true and the conclusion false at the same time* – then the inference fails. To set this out in the fairly broad terms in which we have been dealing with arguments, the test to apply when judging an inference is:

> *Could the reason(s) be true (or otherwise acceptable) and the conclusion*
> *false (or otherwise unacceptable) at the same time?*

If the answer is 'No' then the inference – the move from reasons to conclusion – is a good one and compels you to accept the conclusion if the reasons are true. However, if the answer to that question is 'Yes', then the inference fails (or is not justified).

To return to our example, the reason is in fact **true** (if you check this in a given community, say the UK, you will find that women's brains are on average smaller). However, even allowing for the vagueness of the conclusion that women are less intelligent than men, it is clearly false (and this is obvious in any society in which men and women have equal opportunities to develop their abilities).

So this is an example of an argument where the reason is true but the *inference* from reason to conclusion is unjustified. And the inference is unjustified because the reason could be true and the conclusion false at the same time (they are). Taking this as an initial test to apply when trying to decide whether an inference is justified, it is clearly *quite different* from the tests you should apply when trying to decide whether reasons are acceptable.

Question 8.3

Apply the test we have just explained to decide whether the inferences you identified in the passages given in question 8.1 are justified.

8.3.1   Questions appendix, passage 1.
8.3.2   Questions appendix, passage 3.
8.3.3   Questions appendix, passage 10.
8.3.4   Questions appendix, passage 17.
8.3.5   Questions appendix, passage 36.
8.3.6   Questions appendix, passage 39.

As we have just seen, sometimes an argument fails because, though its reasons are acceptable, the inferences based upon them fail. By contrast, sometimes an argument fails because its reasons are *unacceptable* even though the inferences based upon them meet our test for being good inferences. Here is an example:

> If you have memorised the key points in this book you will do
> well in the critical thinking examination and you have memo-
> rised them **so** you will do well in the exam.

It is reasonably clear that **if** the reasons are true, the conclusion must be too, so this is a good inference by our test. However the reason which says you only need to memorise the key points in this book to do well in the exam is certainly false (and perhaps the claim that you have memorised them is false too?), so this is an argument which fails to justify its conclusion not because it makes a poor inference, but because at least one of the reasons on which it is based is false.

Of course, some arguments fail because they are based on unacceptable reasons **and** make poor inferences from them, but the point we want to make here is the process of deciding whether the reasons are acceptable and the process of deciding whether the inferences are justified are quite different – and use quite different tests. If an argument **fails either or both** of these tests it fails to justify its conclusion. However, if it **passes both** it succeeds in justifying it. This is such an important point that it is worth setting out for reference.

*For an argument to succeed in justifying its conclusion it must meet **two** conditions:*
(i) its reasons must be true or otherwise acceptable, and
(ii) the inferences which are then drawn from those reasons must be good ones.

8.3 Some different standards for evaluating inferences and arguments

We saw earlier that there are different kinds of reasons, which have to be judged differently (for truth, credibility, acceptability as values, definitions or whatever). In the same way, different kinds of inferences have to be judged by quite different standards. The standard/test we just introduced is one, but not the only one, as we shall now explain.

Although, of course, every argument aims to provide support for its conclusion, some arguments are meant to be much more 'conclusive' than others; they mean to leave less room for objection than other arguments. Thus, some reasoning is meant to be what is called **'deductively valid'**. This is the fiercest standard of all for judging inferences.

Using language similar to that in our test above, the test to decide whether an inference is deductively valid is this:

Can you think of *any way* the reason(s) could be true and the conclusion false (however unlikely)?

If the answer to that question is 'No', then the inference – the move from reasons to conclusion – **is** deductively valid. If the answer is 'Yes' then the inference **is not** deductively valid.

Thus, if an argument is deductively valid, the truth of its reasons **absolutely guarantees** the truth of its conclusion; if the reasons are true, the conclusion **must** be true, there are no other possibilities. For example, if it is true that 'all whales are mammals' and 'all mammals give birth to live young' it **must** be true that 'all whales give birth to live young'. There is no way the reasons could be true and the conclusion false. So this is a deductively valid argument.

Other arguments have to be judged by quite different standards. For example in a criminal court the question is whether the case against the accused has been '**proved beyond a reasonable doubt**'. This is quite a fierce standard for an argument to meet; both the reasons and the inferences in the case must be 'proved beyond a reasonable doubt'. Thus, in this case the test to apply to the inferences is:

> If the reasons are true (or otherwise acceptable), is there a reasonable doubt about whether the conclusion is true (or otherwise acceptable)?

Such a test is clearly not as fierce as that of deductive validity. Consider the following case:

> Abe has confessed to murdering Bert. The murder weapon was Abe's hand gun and it is covered in Abe's fingerprints. It was well known that Abe hated Bert. Despite a thorough police investigation, there is no evidence to suggest that anyone else was involved. **Therefore** Abe must have been the murderer.

Clearly, this argument is **not** deductively valid. One can imagine ways in which the reasons could be true and the conclusion false (perhaps Abe is covering for his brother Cain for some reason). However, a court case which culminated in this summary might well find the case against Abe 'proved beyond a reasonable doubt'.

In civil legal cases the standard which has to be applied is still less fierce; here the case has to be shown to be '**more likely than not on the balance of evidence**'. Thus, a juror or judge in such a case has to apply a still weaker standard when reaching their conclusion.

Yet again, in many everyday situations we present arguments which are meant to be judged by still less fierce standards. For example, they are meant to be '**reasonable**', but not at all conclusive, because the issue is not sufficiently important or is not very controversial – and usually leaves an enormous amount unsaid and assumed. Indeed, in most real arguments, a great deal is left unsaid, so it will turn out to be very important to think carefully about the assumptions which lie behind most arguments when judging how persuasive they are. We now explain these ideas in more detail in successive sections (dealing with assumptions in due course).

8.4 Deductive validity

We deal first with the standard of 'deductive validity', not because it is the most important in our context, but because it is the easiest to grasp and understand. Once you are clear about this idea, you will find the other standards relatively easy to understand.

Here is another example of a deductively valid argument:

Example 2

Andy is taller than Bessie and Bessie is taller than Charlie, **therefore** Andy is taller than Charlie.

If you imagine these three people, you can see that if Andy is taller than Bessie and Bessie is taller than Charlie, then Andy **must** be taller than Charlie; if the reasons are true, the conclusion **must** be true. It is **impossible** for the reasons to be true and the conclusion false. That is all it means to call an argument 'deductively valid'.

Here is another example:

Example 3

We must either take the left turn or the right turn here. If we go left we shall be delayed by road works and if we go right we shall be delayed by a road accident. So, either way we shall be delayed.

Clearly, in this example, if it is true that we must go left or right (that there are no other options) and that the other claims are true, then we **must** be delayed. There is no escaping this conclusion if the reasons are true. It is **impossible** for the reasons to be true and the conclusion false.

In the previous section we gave an example of an argument which was **not** deductively valid (the one about Abe being a murderer). Let us look at another example:

Example 4

The painting known as the *Mona Lisa*, which is in the Louvre in Paris, is one of the most famous paintings in the world. The way the painter paints flesh colours is so unique the painting could almost be identified from that alone, if we were uncertain of its provenance. However, there has never been any doubt that the painting is by Leonardo Da Vinci, **so** it must be.

Clearly, this argument is **not** deductively valid. Although, 'there has never been any doubt' one could imagine some great fraud having been perpetrated, so the argument is not deductively valid (it is *possible* for the reasons to be true and the conclusion false, however unlikely).

Question 8.4

Judge which of the following arguments is deductively valid and which is not. Explain in each case why you make your decision:

8.4.1   Tom hates everyone Mary loves and Mary loves Tom. So Tom must hate himself.
8.4.2   The butler was in the pantry. In that case he couldn't have shot the master, who was in his study. So the butler couldn't have done it!
8.4.3   Questions appendix, passage 3.

As we have explained, to decide whether an argument is deductively valid you have to ask whether it is *possible* (however unlikely) for the reasons to be true and the conclusion false at the same time. Sometimes this is easy to judge (as in most of the immediately preceding examples) but it is worth noting that it is sometimes very difficult to judge; for just such an example see the Galileo argument in the Questions appendix, passage 51, which is fully discussed in Fisher (1988, chapter 6).

8.5 Deductive validity and patterns of argument

We mentioned earlier that there are different patterns of argument – that arguments can display different structures (chapter 3). Interestingly, some patterns of argument are such that any argument which has that structure will be deductively valid whatever its subject matter – whatever it is about. Here is an example of such a pattern/structure:

> If the consumption of petrol by cars across the world is not significantly reduced soon, exhaust emissions will continue to damage the ozone layer. If this happens the incidence of skin cancer will increase considerably and if this happens deaths from skin cancer will increase so if worldwide petrol consumption is not reduced skin cancer deaths will increase.

This argument has the shape:

> If A then B and if B then C and if C then D, so if A then D.

Though the original argument was quite long, once you display the structure of its reasoning using the letters A–D to stand for sentences in the original, it is not too difficult to see that if the reasons are true, the conclusion **must** be too. Indeed, it is easy to see that this will be equally true of any other argument which has the same shape.

Here are two arguments which exhibit other patterns which are deductively valid:

If the consumption of petrol by cars across the world is not significantly reduced soon, exhaust emissions will continue to damage the ozone layer. Since petrol consumption will not be reduced, car exhaust emissions will continue to damage the ozone layer.

Its pattern is:

> If A then B and A is true, **so** B must be true,

a pattern which is clearly deductively valid; if the reasons are true the conclusion must be. This is such a common pattern of argument that it has a special name – 'modus ponens' or 'affirming the antecedent'.

Here is another argument, with a different structure:

> If some words really did resemble natural sounds (as some theories about the origin of human language suggest), you would expect them to be the same or similar in every language. Interestingly enough, careful inspection shows that they are not. Therefore the theories must be wrong. (Cf. Questions appendix, passage 31)

This argument exhibits the pattern:

If A then B but B is false, **so** A must be false too.

This pattern is also clearly deductively valid. It, too, is so common that it has a special name, 'modus tollens' or 'denying the consequent'.

In fact both these argument patterns are very common and very simple; and they are so simple that people often leave out one of the premises when arguing, taking it for granted. When you are looking for assumptions, it can be important to remember this.

Question 8.5

Look at the following examples and decide which ones exhibit a pattern which is deductively valid and which do not.

8.5.1　If the world's climate was getting warmer, we would find that some of the ice at both the North and the South Pole was melting at an unusually high rate. If the ice was melting, we would see its effect in the raising of the level of the sea. The world's climate is getting warmer so we should find evidence that sea level is rising. (See Questions appendix, passage 3)

8.5.2　If people who claim to have been abducted by aliens really have been abducted, then we would need to take reports of UFO sightings very seriously. However, such claims are very unlikely to be true. Therefore, we do not need to take reports of UFO sightings seriously. (See Questions appendix, passage 7)

8.5.3　A group of reputable European scientists has reported that studies they have conducted do not demonstrate that there is a significant risk of lung cancer from passive smoking. But this analysis was commissioned by the tobacco industry. So findings of the analysis are likely to be incorrect. (See Questions appendix, passage 11)

8.5.4　If it was true that animals have benefited from toxicity tests on animals more than the test animals have suffered, these tests might be justified. Unfortunately for those who countenance such tests, the benefit to animals cannot be established, so toxicity testing on animals is not justified. (See Questions appendix, passage 16)

There is much more that could be said about the standard of deductive validity (and those who want to learn more could read the 'Appendix: Elementary formal logic' in Fisher (1988) or the 'Logic appendix' in Everitt and Fisher (1995)) but it is not enormously important in the context of everyday argumentation, so we are happy to leave you to rely on your intuitions in this area, and move to a less severe standard. If an argument does not meet the standard of deductive validity it might nonetheless be a good argument for its intended purpose, so let us look now at arguments which prove their conclusion beyond a reasonable doubt.

8.6 Proved beyond a reasonable doubt

As we noted, the standard of proof which applies in the criminal courts is 'proved beyond a reasonable doubt'. This is a matter which juries have to decide. They are not expected to require deductive validity when deciding whether the evidence proves the case. It will normally be possible to imagine ways in which the evidence could be true but the conclusion false (so that the case is not deductively valid) but that is not the test they have to apply; they have to ask whether there is a 'reasonable doubt', not whether there is a 'possibility' that the reasons are true and the conclusion false. Thus, in the example we described in section 8.3 about Abe and Bert, it is not difficult to see that the argument is not deductively valid but could well be 'proved beyond a reasonable doubt'. Here is another example:

> On a lovely sunny evening in 1989, Linda Russell and her two daughters, Megan and Josie (aged 9), were walking home from school along a lonely country lane near Canterbury, in England, when they were confronted by a strange man. He tied them up and attacked them about the head with a hammer, leaving them all for dead (though Josie survived). After a lengthy police investigation and subsequent trial, a man called Michael Stone was convicted of the murders. There was no forensic evidence against him (blood, hairs, fingerprints, and such evidence). He was convicted partly because he had no alibi for the time of the murder but mainly on the basis of the testimony of two people who had conversations with him when he was being held as a suspect. One, Damien Daley, had convictions for robbery, burglary and assault; the other, an orderly, was Barry Thomson. Both testified at Stone's trial that he had confessed to the murders in their hearing in prison. They were able to give details which were convincing to the jury.

If you think about this example, it is not too difficult to think of the sorts of evidence that Daley and Thomson would have to produce which would convince a jury 'beyond a reasonable doubt' that they were telling the truth.

Question 8.6

Discuss with fellow students (or friends if you are engaged in self study) what this might be and write a summary of your deliberations.

As it happens, Stone's conviction was quashed in early 2001, after Thompson confessed in a national newspaper that his testimony was a pack of lies! But it is not difficult to imagine evidence that would establish Stone's guilt 'beyond a reasonable doubt'.

Question 8.7

In each of the following examples, assume the reasons given are true or otherwise acceptable and judge whether you think the conclusion is established 'beyond a reasonable doubt' – giving your reasons.

8.7.1 Although the Earth looks 'flat' to us when we are on its surface, and people believed it was flat until quite recently, we have accumulated an enormous amount of evidence in the last few hundred years that it is roughly spherical. We can watch ships disappear over the horizon; ships and planes navigate successfully on the assumption that the world is roughly spherical; and more recently we even have pictures taken from space which show that the Earth is spherical. So it must be roughly spherical.

8.7.2 John has just slipped and fallen about 25 feet from a ladder on to a concrete path beside his house. Although he seemed to hit the ground hard, he is still conscious. He is motionless but groaning horribly and there seems to be blood coming out of his mouth. He must be seriously hurt.

8.7 Shown to be more likely than not on the balance of evidence

In civil courts the standard of proof which is used in the criminal courts does not apply, but a less fierce standard applies, namely that the case has to be proved on the balance of the evidence or on the balance of probabilities. Thus a civil court can find against someone even though there are doubts about the case which would require the cost to find them not guilty if it were a criminal charge.

Similar reasoning occurs in many contexts. For example, in *The Science of Deduction* Sherlock Holmes is subjected to a test by Dr Watson. Watson has heard Holmes say that it is difficult for someone to use an object daily without leaving evidence about his character and habits on it that a trained observer could read. He hands Holmes an old watch 'which has recently come into my possession' and asks Holmes to tell him what he can about its late owner. Holmes looks at the watch carefully, opens it and inspects the works, using the inevitable magnifying glass. Then, after remarking that there is very little evidence because the watch was recently cleaned, he says:

> 'Subject to your correction, I should judge the watch belonged to your elder brother, who inherited it from your father.'
>
> 'That you gather, no doubt, from the HW upon the back?', says Watson.
>
> 'Quite so', Holmes replies, 'The W suggests your own name. The date of the watch is nearly fifty years back and the initials are as old as the watch; so it was made for the last generation. Jewellery usually descends to the eldest son, and he is most likely to have the same name as the father. Your father has, if I remember right, been dead many years. It has, therefore, been in the hands of your eldest brother.'
>
> 'Right, so far', says Watson 'Anything else?'
>
> Holmes continues, 'He was a man of untidy habits – very untidy and careless. He was left with good prospects, but he threw away his chances, lived for some time in poverty with occasional short intervals of prosperity, and finally, taking to drink, he died. That is all I can gather.'

Watson is amazed and affronted by the accuracy of Holmes' description, believing Holmes must have known all this from some other source, but Holmes assures him he never knew Watson had a brother until he inspected the watch. 'Then how in the name of all that is wonderful did you get these facts?' asks Watson, 'They are absolutely correct in every particular.' Holmes says he was lucky and remarks that he could 'only say what was the balance of probability'. He then explains his reasoning:

> 'I began by stating that your brother was careless. When you observe the lower part of that watch case you notice that it is not only dinted in two places, but it is cut and marked all over from the habit of keeping other hard objects, such as coins or keys, in the same pocket. Surely it is no great feat to assume that a man who treats a fifty-guinea watch so cavalierly must be a careless man. Neither is it a very far-fetched inference that a man who inherits one article of such value is pretty well provided for in other respects.'

Watson nods as Holmes continues:

> 'It is very customary for pawnbrokers in England, when they take a watch, to scratch the number of the ticket with a pin-point upon the inside of the case. It is more handy than a label, as there is no risk of the number being lost or transposed. There are no less than four such numbers visible to my lens on the inside of this case. Inference – that your brother was often at low water. Secondary inference – that he had occasional bursts of prosperity, or he could not have redeemed the pledge. Finally, I ask you to look at the inner plate, which contains the keyhole. Look at the thousands of scratches all round the hole – marks where the key has slipped. What sober man's keys could have scored those grooves? But you will never see a drunkard's watch without them. He winds it at night, and he leaves these traces of his unsteady hand. Where is the mystery in all this?'

Notice that there is nothing conclusive about his reasoning, however impressive it may be. Holmes' reasoning is certainly not deductively valid. What Holmes and Watson call deductions are not what we have called deductively valid inferences, but what many people call 'inductions'. Holmes is arguing from past experience to present judgements, or arguing , as he says, on the basis of 'the balance of probabilities'. This kind of reasoning is not deductively valid and it does not prove its conclusions 'beyond a reasonable doubt', but it can obviously get you quite a long way in many situations!

The same kind of reasoning occurs in many other everyday contexts. It is also common in scientific contexts, when scientists are struggling to understand something. For scientific examples look in any edition of *The New Scientist*, *Scientific American*, *Nature* or the like; for an engaging semi-scientific example (originally published in *The New Scientist*) see the Questions appendix, passage 54 [Leonardo da Vinci].

How should we judge reasoning like Holmes's? Well, it is not easy to say in general. It will often depend on the context. There is no doubt that arguments which do prove their case 'to be more likely than not on the balance of the evidence' are common enough in the civil courts. This is a standard which is frequently applied in the courts without controversy; of course there are civil cases where judgments are reached which are controversial, but many are reached which are not. This suggests, given what we said in chapter 5 about clarifying ideas, that though 'shown to be more likely than not on the balance of the evidence' may be a vague idea, it has a reasonably clear meaning at least in some contexts.

In particular cases the tests to apply to decide whether the inferences are acceptable may depend not only on the context, but also on background assumptions and on the particular subject matter. For example, where the reasoning aims to explain the cause of something, this has to be judged by special standards (and with the aid of some distinctive questions); similarly, where the reasoning aims at recommending a course of action, this too has to be judged by special standards (with the aid of some distinctive questions). Thus, although it is not easy to say much in general, about making the judgement that a case is 'shown to be more likely than not on the balance of the evidence', we discuss reasoning to causal explanations and to recommendations in chapters 10 and 11 respectively, because they are so common and important. This will go some way to provide guidance about whether such reasoning shows its conclusions to be 'more likely than not on the balance of the evidence' in these cases. In short, if you want to decide whether reasoning of this kind is persuasive, you have to decide whether reasonable alternatives have been ruled out and whether what is concluded fits reasonably well with everything else we know in this area. We shall say much more about this later, but, before we do, we need to say more about the importance of assumptions and context where judging inferences is concerned, and we shall do this in the next chapter.

Question 8.8

The following arguments are both weak. In each case, say what you can about whether this is because they have unacceptable reasons or make unjustified inferences – or both.

8.8.1   Although not all single-parent families are the result of divorce, in the UK almost a quarter of families with dependent children are headed by a single parent. This compares with an average figure of only 14 per cent in the rest of the European Union. These figures show that divorce has been made far too easy in this country. (Questions appendix, passage 48)

8.8.2   When a couple works hard at their marriage, they are very unlikely to find themselves in the divorce court. A low rate of divorce in a country will therefore indicate couples taking their marriage seriously, both for themselves and for their children. A low rate of divorce is more easily achieved when divorce is made more difficult. Therefore the Government should change the law accordingly. (Questions appendix, passage 48)

8.8 To summarise

We commonly infer all sorts of things from other things we know. Inferences are the moves we make from reasons to conclusions (where we take the reasons to *support* the conclusions), moves we make with varying degrees of confidence.

For an argument to justify its conclusion its reasons must be true or otherwise acceptable **and** the inferences which are then drawn from those reasons must be good ones.

For an inference to be a good one, we expect to be able to see some reasonably secure *connection* between reason(s) and conclusion – a *link* we can understand and accept in the light of everything else we believe. The test to use is some suitable variation on:

> *Could the reason(s) be true (or otherwise acceptable) and the conclusion false (or otherwise unacceptable) at the same time?*

where the variation depends on the standard which is to be applied.

There are several different standards for judging inferences and arguments, including 'deductively valid', 'proved beyond a reasonable doubt', 'shown to be more likely than not on the balance of probabilities' and 'reasonable'.

Thus, the standard for judging whether an inference is deductively valid is:

> Can you think of *any way* the reason(s) could be true and the conclusion false (however unlikely)?

but the standard for deciding whether an inference is 'proved beyond a reasonable doubt' is:

> If the reasons are true (or otherwise acceptable), is there a reasonable doubt about whether the conclusion is true (or otherwise acceptable)?

and the standard for deciding whether an inference is 'shown more likely than not on the balance of probabilities' is similarly reformulated.

'Deductive validity' is an easy idea to work with (though inferences which meet this standard, or aim to, are not very common in ordinary argumentation), so we begin with this idea since it helps people to grasp the other standards for judging inferences.

Some arguments are 'deductively valid' just because of the pattern they display and we explain some examples in which this is the case.

We do not say anything much about the standard of 'reasonableness'; it is too general to say much of substance except in particular cases and contexts.

Question 8.9

If you would like a difficult concluding question consider one of the following passages, identify the inferences being discussed and comment on how strong they are.

8.9.1   It is often said that although there is no positive evidence for the existence of a God, nor is there evidence against His existence. So it is best to keep an open mind and be agnostic. At first sight that seems an unassailable position. But on second thoughts it seems a cop-out, because the same could be said of Father Christmas and tooth fairies. There may be fairies at the bottom of the garden. There is no evidence of it, but you can't *prove* that there aren't any, so shouldn't we be agnostic with respect to fairies? The trouble with the agnostic argument is that it can be applied to anything. There is an infinite number of hypothetical beliefs we could hold which we can't positively disprove. On the whole, people don't believe in most of them, such as fairies, unicorns, dragons, Father Christmas, and so on. But on the whole they do believe in a creator God. (See Questions appendix, passage 57 [Dawkins])

8.9.2   It is important not to confuse my view that religious claims are *meaningless* with the view that is adopted by atheists, or agnostics. Atheists deny that God exists and agnostics say they do not *know* whether He exists. Thus, my view that all claims about the nature of God are meaningless is actually incompatible with each of these familiar positions. For if the sentence 'God exists' is meaningless, then the atheist's claim, 'God does not exist' is meaningless too, since only meaningful claims can be meaningfully denied. As for the agnostic, although he says he does not know whether 'God exists' or 'God does not exist' is true, he must think both claims are meaningful because he thinks that the question 'Does God exist?' is a genuine, meaningful question. Since I have insisted that such claims (and questions) are meaningless, my view is incompatible with the agnostic's position too. (Adapted from the writings of A. J. Ayer, *The Existence of God*, ed. Hick

Further reading

See Fisher (1988, *passim*), but especially chapter 2 and the Appendix. Also Ennis (1996, chapters 5–7).

Evaluating inferences: assumptions and other relevant arguments

As we have already seen, when evaluating arguments, explanations and so on, we have to decide both whether the reasons are acceptable and whether the inferences are justified. In simple cases, such as many of the arguments we saw earlier, judging to what extent reasons support their conclusions – to what extent the inferences are justified – is relatively straightforward. But in most real arguments there are two complications with which we must now deal. The first is that there are assumptions lying in the background (and perhaps general background information) which may be very relevant to what is being argued and which may need to be elicited if we are to have a full view of the argument. The second is that there are often different, perhaps opposing, considerations from those which have been presented by the author and which need to be taken into account if one is to evaluate the argument skilfully. Clearly these two complications may well be related in a given argument since the author may well be assuming things which are relevant considerations or which conflict with other relevant considerations.

9.1 Implicit assumptions

The reader may find it helpful to look back to sections 4.1 and 4.2 before proceeding.

It is often quite easy to know what someone is assuming. For example, it is reasonably safe to assume that an environmentalist who is arguing against building some new motorway across a site of special scientific interest will believe various commonly held views about car emissions and some less common ones about the importance of distinctive species and habitats, which she takes to be relevant to the issue. It can be easy to spot assumptions in texts too; for example, consider the following:

> Being a driving instructor is a challenging and rewarding occupation. One has a great freedom in working for oneself, and it is unnecessary to have passed any 'A' levels. Therefore, a suitable job for anyone without 'A' levels is that of driving instructor. (Questions appendix, passage 1)

It strikes most readers very quickly that this piece assumes that if a 'challenging and rewarding job with freedom to work for yourself' appeals to you, then to be a driving instructor you need little more than to 'have no A levels'! So the implicit assumption here is very obvious. Furthermore, given that driving instructors need all sorts of special qualities, like patience and teaching ability, it strikes most people very quickly that the inference is a poor one because the reasons could be true and the conclusion false judging by any reasonable standard. (Incidentally this is clearly an example which bears out what is said in the last sentence of the opening paragraph above, since this argument assumes something which is false and which conflicts with other relevant considerations.)

Sometimes, of course, it is not so easy to tell what is being assumed. In those cases, how should we proceed to elicit assumptions, especially when we are concerned about the quality of inferences?

In short, the general strategy is that we should attribute to arguments/explanations and so on those assumptions which:

(a) *seem likely in the context (see the environmentalist example), or*
(b) *which make sense of what is said, or*
(c) *which seem necessary to make the reasoning as strong as possible (if true).*

The rationale for this strategy is that we are interested in discovering the truth about issues rather than scoring points off people, so we interpret reasoning as constructively as we can; this is part of what is generally known as the Principle of Charity in the critical thinking tradition (contrast what goes on in Parliamentary debates!). Let us begin by explaining how the general rule works with an easy question which you should answer before continuing.

Question 9.1

Consider the following argument:

> If the world's climate was getting warmer, we would find that some
> of the ice at both the North and the South Pole was melting at an
> unusually high rate. If the ice was melting, we would see its effect
> in the raising of the level of the sea. There is evidence that this level
> is increasing, so the world's climate must be getting warmer.
> (Questions appendix, passage 3)
>
> What do you think this argument is implicitly assuming (do you
> still agree with your answer to 4.1.1)?

The obvious 'problem' with this argument is that there might
be other plausible explanations for the rising sea level. However,
it is also reasonably clear that it is implicitly assuming something
like 'the [or *the only plausible* or perhaps even *the only possible*]
explanation for the rise in sea-level is that the world's climate is getting
warmer'. So, given our general principle, we should attribute to this
argument one of the implicit assumptions mentioned above. Probably
those who would advance this argument would grant that they are
assuming that this is *the only plausible* explanation, but we do not need
to worry too much about that detail; the point is that this assumption
makes the reasoning as strong as possible, it makes sense in the
context, and thus it seems reasonable to attribute it.

Here is a rather different example (derived and adapted from a text
on British history) about King William Rufus:

> Little primary evidence from the reign of William Rufus exists
> that enables historians to say exactly why he was detested by all
> classes of his subjects. However, by comparing the remedial
> measures contained in the coronation charter of Henry I, who
> succeeded Rufus, with what is known of the law and custom of
> the preceding reign of William the Conqueror it is possible to
> form some idea of the tyranny of William Rufus.

This seems to be assuming that William the Conqueror was not
'detested by all classes of his subjects', that the prevailing law and
custom was changed by Rufus (could he have been hated for quite
different things?) and that the coronation charter of Henry I contained
some measures which we can pick out and say, 'these were put in

specifically to remedy some of the things for which Rufus was hated'. If we attribute these assumptions to the piece, it makes perfectly good sense and makes a reasonable case for thinking that we might be able to work out something about the nature of Rufus' tyranny from this evidence. If, we think any of these assumptions is false the argument does not make sense and does not make much of a case for its conclusion, tentative as it is.

Question 9.2

In each of the following examples identify something which is implicitly assumed and say how making that assumption affects the inference (does it make it more acceptable or show that it is weak)?

9.2.1   Questions appendix, passage 16.

9.2.2   Questions appendix, passage 33.

9.2.3   If the building burned to the ground there will be only a pile of ashes and rubble. There is only a pile of ashes and rubble. Therefore the building burned to the ground.

9.2.4   A teacher is speaking to a colleague about a particular student just before an exam and says, Jones has worked hard so he will pass the exam.

9.2.5   Widespread outcrops on Mars of a green rock called olivine suggest the planet has long been too dry and cold for life to flourish on its surface.

  A blend of iron and magnesium silicates, olivine is found inside some volcanic deposits on Earth, but it does not last long once it has been exposed. In warm, moist environments it starts weathering in months, says Roger Clark of the US Geological Survey in Boulder, Colorado. Yet spectroscopic data shows that olivine covers over 2.5 million square kilometres on Mars, including some ancient regions that are heavily cratered or eroded, he told a meeting of the American Astronomical Society last month in Pasadena, California.

  That means that Mars cannot have been warm and moist since the olivine was deposited about 1 to 3 billion years ago. ('Parched planet', *New Scientist*, 11 November 2000, p. 31)

9.2.6   Questions appendix, passage 59 [the Noodle's Oration] considering only the arguments contained in the first and fourth paragraphs.

Question 9.3

James Lovelock, author of the Gaia hypothesis (that the Earth is a self-reg-ulating biosphere geared to preserving life) has recently argued that the way to power economies without the damage being done to the biosphere by polluting greenhouse gases is to adopt nuclear power. Look at his argu-ment in the Questions appendix, passage 52, identify any assumptions he makes and say how they affect the strength of any inferences he makes.

9.2 Assuming 'if the reasons are true the conclusion is'

Before leaving assumptions and how they affect inferences, we should note that one strategy for attributing assumptions to arguments is less helpful than you might think. Consider the argument:

> Some people have solved their own unemployment problem by great ingenuity in searching for a job or by willingness to work for less, so all the unemployed could do this.

It is clear that you *could* add the assumption 'if some people have solved their own unemployment problem by great ingenuity in searching for a job or by willingness to work for less, then all the unemployed could do this', which would convert this argument into a deductively valid argument. This resulting argument would have the shape, 'A and if A then B, so B' which, as we already saw (section 8.5), is deductively valid.

However, notice that this addition has not changed the argument from one which raises doubts to one which does not. If we thought the original inference was questionable, our doubts must apply equally to the added, hypothetical assumption. The 'locus' of our questions may have moved to the hypothetical, but they are exactly the same ques-tions we had about the original inference. So adding such an assumption does not greatly advance the process of evaluating an infer-ence (though people sometimes find it easier to see what is going on when they do this). Notice also that adding such a hypothetical assumption does nothing to make the original argument any stronger (old doubts are simply relocated) so it does not have to be done under **(c)** of our general strategy. To summarise this point, **any** inference, **however illogical**, can be converted into a deductively valid one just by adding the hypothetical assumption 'if the reasons are true so is the conclusion', but this does not strengthen the argument.

9.3 Other relevant considerations

Working out what someone is assuming is often quite 'creative', because you have to be imaginative about what they might have assumed or you have to do some research into their views (asking them or reading their other writings). However, thinking of 'other considerations' which are relevant to an argument is certainly where critical thinking becomes the **critico-creative** thinking we spoke of earlier (section 1.6). Consider an example we looked at earlier (section 3.5):

> R1<Most prospective parents would prefer to have sons>. **So** C1[if people can choose the sex of their child, it is likely that there will eventually be more males than females in the population] **and** R2<This could produce serious social problems>, **therefore** C2[we should prohibit the use of techniques which enable people to choose the sex of their children].

Question 9.4

Answer the following questions before reading on:

9.4.1 Briefly note whether you think this argument is persuasive or not, saying why?

9.4.2 List any other arguments you can think of which are relevant to the issue (perhaps you can extend the list you gave in answering question 6.2).

This argument seems quite telling to many people when they first encounter it. However, if we try to think of other relevant considerations, to 'think outside the box' so to speak, we soon get a different view. Here are some other considerations which have occurred to students with whom I have discussed this example:

(i)   Freedom of choice is very important in some societies and they might prefer to give people the choice and then deal with any resulting social problems.

(ii) If prospective parents can choose the sex of their child this may reduce the tendency in some societies to go on having children until parents have the sons or daughters they want. This could reduce the number of 'unwanted' children and might also reduce the rate of population growth (for example in India?).

(iii) Some diseases are inherited only through the female line (or male line). Perhaps these techniques could be used to eliminate (or reduce the risk of) such illnesses.

These are all reasons which weigh *against* banning these techniques. There might be other lines of argument which would count *for* banning them; for example:

(i)   They might have unwelcome side effects,
(ii) They might be very expensive,
(iii) There might be religious arguments against them (for example, interfering with God's will),

and so on. (How many of these did you think of?)

Issues like this are rarely simple. If we are to judge them wisely we need to be imaginative about what they are assuming and what other considerations are relevant and make our judgements on the basis of all of these.

Thus, if you are asked to respond to an argument like this, you first need to be clear what it says (and assumes) and then you might respond to its basic reasons (challenging or agreeing with those) and then ask yourself how well they support their conclusions, but in doing this it is essential that you think around (or research around) the subject to take into account all the other relevant considerations.

Here is another example as an exercise (the argument is usually greeted with raised eyebrows when students first encounter it but they have great difficulty in saying what is wrong with it! See what you think):

Question 9.5

Consider the following argument and think of as many 'other relevant considerations' as possible to help you evaluate it:

> Young people in Britain should not get married. Current statistics show that 40% of marriages end in divorce and one can safely assume that many of those couples who remain together are unhappily married. Therefore, it is more likely than not that young people who marry will divorce or be unhappily married. These are daunting odds for any young couple.

I sometimes find that when students are trying to think of 'other relevant considerations' they are slow to produce ideas or they struggle because they somehow feel they must only come up with 'good' or 'correct' ideas. It can help you overcome this difficulty if you allow yourself to 'brainstorm' possible answers. When you brainstorm, you just quickly jot down as many 'possible' answers as you can, even if they seem silly.

Later you sift though them deciding which deserve to be taken seriously. The point about brainstorming is that there are no 'wrong' answers. Your objective is simply to produce as many answers as possible in a short time – and brainstorming helps to 'free up' your thoughts. Many students find it easier to do this, and then quickly select the useful ones from their list, than to think of 'good' suggestions straight off.

You might like to try this technique on one (or more) of the following questions:

Question 9.6

Think of as many 'other relevant considerations' as you can which might help you weigh the following arguments:

9.6.1   Questions appendix, passage 21.
9.6.2   These big art exhibitions, which collect paintings from all over the world, are bad for the paintings. However they are transported, there is a danger of accidents and resultant damage or destruction and it can't be good to subject paintings to the changes of pressure and humidity that even carefully controlled travel is likely to bring. (Cf. question 4.4.4)
9.6.3   Questions appendix, passage 39.

9.5 Overall argument evaluation and presenting a well-argued case

We have now explained in detail nearly all the steps contained in our basic thinking map (in section 4.3). We have looked at characteristic ways in which we reason poorly, we have presented better models and we have given ourselves practice in adopting these. We have also been given extensive practice in using the language which is central to the process of presenting and evaluating reasoning. The result is that we should now be able to look at arguments and (perhaps after suitable research) write much better argued responses to them than we could have done previously – because we know what questions to ask and how to answer them. Referring back to our analogy with the basket ball game, now is the time to play a whole game.

So let us try applying all the lessons we have learned in a few realistic examples. Once you are comfortable with writing out the structure of some reasoning you will find you can spot the structure of an argument quite quickly and easily, so you may not need to write it out. In what follows I shall discuss examples without spelling out their reasoning structure, but what I say should show that I have understood them.

Here is a (rather British) example. A tabloid Sunday newspaper, the *News of the World*, revealed that a senior judge, Anthony Thornton, had been involved in a 'drugs and sex romp with jailbird hookers'. The judge was immediately summoned to see the Lord Chancellor, Lord Mackay (the head of the British judiciary), who decided not to dismiss or discipline him. The following leading article then appeared in a 'quality' British newspaper:

Example 1

One thing is certain: the Lord Chancellor would not have read the *News of the World* last Sunday. No minister has a more austere approach to Sunday. As a former elder of the Free Presbyterian Church of Scotland, Lord Mackay is a strict Sabbatarian. Not only does he not use the telephone on a Sunday but he will not grant interviews to reporters whose work will be published on a Sunday. Even so, his office read the Sunday tabloid's front page splash about a top judge's 'drugs and sex romp with jailbird hookers'. Not surprisingly there was a meeting between the judge, Anthony Thornton, and Lord Mackay on Tuesday. Somewhat surprisingly, Lord Mackay has backed the judge.

His initial support is important. It is not an offence for adults to consort with prostitutes in private. A sensible judge would avoid such contacts, not least because of blackmail threats, the risk of ridicule, and the danger of the prostitutes appearing before his court. But what is unwise should not necessarily be dismissable. There was no risk in Judge Thornton's case of any prostitutes appearing before him. As an Official Referee, he specialises in technical civil cases. By backing the judge, who denied he had taken drugs or known the women involved had criminal records, the Lord Chancellor signalled his support for protecting privacy. He also reduced the risk of future blackmail. The issue is not over yet. Lord Mackay declined to invite the newspaper to submit evidence. That was a mistake. He has only heard the defence. Now the tabloid is threatening further disclosures this Sunday. This may require a resignation, but Lord Mackay's initial instincts were brave and right. Lord Mackay's personal integrity is firmly established. This week's decision demonstrates his humanity.

What should one make of this argument? It is clear what is being argued, that Lord Mackay was right to support Judge Thornton. The reasoning is clear too; the judge may have been 'unwise' but what he did was not a legal offence; there was no danger that his professional position would be compromised; and it is important to protect the right to privacy. The paper criticises Lord Mackay for not inviting the *News of the World* to submit evidence, but apart from that it supports him.

This matter arose in British context, with all that means for underlying assumptions. You will have your own perspective on what that implies. Some people think British society has a prurient obsession with sex which is quite different from attitudes in many other societies. Some think the British Establishment takes care to protect its own members if at all possible. Whatever the truth about these claims, the problem here is essentially whether Judge Thornton has done anything 'wrong' so far as his position as a judge is concerned. So the relevant considerations are about whether he damaged his or others' capacity to enforce the law. Merely engaging in the 'romp' did not prejudice his work as a judge (because he specialised in a very distinctive kind of case) unless there was a risk of blackmail. However, the publicity given by the *News of the World* may have done something to discredit Judge Thornton as a judge or perhaps the judiciary in general, so we need to consider that possibility. It seems unlikely that this publicity will have affected his work as a judge (because he doesn't have to make judgements in situations in which it might) and the publicity will surely have removed much scope for blackmail. Perhaps the story shows some judges to be more ordinary, more possessed of ordinary human frailty, than the image they might prefer to project, but that does little to discredit the judiciary in general. Some people may take the view that judges should be dismissed or disciplined if they engage in 'immoral' activities like these, but that is not a widely held view. Furthermore, it is certainly true that the right to privacy is a problem area for many people in modern British life, so it seems right to assert that in a case like this and to praise Lord Mackay for doing so. Overall, it seems that this is a reasonable argument.

In responding to this argument I asked the questions in our thinking map (section 4.3), analysed it carefully and evaluated it according to the questions which should be asked, but I could find no real ground for objecting to it, so, after careful consideration, I agreed with its judgement. Of course, other people might take a different view, but that would need to be argued in a similar way.

Let us look at another example, an argument we saw earlier about 'joyriders' (young people who steal cars and drive them fast and dangerously round British cities):

Example 2
The police force should ban their officers from driving at high speed in

pursuit of young joyriders who steal cars. Many deaths, both of joyriders and of innocent bystanders, have occurred as a result of such chases. The police say that they have policies which are aimed at preventing danger to the public during car chases, by requiring police drivers to abandon the chase when speeds become too high for safety. But the excitement of the chase inevitably makes the police drivers forget the policy, and disregard public safety. No stolen car is worth a human life. (Questions appendix, passage 36)

If you wish to respond to this argument you need to understand it – what it is arguing for, its reasoning, its assumptions and so on – and you need to ask the right questions about it. If you mark it up in the ways we have described earlier it is easy to see what it is being argued and if you ask the right questions it is surprising what a lot you can say in response to this reasoning. Here is a possible response:

Joyriders: Don't blame the police

The author argues that the police should ban their officers from driving at high speed in pursuit of young joyriders who steal cars. She argues this essentially on the ground that many deaths of both joyriders and innocent bystanders have occurred as a result of such chases. Furthermore, she claims that these have occurred because the excitement of the chase inevitably makes police drivers forget the requirement to abandon pursuit when speeds become too high and thus disregard human safety.

But the problem is what should replace present policy and practice. Whilst it is easy to agree that no car is worth a human life, this is not the issue. The issue is what should be done about joyriders? If they are not pursued by the police they drive dangerously, risking harm to themselves and others, and if they are pursued the same thing happens; the problem is that they steal and wreck cars and injure themselves and innocent bystanders as a result of their reckless driving *whether they are pursued by the police or not*, so whatever is done, there will be serious risks.

It would help if we had some reliable figures about joyriding; in particular, how many and what sort of accidents occur when these drivers are **not** pursued and what are the comparable figures when they **are** pursued? These might help us to decide whether police pursuit *increases* the likelihood of accidents resulting in injury or death –

or *reduces* it. They might also help us decide the extent to which unreasonable risks are being taken by the police when they pursue these drivers.

The author claims that 'the excitement of the chase inevitably makes police drivers forget the policy (of abandoning the chase when speeds become too high for safety) and disregard public safety'. An equally plausible explanation is that police officers have to make difficult decisions very quickly in dangerous situations and, whatever their training, mistakes are inevitable. *Lives are at risk anyway*. The figures might help us decide whether the present policy is making things worse.

Of course, the present figures will not tell us all we need to know because if joyriders knew they would not be pursued the problem would surely get worse, so there are still difficult judgements to be made. It is all too easy to blame the police for present problems. Why not blame doctors for the sick and injured people who die in their care? The real question is, 'Would we be worse off without their imperfect efforts?'.

Perhaps there are other alternatives which involve less risk. For example, perhaps cars could be made more secure or perhaps police pursuit by helicopter would be safer or perhaps 'spiked mats' could be placed in the path of stolen cars. Perhaps we should experiment with these alternatives.

I have set both these preceding questions as exercises to students in the past and since they have studied the methods presented earlier in this book, many have produced well-reasoned cases like these – and most agree that they would have found this very difficult before studying these techniques. The point is that if you ask the right questions you may see that an argument is quite reasonable or you may see problems with a piece which otherwise looks quite powerful. Remember, of course, that it is important to apply the thinking map to your own arguments too.

Question 9.7

Now, for an exercise which requires you to apply all the lessons you have learned so far, answer one of the following questions:

9.7.1   The Questions appendix contains a piece by Richard Dawkins which concludes as follows, 'Science offers us an explanation of how complexity (the difficult) arose out of simplicity (the easy). The hypothesis of God offers no worthwhile explanation for anything, for it simply postulates the difficult to explain and leaves it at that. We cannot prove that there is no God, but we can safely conclude that He is very, very improbable indeed.' Using all you have learned so far, write a response to Dawkins' argument in no more than 1,000 words.

9.7.2   Choose any topic which interests you and then write a well-argued case in support of your view on that subject in no more than 1,000 words. You may use any of the passages in the Questions appendix as a starting point, or write on some other topic or choose an essay which you have to do in some other subject you are studying. The point is to use the language of reasoning and to ask yourself the right questions to produce as well-argued a case as you can.

You can get a long way with examples like those we have been considering using our thinking map from section 4.3. However, many arguments aim at establishing explanations or recommendations and there are thinking maps which can help focus your questioning in these cases. For this reason, we shall conclude our introduction to critical thinking skills, with two chapters which explain the special questions which can be especially helpful in these contexts.

9.6 Summary

If you are going to evaluate reasoning skilfully you need to judge whether the inferences are good ones and to do this, besides using the appropriate standards, you need to look carefully for implicit assumptions which it is reasonable to attribute to the arguer or argument and you need to ask whether there are other relevant considerations which need to be taken into account.

Where assumptions are concerned you should attribute those which seem likely in the context, make sense of what is said and/or make the reasoning as strong as possible (since we are interested in getting at the truth of things rather than in scoring points off people). It does not strengthen an argument to add the assumption that 'if the reasons are true, the conclusion must be' though it may help you in analysing what is being argued.

We could summarise the lessons of the previous two chapters in the following 'thinking map' which derives from and slightly expands our thinking map in section 4.3.

JUDGING INFERENCES SKILFULLY

3 Does the reasoning include some important **assumptions**?
6 (a) Does the reasoning **Support** its conclusion(s)?
  (b) Are there **Other Relevant Considerations/Arguments** which strengthen or weaken the case?
7 What is your **Overall** Judgement?
    Are the reasons acceptable and are the inferences deductively valid?
    Is the case proved beyond reasonable doubt?
    Is the case shown more likely than not on the balance of probabilities?
    Is the argument reasonable?

Of course, you need to remember to apply all the questions and standards we have discussed throughout the book **to your own reasoning**, and I concluded this chapter with two examples where I tried to be careful to do precisely this in arguing my own response to two pieces of reasoning. You will have to be the judge of how well I managed to follow my own injunctions!

Reasoning about causal explanations

Much of our reasoning is concerned with causal explanations for events or states of affairs. For example, the detective in a murder enquiry wants to know what caused the victim's death. Government advisers might want to know what caused a rapid increase in the inflation rate during a particular period. Doctors want to know what causes various illnesses in human beings so that they can treat their patients. Seismologists want to know what caused the San Francisco earthquake in 1906 so that they can predict future earthquakes. Plant scientists want to know what causes crops to thrive or succumb to disease so that they can breed disease resistant strains. Historians want to know what were the causes of the American Civil War. And so the examples could go on.

Whether we are trying to work out an explanation for ourselves or wishing to assess an explanation which has been offered by someone else, we need to be clear about the kind of reasoning which is appropriate where causal explanations of various kinds are concerned, and that is what this chapter is about.

10.1 The pattern of reasoning in most causal explanations

Sometimes it is not at all difficult to identify the cause of something because we just see what happens (or observe it with other senses) and the cause is obvious. For example, if we hit the gatepost with our car we just *see* what knocks the post over and what causes the dent in the car. In this kind of case the pattern of reasoning which is appropriate to justify the causal claim is simply, 'I saw (and/or felt) the crash so I know that I knocked the gatepost over and dented the car.'

However, most causes are less obvious and the reasoning which justifies accepting less-obvious causal claims needs to be more complex. Suppose the police find a woman's body at the bottom of a lake. They will want to know the cause of death and this may be far from obvious. Perhaps the obvious suspicion (hypothesis) is that she drowned but there are other possibilities too and the police will need to be certain – or as certain as possible about the real cause of her death – so they will need evidence which rules out other possibilities and supports just one. For this reason they will need a pathologist's report; a pathologist is an expert who knows what evidence to look for in a case like this. Perhaps the woman simply fell into the lake and drowned, perhaps she had a heart attack first and fell into the lake, or perhaps she was murdered first and then dumped in the lake – and no doubt there are other possibilities. The expertise of the pathologist consists in knowing what sort of evidence will show the cause of death – what evidence suggests drowning, what evidence suggests a heart attack and so on. Thus, after carefully inspecting the body and subjecting it to various tests, which are standard in his profession, he will write a report for the police saying what evidence he has found and what this leads him to conclude about the cause of death and how confident he is of his conclusion.

His report might be very straightforward. For example, if the body has not been in the water for long and all the evidence is clear and points in the same direction, he may be able to conclude with great confidence that the cause of death was X (drowning, a heart attack, a gunshot wound to the head, or whatever). On the other hand, it might be more complicated. If the body has been in the water for longer, some of the evidence might be lost or the evidence might point in different directions; in that case he may be unable to be sure of the cause of death and his report will again give the evidence, but will explain his degree of uncertainty.

In either case the pathologist will use a combination of observation and theory (including hypotheses). On the basis of what he sees initially (some initial observations) he will guess (hypothesise) some possible causes of death and will then look for further evidence which supports or excludes those possibilities. This is fundamentally the pattern in reasoning about all causal explanations where the cause is not immediately obvious; there will be many differences of detail in detective work, historical enquiries and scientific investigations but this pattern is common: *given what you want to explain, what are the possible explanations and what evidence will support/rebut each of these? Then, given the evidence you have or can find, which explanation is rendered most likely and fits best with everything else we know and believe? And how confident can we be that it is the right explanation?*

Question 10.1

Say what you can at this stage about the reasoning in Questions appendix, passage 5.

10.2 An example of causal explanation

Following on from our example of how the pathologist works, let us imagine that an historian has produced the following argument:

> Napoleon must have died of arsenic poisoning whilst in exile on St Helena. Arsenic can be administered in small doses which will not be noticed, but will eventually kill the victim. Arsenic poisoning leaves traces of arsenic in human hair, and reliable tests recently showed that Napoleon's hair contained abnormally large amounts of arsenic. It had been thought that he died of cancer, but his symptoms included nausea, chills, weakness and increasing corpulence, which cancer specialists say are not symptoms of cancer. However, these are typical symptoms of arsenic poisoning according to specialists.

This is typical of the kind of reasoning which occurs in causal explanations. The occurrence of the word 'must' shows the intended conclusion and 'died of arsenic poisoning' is clearly a causal claim. The reasoning then presents evidence for this claim. And, in this case, it also considers a possible alternative explanation (that cancer caused Napoleon's death) and argues that the evidence conflicts with this alternative hypothesis, but supports the favoured one.

Using the notation we introduced earlier, plus a new symbol AH for 'alternative hypothesis', we could make the structure of the reasoning explicit as follows:

> C[Napoleon **must** have died of arsenic poisoning whilst in exile on St Helena] **for the following reasons**. R1<Arsenic can be administered in small doses which will not be noticed, but will eventually kill the victim>. **and** R2<Arsenic poisoning leaves traces of arsenic in human hair>, **and** R3<reliable tests recently

showed that Napoleon's hair contained abnormally large amounts of arsenic>. It had been thought AH[that he died of cancer], **but** R4<his symptoms included nausea, chills, weakness and increasing corpulence>, **and** R5<cancer specialists say these are not symptoms of cancer>. **However**, R6<these are typical symptoms of arsenic poisoning according to specialists>.

Then R4 and R5 are the evidence against the alternative hypothesis and R1, R2, R3, R4 and R6 provide support for C.

We shall shortly explain how to judge whether this is good and compelling reasoning, but before we do let us point out some characteristic weaknesses we tend to display when thinking about causes.

10.3 Characteristic weaknesses in our thinking about causes

When the cause or causes of an event are not immediately obvious we may need to work things out by doing some detective work, a historical study, a scientific experiment or some other kind of investigation. Unfortunately, we often do nothing of the kind. We do not proceed scientifically, historically or whatever; in fact we do not do anything remotely systematic. Instead, we **jump to a conclusion** and accept the first explanation which comes into our heads; we do not even entertain any alternative explanations. Most of us do this sometimes; for example, we jump to a conclusion about why the car will not start, instead of considering possible alternatives – could it be out of petrol, could it be an electrical fault and so on. Or we hear a TV news report of a car bomb explosion in the heart of London and we immediately jump to a conclusion about the likely perpetrators – without even considering possible alternatives. Whether jumping to a conclusion matters depends on the case.

The second weakness we sometimes display when considering the causes of events is that we fail to consider all the relevant evidence; we take the bits of evidence which support our favoured explanation and ignore the others – or we do not even look for conflicting evidence. For example, cigarette smokers commonly pay more attention to the cases of smokers who have lived long and healthy lives than to the much larger percentage of smokers when compared with non-smokers who have suffered ill-health or died early from smoking-related diseases.

It is worth spelling out these characteristic faults in a way which is easy to remember, because these are the faults we will be inclined to slip into and we want to guard against:

Common faults in thinking about causes

---

1 We consider only one possible cause and accept it without considering other possibilities.
2 We attend to only some of the relevant evidence in determining what causes or caused something.

The answer is clearly to consider several possible causes of the event or phenomenon in which you are interested and to ask yourself what evidence would favour these various alternatives and then look for the evidence.

Remembering the basket ball analogy we used in chapter 1 to explain how to change your ways of thinking, we now need a model of good thinking about causes. The key is to ask the right questions and in the light of what we have said earlier it is fairly obvious what these should be.

10.4 The basic questions for skilful causal explanations

It follows from what we have been saying that the basic questions we need to ask ourselves when handling causal explanations are these:

'Thinking Map'   SKILFUL CAUSAL EXPLANATION

1 What are the **possibilities** in this case?
2 What evidence could you find that **would** count for or against the likelihood of these possibilities (if you could find it)?
3 What **evidence** do you have already, or can you gather, that is relevant to determining what causes what?
4 Which possibility is rendered **most likely** by the evidence? (What explanation fits best with everything else we know and believe?)

The first question, 'What are the **possibilities** in this case?', may require us to be quite imaginative about other possible explanations. How imaginative depends on the case. For example, if the question is relatively unimportant, like what caused your current headache, we might be content to think of very few possibilities, but if the question is what caused a serious epidemic of some disease we might need to be much more imaginative about the possibilities. Notice that this is one of those points where critical thinking has to be 'creative' and imaginative to be good thinking.

Often, in deciding which possibilities need to be considered, we need to take into account whatever else is known about the subject. For example, the pathologist investigating the death of the woman found at the bottom of the lake needs to bring his experience and expertise to bear to decide whether it is necessary to consider the possibility that she killed herself somehow. Our answer to this initial question may well build in various assumptions so, depending on the importance of the case, we may need to note these too.

With the second question, 'What evidence could you find that **would** count for or against the likelihood of these possibilities (if you could find it)?', again, this may require you to be quite imaginative or may require you to draw on expertise in the area. Again, how much care you should give to thinking about the evidence which tells for or against the various possibilities will also depend on the seriousness or importance of the case and again you may need to be alive to the assumptions you build into your thinking. In short, if the case matters, we must not only think of alternative possible explanations, but we must also list some of the things that would support or tell against these alternatives. This second question may prompt us to look for information we would otherwise not have considered and this will help us to avoid making causal judgements on the basis of too little evidence (one of the characteristic weaknesses we want to guard against in thinking about causes).

Question 10.2

Consider the claim that 'working systematically through this text will increase your critical thinking ability'. What evidence do you think would show this to be true or false?

The third question, 'What evidence do you have already, or can you gather, that is relevant to determining what causes what?', is crucially different from the second. To answer the second question, you should so-to-speak 'look away' from the rest of the argument which is presented to ask yourself what on earth **would** prove the claim you are interested in (see Fisher (1988) *The Logic of Real Arguments* on the Assertibility question). However, once you know what you are looking for, you have to actually look for it – and of course the evidence may be very hard to find. Detectives know what would prove that Jones shot Smith (forensic evidence about the bullet linked to Jones's fingerprints on the murder weapon and so on) but it may be very difficult to find the evidence. Similarly, it is commonly very difficult to find the evidence we need in science; it was one thing to say what evidence **would** support Einstein's theory of relativity but it was another thing for the Michelson–Morley experiment actually to provide the evidence.

The fourth question, 'Which possibility is rendered most likely by the evidence?', requires you to pull together what evidence you have, given the alternatives you are considering, to come to the best judgement you can. This will often mean that you have to come to a tentative conclusion, signalled by saying something like, 'This seems most likely but the evidence is not at all strong.' Sometimes, of course, you will be able to come to a confident conclusion, for example the pathologist might report, 'I am absolutely confident that she died from a heart attack before falling into the lake.' In the pathologist's case, he will be able to bring all kinds of expertise to bear, and often the confidence you can place in a judgement about what causes what will depend on how much else you know about the subject matter and how well the evidence fits together with everything else you know or believe. Judging causal connections with any degree of confidence often requires bringing together a lot of related knowledge and belief, which is why the last question is supplemented with the question, 'What explanation fits best with everything else we know and believe?', to remind us to consider the evidence in that context.

To summarise, for explanatory reasoning to be successful it must:

(i)   consider reasonable alternatives, and
(ii) find evidence which (a) rules out other possible explanations and (b) supports the favoured explanation,
(iii) fit well with everything else we know.

These are the tests to apply when judging the reasoning used in justifying causal explanations. In this chapter we shall discuss only relatively simple and easily accessible examples but the same principles apply if you are considering much more complex or arcane examples.

Question 10.3

In the light of the previous guidance, look again at the example about Napoleon's death (section 10.2) and write a brief evaluation of the argument saying whether it is convincing or not (or what its strengths and weaknesses are).

To reinforce the points we have just been making, let us look at another example:

> It is widely believed by experts in the field that the dinosaurs died out quite suddenly about 65 million years ago. The most likely explanation for their destruction seems to be that a large meteor hit the Earth at about that time. The resulting explosion would have sent a huge cloud of dust into the upper atmosphere which would have circulated the Earth for some years. This would have shut out the sun, thus stopping photosynthesis in plants and destroying the dinosaurs' food supply. It is also believed that the dinosaurs were cold-blooded so they needed the sun to keep warm. Either they froze to death or they starved. The best evidence for this is that an exceptionally large amount of iridium is found in layers of the sea thought to have been formed 65 million years ago and iridium is found in meteors in much higher concentration than on the Earth's surface.

If we consider this reasoning with a view to evaluating it skilfully, we have to ask ourselves whether there are other possible explanations for the extinction of the dinosaurs and what sorts of considerations would favour or tell against the various options? We then have to draw on whatever evidence we have to make the best judgement we can.

Question 10.4

10.4.1 What other possible explanations can you think of?

10.4.2 What evidence **would** support or refute the possibilities you envisaged in 10.4.1?

10.4.3 Assume that what the passage says is true; how strongly does it support the explanation it offers?

10.4.4 Assume that what the passage says is true and bring in anything else you know about the death of the dinosaurs to produce the best argument you can to explain their extinction.

10.4.5 Suppose we discovered in the fossil record that some species of plants which require very little light did **not** die out at the same time as the dinosaurs. What does that tell us?

10.4.6 Suppose we discover that in fact different species of dinosaurs died out at different times separated by intervals of hundreds of thousands of years. What does that tell us?

10.4.7 Suppose we discover that there have been other mass extinctions of species at other periods in the Earth's history. What does that suggest?

The last question (10.4.1–10.4.7) should help to emphasise the importance of being **imaginative** in evaluating the reasoning provided in support of causal explanations. As we have said before, good critical thinking often requires creativity and imagination.

Question 10.5

Using the thinking map for Skilful Causal Explanation to guide you, write a brief evaluative response to the following passage:

An underwater survey of the Witch Ground, in the North Sea off Aberdeen [Scotland], has discovered a trawler which was probably sunk by a sudden burst of methane gas escaping from a vent in the sea floor – known as the Witch's Hole. When methane – or natural gas – bubbles through the sea in big enough volumes, it lowers the density of the water around it to a point at which objects, including ships will no longer float. 'Any ship caught above [such a blow-out] would sink as if it were in a lift shaft', said Alan Judd, a marine geologist from the University of Sunderland who led the Witch Ground survey expedition. In this case the trawler had sunk 'flat' with its hull sitting horizontally on the sea bed exactly over the Witch's Hole vent. This was consistent with the vessel being sunk by a methane blow-out; if she had been holed she would have sunk with the holed end lowest. Even sailors who jumped overboard wearing life-jackets would sink like stones. The Witch Ground and the Witch's Hole in particular, have long been known among fishermen as treacherous waters. Methane blow-outs are thought to have destroyed about 40 oil platforms around the world; the Witch Ground is just 22 miles from the Forties oil field. (Adapted from article in *The Times*, 30 November 2000 by their Science Correspondent Mark Henderson)

Question 10.6

Using the thinking map for Skilful Causal Explanation to guide you, briefly evaluate the following reasoning:

> Studies on individuals have attempted to determine whether raising the consumption of cholesterol affects the level of blood cholesterol. For example, volunteers drank four pints of milk a day for a period: their blood cholesterol levels were unaffected. Even more damaging to the hypothesis that ingested cholesterol can damage the heart are the results of two recent and independent studies funded by the British Medical Research Council. One found that men who drink no milk have ten times as many heart attacks as men who drink more than a pint a day. The other discovered that men who eat margarine have twice as many heart attacks as those who eat butter. There are in fact good reasons why one would not expect blood cholesterol to vary with diet. First, the liver manufactures three or four times as much cholesterol as is normally ingested. Secondly, the body itself regulates the amount of cholesterol in the blood: its level is normally kept constant regardless of what is eaten, though some unfortunate people have too high a setting and are likely to die young through heart attacks. The true causes of high blood cholesterol are not known. What is known is that although reducing blood cholesterol levels by drugs reduces heart disease, it does not increase longevity: people die of cancer instead. There is no solid evidence that cholesterol intake affects blood cholesterol levels, yet jumping to conclusions on the basis of insufficient evidence has caused a considerable scare. (Sutherland, 1992, p. 184)

10.5 The language of causal explanations

At this point you should probably look back at section 3.7 to remind yourself again of the points made there in some detail. Remember, it is easy to confuse arguments and causal explanations because of the ambiguity of certain words and phrases like 'because' and 'that's why'. These words sometimes signal that a reason is being given for a conclusion but sometimes signal that the author is giving a causal explanation and we provided a test to help you decide which is the case. With a little practice however, explanations leap to the eye and you will quickly learn to ask the right questions.

In general, the language we use in reasoning about causal explanations is very similar to the language we use in other kinds of reasoning (cf. sections 2.3 and 2.5); thus, we use the same language mentioned there to signal the confidence we have in claims, to criticise reasoning and so on. But in explanatory contexts, there is special emphasis on 'hypothesis', 'explains', 'causes' and 'evidence', so the language we use tends to include these and related words, like 'the theory says', 'the facts/data are/suggest/imply', 'is consistent with (or not)' and so on. It is also common to use verbs or phrases which imply a causal relation-ship without using the word 'cause', like 'drown', 'died from arsenic poisoning', 'died out', 'hit', 'sunk', 'affects the level of blood choles-terol' to give some examples we have encountered in this chapter. It is also quite common to reason 'by analogy' and to refer to what experts in the field believe when reasoning about causal explanations. Often, of course, such language is absent, but it is often implied and it could be helpful to write it in as we did with the 'therefore test'.

Consider the language of the following passage:

> The distinctive yellow-green colours of Van Gogh's paintings of landscapes and domestic interiors may be due to the side effects of his taking the drug digitalis. Although there are few medical records to prove the point, it is generally known that digitalis was commonly prescribed during the time Van Gogh lived. Also, Van Gogh's portraits of the doctor who treated him show the doctor holding a stem of foxglove, the very plant from which digitalis is made.

Once you think about it you can see that the author is offering a pos-sible causal explanation for Van Gogh's distinctive use of colours ('due to the side effects'). It is tentatively put forward ('may be . . .'). We could call this claim her hypothesis or her conclusion – either way it is very tentatively advanced and the reasons (or pieces of evidence) offered in its support are presented as only weak evidence for her the-ory ('Although there are few medical records to prove the point . . .'), so overall it is a very tentative argument in support of a thesis.

However, it is an interesting idea; perhaps a painter's way of paint-ing could be influenced by taking certain drugs and perhaps this was the case with Van Gogh. Of course, as it stands, the case is extremely weak, but if we wanted to consider the hypothesis seriously it is clear from our thinking map what questions we should ask. We need to con-sider whether there are other possible explanations for Van Gogh's use of those colours (he mixed them himself from unusual ingredients; he was partly colour blind), and we would need to consider what evidence would support or conflict with these ideas and then we would need to look for it, for example, did Van Gogh suffer from any illnesses for which digitalis was commonly prescribed, is there any other evidence that he took digitalis, does taking digitalis have a similar effect on painters' choice of colours now, do we understand the mechanism at work, and so on.

Though the language of the passage is not completely transparent a little thought shows what is being suggested. ('Perhaps Van Gogh used those distinctive yellow–green colours in his paintings of landscapes and domestic interiors because he took the drug digitalis.') By the criterion we explained in section 3.7 it is clear that this is an explanation (since it is known that Van Gogh used distinctive colours – that is clear for all to see – but it is not known whether he took digitalis). Furthermore, though it takes a bit of imagination, it is also reasonably clear what questions we should ask if we want to determine whether it is a good explanation.

Question 10.7

Bearing these remarks in mind, decide what is being explained and what is being argued for in the following passage. Is the argument convincing to you?

> Since 1980 [the number of human twin births has] been increasing – they are up by 42 per cent since that date throughout the developed world. For every 1,000 births in the developed world 29 are now twin births. This figure is likely to continue to increase because many of the extra twin births are caused by fertility treatments which result in the release of more than one egg during ovulation. This is also why the whole increase in twin births is taken up by fraternal twins who come from separate eggs. The rate of identical twins, from division of the same egg, has remained constant at 4 for every 1,000 births.
>
> So, while the number of twin births is set to increase even further in the short term as more women seek fertility treatments, there will be a limit to the number of extra twin births because, first, not all will seek this treatment and, second, not all women who do will have twins.
>
> At what point the figure will stabilise we do not yet know, but we can rest assured that the majority of births will remain as single births. ('Twin sets', *New Scientist*, 18 November 2000, p.121)

This neat example illustrates the difference between explaining and giving reasons for a conclusion; the first paragraph explains a phenomenon, the second gives reasons for a conclusion. It arose from a question about the increase in twin births and whether this would continue until all human births were twin births.

10.6 Making things fit together

The thinking map for Skilful Causal Explanation included the question, 'What explanation fits best with everything else we know and believe?'. In general scientists are trying to construct a 'web' of beliefs which best explain how things happen in the world, which make the best possible sense of our experience, so everything is intended to fit with everything else. The implication is that the more science you know the better you are able to judge whether a given explanation is plausible or not. But you can practise this skill with whatever level of knowledge you happen to have. Let us look at an example to illustrate this:

> Compasses will not always point north. Every 500,000 years or so the earth's magnetic field flips, swapping the positions of the magnetic poles. The last time this happened was 780,000 years ago so we are long overdue for another flip. When it comes it could be faster than anyone expected.
>
> Geophysical processes tend to be slow, and until recent times most geophysicists believed that a complete flip would take around 5,000 years. But last year a team of scientists announced they had found evidence in the magnetism of some rocks that parts of the flip might happen so quickly you could almost see the compass needle move. So fast indeed that long-haul flights could be thrown completely off course, and migrating birds, used to trusting their inbuilt compasses, could be left perplexed. ('When North Flies South', *New Scientist*, 30 March 1996, pp. 24–8)

Question 10.8

Before reading on, note what evidence you can think of which might support/refute what is claimed here (which incidentally is not a straightforward causal claim – but a claim about a scientific phenomenon)?

The most dramatic evidence for this comes from a pile of successive lava flows almost one kilometre thick (and 16.2 million years old) on Steens Mountain in eastern Oregon, USA.

Lava flows erupting on to the surface of the Earth contain particles of [iron and other] metal and when the lava cools below about 580 degrees C these particles become magnetised by the ambient field. This freezes the direction of the prevailing geomagnetic field into the rock, and from this the scientists can work out the position of the geomagnetic pole at the time the rock cooled. Most lava flows take only a matter of weeks or months to cool – much shorter than the time taken for a complete flip – and from the flows that formed while a reversal was under way scientists have concluded that the reversing field moved fairly slowly. But Steens mountain contains two flows that appear to have caught the moving field racing from one position to another.

When a lava flow is deposited, it cools first at the top and bottom, and only later towards the centre. If the [Earth's magnetic] field is stable while the lava is solidifying, the orientation within the magnetic particles is the same throughout. But the key

Arrows show direction of magnetic orientations within three successive lava flows

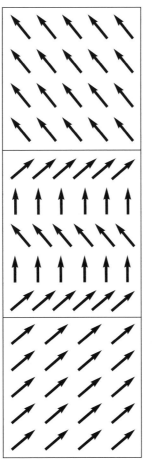

Youngest lava flow showing stationary pole

Intermediate lava flow showing moving pole

Oldest lava flow showing stationary pole

flows at Steens mountain look very different. The top and bottom
of the flows have exactly the same orientation as the underlying
lava. As you move towards the centre of the flows, the polarity
slowly changes orientation until in the very centre it exactly
matches that of the overlying flows. This is just what you would
expect if the lava flows had caught the field in the act of moving.

The scientists who studied these lava flows and published their
results in *Nature* concluded that:

at the time the lava was solidifying, the geomagnetic pole
shifted as much as six degrees a day over a period of 13 successive days.

Extrapolating from these figures the North and South magnetic poles
could flip completely in two to three months – a dramatic contrast with
the 5,000 years scientist formerly believed it took. The scientists who
published these results are very reputable 'the best people there are for
this sort of work' said another geophysicist from the University of Leeds,
and their work was published in a reputable scientific journal, *Nature*.
The problem for geophysicists is that it is very hard to reconcile this evidence, and the conclusion drawn, with other things they believe about
the Earth's core and what causes the Earth's magnetism. But other possible explanations of the Steens Mountain evidence, say the occurrence
of one of the Sun's periodic magnetic storms, just don't seem to fit
either. To make things even more puzzling further similar evidence has
now been found in 12 million year old rocks in New Mexico.
This is an interesting example, partly because it shows how instructive it can be to ask 'what would show X?', but also because subsequent
reasoning by the scientists concerned has been largely about what 'fits'
with everything else we know and believe.

Question 10.9

Review your answer to question 10.1 to see if you wish to revise it in the
light of your work in this chapter.

Question 10.10

Using the lessons of this chapter, write a brief response to the following
passage:

There is a small area in the middle of the right-hand side of the brain which produces a curious effect if an epileptic focus develops there. In such a focus the nerve cells from time to time all fire together: when they do so, they cause an epileptic seizure. A focus in this particular area can render the person highly religious, and cause him to avoid sex in any form and to give up all addictions such as smoking and alcohol. Remarkably, when the focus is removed and the person goes back to his previous existence, he may become an atheist, and return to cigarettes, alcohol and the pursuit of sex. It may be that the form the Christian religion has taken was in part caused by St Paul suffering an epileptic attack on the road to Damascus. (Sutherland, 1992, pp. 10, 11)

10.7 Summary

Much of our reasoning is concerned with causal explanations. Sometimes we just see what causes something, but mostly we have to work it out. In the latter case it is common for us to slip into one of two errors; either we consider only one possible cause or we attend to only some of the relevant evidence.

To remedy these faults, we need to ask the right question when considering reasoning to a causal explanation. These are:

1 What are the **possibilities** in this case?
2 What evidence could you find that **would** count for or against the likelihood of these possibilities (if you could find it)?
3 What **evidence** do you have already, or can you gather, that is relevant to determining what causes what?
4 Which possibility is rendered **most likely** by the evidence? (What explanation fits best with everything else we know and believe?)

Examples of reasoning to causal explanations show how these questions can help us think better about such cases.

Of course scientists, detectives and many others have to ask themselves questions very like the ones we have presented here if their reasoning about causal explanations is to pass the scrutiny of others.

Further reading

Ennis (1996, chapters 8 and 9). Swartz and Parks (1993) and (1994) on causal explanation.

Decision making: options, consequences, values and risks

How often have you said, or heard someone else say, 'How could I have been so stupid?' after making a decision which turned out to be a disaster. As with causal explanations, the thinking involved in deciding what to **do** – or **recommending a course of action**, or **weighing someone else's recommendation** – needs special attention because it is very common, is often important, and has to be evaluated in a distinctive way. In earlier chapters we already encountered numerous examples of reasoning which recommended a course of action, for example the argument that we should not permit prospective parents to choose the sex of their child, the argument that young people should not get married and numerous others.

We are all used to making decisions (or recommending a course of action), but sometimes we do that less skilfully than we might and the purpose of this chapter is to explain how to do it better and to give you practice in doing so.

Of course, we make decisions and recommendations about many matters which are not very important, like what clothes to put on in the morning before lazing about at home, or what to have for breakfast on such a day, but in this chapter we are mainly concerned with decisions and recommendations about more substantial matters, such as personal ones like which university to go to, which subjects to study, whether to take a job, whether to become vegetarian and so on, and more 'policy' ones like whether cannabis should be legalised, whether boxing should be banned, whether fox-hunting with hounds should be illegal, whether parents should be punished if their children break the law and so on. In short we are more concerned with decisions of a significant kind –

which merit careful consideration but which we often decide rather hastily. Sometimes, of course, decisions have to be taken very quickly – perhaps to deal with an emergency – and then one just has to act. But often, we do have time to think, and if the decision matters, the question is how to make a good decision rather than a poor one. Most of us have never been taught how to take decisions well – in particular what questions to ask before deciding – but this is a skill which can be taught, as we shall show. Whether we are trying to make a decision ourselves or are wishing to evaluate someone else's decision or recommendation, we need to be clear about the kind of reasoning which is appropriate in such contexts, and that is what this chapter is about.

Question 11.1

Think of a poor decision you made (about a significant matter) and write down anything you did – **or failed to do** – in the process of coming to that decision which caused you to make a poor decision. (For example, perhaps you did not really think about the decision at all!)

11.1 Common flaws in our thinking about decisions

Most of us have made a poor decision at some time and can put our finger on some flaw in the process which lead to that decision; either we simply did not think, or we did not find out some relevant information, or we listened to our heart and not to our head, and so on. I have often asked this question in workshops on decision making, and participants usually come up with a list very like the following:

> Did not give the matter enough thought.
> Did the first thing I thought of.
> Didn't think of possible alternatives.
> Didn't consider the consequences of various courses of action.
> Needed to get some more information.
> Didn't really consider what mattered to me.
> Was too hasty.
> Was too emotionally involved.
> Did what the 'boss' said.
> Accepted what others recommended without thinking about it.

Maybe your answer to question 11.1 above is included in this list or maybe you mentioned some other problem. Either way, most people have no difficulty in recognising these problems where decision making is concerned. The question is, 'What can be done to combat these weaknesses?', and the answer is surprisingly simple: if you recognise problems in the process of making decisions then you are half-way to being able to remedy them. If you think back to our basket ball analogy in chapter 1, you will realise that you then need a model of good decision making to emulate. So let us present such a model now.

11.2 A model for good decision making

The model we present here arises out of the list of weaknesses we identified earlier. There is nothing very controversial about this model; the ideas behind it have been around – in what is sometimes called 'decision theory' – for at least fifty years, but most people find that it is a great help to their own decision making and to responding to other people's reasoned recommendations.

11.2.1 Be clear why the decision is necessary

Suppose you are considering whether to become a vegetarian. You might consider this issue for at least two quite different sets of reasons. On the one hand, you might feel this is essentially a moral issue – about the rights and wrongs of treating animals in a particular way and eating them. Or you might see it mainly as a health issue – about the benefits and health risks associated with eating meat. Of course, you might think both sets of considerations are relevant, but it is very common for people to adopt one perspective or the other. The point is that you need to be as clear as possible about the background to the decision, the assumptions which lie in the background, the context and so on if you are to weigh the case wisely. Although models of good decision-making often fail to mention this requirement explicitly, it is implicit and getting clear about why a decision is necessary helps to focus one's thinking.

Sometimes being clear about why a decision is necessary means identifying a problem and sometimes it will require you to think carefully about *objectives* – what you, or others want to achieve. So, for example, if you are considering which university to attend, you might realise you know very little about the institutions you could attend, so that is a problem. Alternatively someone might advise you to apply for university A 'because that is the most prestigious place for the subjects in which you are interested', but you may feel that this is not necessarily right for you, so you may need to think carefully about what you want to get from your university education, what you are looking for – what your *objectives* are.

11.2.2 Make sure you consider alternative possible courses of action

One of the commonest mistakes we fall into when we are faced with making decisions or considering recommendations is that we fail to think of some reasonable alternatives. In fact, most people admit that they commonly make decisions by first deciding what they want to do and *then* rationalising that choice (if you reflect on your own decision making, you may be surprised how often you do this). The solution is clear enough. When faced with a decision, you need to pause and ask yourself what the alternatives are. This sounds easy enough, but it is quite hard to change old habits, so some practice will be required to achieve this habit. Not only do most us have the habit of leaping first and producing the justification afterwards, but most of us find it hard to be imaginative about what alternatives there are. How important this is depends on the case.

If the decision concerns something relatively straightforward (like which route to drive between A and B) it might be necessary to think of only one or two alternatives. But if the case is complicated and important it might be necessary to be very imaginative and inventive about possible alternatives (for example, whether Truman should have authorised the use of nuclear weapons on Hiroshima and Nagasaki). This should remind us of what we have said several times earlier, good critical thinking often requires creative thinking, imaginative thinking and 'thinking outside the box'. Sometimes you need just to think of a small number of reasonable alternatives, but sometimes you need to 'brainstorm' to think of unusual possibilities – if the case is very important and knotty – for example, like the case of Truman and the atom bomb. Anyway, when reasoning to a decision which matters it is always important to think what other options there might be.

For an example which illustrates this, look again at an argument we have already seen (question 9.5):

> Young people in Britain should not get married. Current statistics show that 40% of marriages end in divorce and one can safely assume that many of those couples who remain together are unhappily married. Therefore, it is more likely than not that young people who marry will divorce or be unhappily married. These are daunting odds for any young couple.

This can seem a powerful argument until you ask 'What are the alternatives (to getting married)?' Presumably these are something like living together on a long-term basis (without marrying), avoiding long-term relationships and having a series of short-term relationships, or avoiding close relationships altogether! But what are likely to be the consequences of these alternatives? Perhaps we could find statistics showing how individuals in these other relationship patterns fare; perhaps long-term relationships where the partners do not marry break up as often as marriages. Perhaps many of those in a series of short-term relationships suffer in ways they would not wish on others. And perhaps many of those who avoid close relationships suffer considerable loneliness. Until we know how well these alternatives work out statistically this argument does not carry much weight. Perhaps it is just a fact that life is risky whatever you do!

It is not easy to say how many and what alternatives one should consider when faced with making or evaluating a decision or recommendation; it depends on the case, on how important it is, how much time is available, whether relevant information is available (or easy or expensive to obtain), whether you can 'go back' and change your mind if things go wrong, and so on. The important point is that enough alternatives need to be considered in the circumstances if a decision or recommendation is to be adequately justified; this might mean only a small number, or only 'reasonable' alternatives, or perhaps 'imaginative' options too – it depends on the case.

Question 11.2

11.2.1 Imagine you are the teacher who receives the complaint from Hans about the unfair critical thinking test (section 2.2). Why do you need to make a decision about what to do? And what alternative courses of action are open to you?

11.2.2 Suppose you are the Agriculture Minister in the British Government and an outbreak of 'foot and mouth' disease is reported to you. Why is a decision necessary and what alternatives are open to you?

11.2.3 Imagine yourself in President Truman's position as he faced the decision about whether to drop the atom bomb; bearing in mind whatever you know about that event, list as many options as you can which you think need to be considered (brainstorming could help you).

11.2.3 Consider the possible consequences of the various alternatives

It is very common for people to say of a decision they took, 'I just didn't think about what was likely to happen.' But it is often very important not to make that mistake and to think about the possible consequences – both good and bad – of a course of action. For example, suppose you are considering which university to go to; if you do not check out the syllabus of the various courses which interest you and if you do not visit the institutions concerned you may well go somewhere where the course is not really what you want or where you do not really like the place or the people. If you had checked out these possible consequences in advance it could have saved you a lot of disappointment, frustration and perhaps even failure.

Working out the possible consequences of alternatives may require some imagination in order to think of consequences which need to be considered. Some possible consequences will be very obvious and will immediately spring to mind – for example, before choosing a university, it is obvious that you must investigate the course syllabus. But it may require a bit of imagination to think of some possible consequences (for example, do you need to consider the sporting facilities available at the university where you are thinking of studying or don't these really matter to you?).

Question 11.3

11.3.1 Refer back to your answer to question 11.2.1 and write out the possible consequences of two of the alternative courses of action open to you.

11.3.2 Refer back to your answer to question 11.2.2 and set out the possible consequences of two of the alternative courses of action open to you (use whatever background knowledge you have).

11.3.3 Refer back to your answer to question 11.2.3 and, using whatever you know about the bombing of Hiroshima and Nagasaki, think of 'possible consequences' of two important options which President Truman should have considered in deciding whether to drop the atom bomb (since this was an issue of enormous importance you should be as imaginative as you can about possible consequences and perhaps do some reading on the subject if you know little about it).

It is also clear that working out the consequences of possible alternatives will commonly require some investigation – as in the example we have been discussing about which university to go to. This certainly takes time and might cost money (for example, if you have to travel to universities to find out about them and their courses). How much investigation is appropriate depends on the case – on how important the decision is, how sure you want to be (some people like risks and uncertainty) and how difficult it is to find out what you need to know. In general a decision is reasonable if 'enough' of this investigation has been done in the context, but there is no general rule saying how much is 'enough'.

11.2.4 Consider how *likely/unlikely* and how *valuable/undesirable* the possible consequences are

It is very common for people to say things like, 'You should (or should not) do X because otherwise Y *might* happen.' For example, 'You should be vaccinated against tuberculosis because otherwise you *might* catch it.' Here, they are talking about a *possible* consequence of an action but they are making **no** estimate of how *likely* it is, or how *serious* it would be but both of these matter a great deal.

Consider, for example, the British National Lottery; for some time this was advertised with a picture of someone pointing at the viewer; the advertisement resembled the First World War Lord Kitchener advertisement where the caption was 'Your Country Needs You!'; in the National Lottery advertisement the caption was 'It Could Be You!', meaning that **you** could win the National Lottery! Well it is perfectly true that if you buy a National Lottery ticket you **could** win and this would give you millions of pounds which would be **highly desirable** to most people. But what are the chances? How *likely* is it that you will win? If you buy one ticket the chance of winning the National Lottery is about 10,000,000 to 1 against! So, yes, you **could** win but it is very, very **unlikely** (you are far more likely to be killed in a car accident!). This example illustrates the difference between how **likely** and how **valuable** a possible consequence of an action is and how important it can be to distinguish between the two (since they are independent of each other – something may be very desirable and either likely or unlikely, etc.)

Of course, we often have to estimate how likely something is without being able to give figures like those in the National Lottery case. In such cases we use language like 'very likely', 'almost certain', 'extremely unlikely', 'as likely as not' and similar phrases. These are vague but have more content than 'might happen' alone.

Note also that when something **undesirable** might happen it is very common to speak of 'risks'; for example, if you have some medical operation it is common to be told that there is such and such a risk of undesirable side effects – including possibly death!

Question 11.4

11.4.1 What is your view about buying National Lottery tickets for your-self *with your own money* (when you are over 18 – the minimum age for buying them legally). Write a brief case for or against doing this which takes account of alternatives, possible consequences, how likely and how valuable these are.

11.4.2 Refer back to your answer in 11.3.3 and, using what you know about dropping the atom bomb on Hiroshima and Nagasaki, esti-mate how likely and how valuable/undesirable the various possible consequences of your two or three options were.

11.2.5 Take proper account of moral or ethical commitments

Some readers may have found question 11.4.1 (about buying National Lottery tickets for yourself) a bit problematic because you are morally opposed to gambling. This may be something you feel very strongly about or something you believe – but not very passionately. If this is a serious commitment, the only 'possible consequence' which will matter to you is that buying National Lottery tickets would violate your moral code and this is something you regard as highly undesir-able, so you will instantly decide against on that ground alone. Other people, who believe that gambling is immoral but do not feel very strongly about it, might work out the consequences of buying tickets, giving some weight to doing an immoral act, but only some. It would depend on the strength of their commitment.

In general, you can take account of moral and ethical commitments in arriving at a decision by including them in the list of consequences and giving a measure of how undesirable it is for you to violate them. For example, if you were faced with the awful decision about whether you or your partner should have an abortion, this would involve moral considerations for most people (about the 'right to life' of the foetus or about a woman's 'right to choose') and these could be included in the list of consequences with values attached to them which would depend on how strong your moral commitments were. Similarly, perhaps President Truman considered the morality of killing many thousands of innocent civilians if he authorised dropping the atom bomb and the morality of subjecting many more American soldiers to injury and death if he did not.

Question 11.5

What sort of moral considerations do you think would be relevant to deciding the following:

11.5.1 A friend has confided in you, making you promise not to reveal her secret to anyone else. Other friends very much want you to tell them her secret. What should you do?.

11.5.2 As in 11.5.1 but what she has told you could affect your other friends seriously. What should you do?.

11.5.3 You know a school friend is getting deeply into serious drugs. What should you do?

11.2.6 Weigh up which alternative is best in the light of the consequences

Once you have considered a reasonable range of options and worked out their consequences – how likely they are and how valuable/undesirable – then you can make a decision about what ought to be done which is reasonably considered.

Here is an example where this technique was applied in my own case. Some time ago my daughter complained that our old piano was worn out and was preventing her from preparing well for her music exams. There seemed to be a problem, so what was to be done? Here is my reasoning about three options:

Option 1: **Do nothing**. I watched and listened to her playing; there was a small chance that she would simply cope with the piano and continue to enjoy playing; it seemed much more likely that she would become increasingly frustrated and play less, perhaps losing interest. I didn't want to risk this; encouraging her interest in music was very important to me.

Option 2: **Buy a new piano**. I took my daughter to play a wide range of new pianos; she really liked playing some, but these cost far more than I could afford. I felt sure she would love a good piano and would keep playing at least until she went to university (in two years); that was very important to me. But we couldn't afford the ones she liked.

Option 3: **Have the old piano 'restored'**. Three companies looked at it and said it would be very expensive and they could not guarantee success. A fourth said they could guarantee success; their price was reasonable and one I could afford; furthermore, they said they could sell it for twice the cost of restoring it if we didn't like the result of their restoration (because it was special and unusual). On checking with former customers, their credentials were excellent. Furthermore, my daughter preferred to keep her old piano if it could really be restored. Bingo!

It is clear that arriving at this decision involved considerable investigation; it took quite some time and cost some money (telephoning, visiting shops and getting estimates), but looking at the options and working out their likely consequences and the value of these enabled us to arrive at a well-reasoned decision. Not only was it well reasoned, it also turned out well, since the restoration was excellent and my daughter progressed musically as a result!

To conclude this section, if we ask the right questions we have a better chance of making good decisions than most of us do much of the time without the aid of such strategies.

11.3 A thinking map for handling decisions/ recommendations skilfully

If we put together the preceding considerations, we can produce a 'thinking map' which helps us ask the right questions when faced with making a decision or evaluating someone else's case for a recommendation.

'Thinking Map'

HANDLING DECISIONS/ RECOMMENDATIONS SKILFULLY

1 What makes this decision **Necessary**? [Objectives?]
[2 What is **Recommended** and on what **Grounds**?]
3 What are the **Options/Alternatives**? (Realistic or unusual?)
4 What are the **Possible Consequences** of the various options – and **How Likely** are they? (On the basis of what evidence and how reliable is it?)
5 How **Important** are these consequences – for all those affected?
6 When I **Compare** the alternatives in the light of their consequences, which is best? Is the recommended course best?
[7 How can I carry out this decision? (Contingency plans?)]

Let us consider how this thinking map works out with an example. Imagine you are an Inspector of Prisons; a Prison Governor with special responsibility for drugs policy in prisons reports to you as follows:

> Random drug testing of prisoners was introduced in 1995 in order to solve the many problems associated with prisoners taking drugs. Since cannabis can be detected in the body up to a month after having been smoked, prisoners are tempted to switch to heroin, which stays in the system for only 48 hours. As a result, since drug-testing was introduced, cannabis use has declined by a fifth, whereas heroin use has doubled. Heroin is not only a much more damaging drug than cannabis, but it is also extremely addictive. There is evidence that heroin addiction encourages prisoners to intimidate others in order to pay for the drug. (Questions appendix, passage 29)

Question 11.6

Before reading on consider what *you* think should be done.

Following the thinking map your thinking might go something like this:

> There are many problems associated with prisoners taking drugs; the policy we introduced to deal with this has had some unintended and undesirable consequences, so we need to think again. If we abandon random drug testing the old problems will very probably return and we don't want that. If we continue with the present policy we shall probably retain a lower use of cannabis but we shall make some prisoners into heroin addicts and risk increased intimidation. So, what other alternatives are there? We could attempt to make it much harder to smuggle drugs into prisons, with more severe penalties; we could do more drug testing of prisoners and make the penalties fiercer; we could relax our attempts to control drug taking in prisons and try to contain the consequences. Perhaps there are other possibilities too. We probably need some experiments in different prisons to see what the likely effects of these are, but drug taking is a problem for us and we can't just ignore it.

This thinking does not get very far, but it is on the right track so far as it goes. Next we need some evidence about likely consequences, etc. and this will require extensive investigation.

Question 11.7

Refer to your answer to question 11.1 and use the thinking map to see how it would have changed your decision-making process and how (if at all) it would have changed your decision.

Question 11.8

Briefly (about 100 words) review some options and possible consequences in the case of the arguments contained in two of the following:

11.8.1 Questions appendix, passage 8.
11.8.2 Questions appendix, passage 19.
11.8.3 Questions appendix, passage 25.
11.8.4 Questions appendix, passage 35.

These examples do not allow us to get very far in deciding what to do because we mostly need rather more information. If we look back to my 'piano example' (section 11.2.6) it is clear that finding the relevant information can be time consuming and costly. Thus, for example, this would clearly be the case with the example above about drug taking among prisoners. In general, the cost of finding the relevant information, in both time and money, may be a factor you need to take into account when trying to decide what to do, and sometimes it will be too high to be worthwhile. This is a judgement you will sometimes need to make and it will depend on how important the decision is, how serious it would be to 'get it wrong', how costly the extra information would be and whether there is enough time available. Leaving those problems on one side, let us now explain the connection between our model and making the 'right' decisions.

11.4 Decision procedures and making the 'right' decision

We pointed out earlier (chapters 6 and 7) that making judgements about which sources of information are reliable can be done more or less skilfully. But we also pointed out that making these judgements skilfully does not **guarantee** that we arrive at the **truth** (that deciding such issues rationally does not **necessarily** produce the truth). Asking the right questions helps us to avoid falling into some familiar errors and is more likely to produce the truth, but we can still make mistakes. The justification for making credibility judgements in the way we explained earlier is that in general this procedure will produce more reliable beliefs than not doing so; but this does not mean that in a particular case we won't make a mistake.

The same is true with decision making. Most people have had the experience of making some decision carelessly, quickly and without much thought – and have been lucky because the decision has **turned out well**. Equally, it sometimes happens that people have the opposite experience – in which they consider very carefully what to do, following all the procedures we just explained – and their decision **turns out badly**. For example, sometimes people who have taken great care over deciding whether to buy a particular car, have nothing but trouble with it and find that it is just a 'lemon'. Again, the point is that following good decision-making procedures will help us avoid familiar mistakes and generally produces better decisions than doing otherwise (acting on intuition or whatever), but it will not **guarantee** a 'good' decision (since the best laid plans can go wrong). For a dramatic real life example which illustrates the point consider the case of M Raffray and Madame Calment.

> Jeanne Calment, the world's oldest person died on August 4th 1997 aged over 122. In 1965, as a 90 year old widow, Madame Calment agreed to bequeath her flat to M Raffray, her family lawyer in exchange for a monthly pension of 2,500 francs, that was equivalent to about £250. He died in 1995 having paid out £120,000, more than 3 times the flat's value. On the face of it, M Raffray made a very reasonable deal in 1965, since no one could have foreseen that Mme Calment would live so long, but in the event it turned out to be a disastrously expensive deal. (*Daily Telegraph*, 5 August 1997)

Clearly then, there are two ways of assessing the quality of a decision. One is simply in terms of its **out-turn.** The other is in terms of the **quality of the procedures** used in making it. Everyone hopes their decisions will turn out well, but most people also recognise that things can go wrong even with the most rational procedures. The justification for using the procedures we have recommended is not that they will always guarantee a 'good' out-turn, but that they help to save us from error and generally tend to produce better decisions in the sense of better out-turns than any other procedure.

Question 11.9

There are two parts to this question.

11.9.1 Suppose someone offers you the following bet – they will toss a coin and if it comes down heads they will pay you £1,000 but if it comes down tails you will have to pay them £100 (and this will be done only once). Should you take the bet – assuming it is a standard coin, that you can afford to lose £100, would like to win £1,000, and are not opposed in principle to gambling?

11.9.2 With the same scenario as 11.9.1, what should you do if they agree to do it five times?

Question 11.10

Bearing in mind how decision making can go wrong, try to put yourself in Admiral Kimmel's shoes (without the benefit of hindsight) and say what questions he should have asked at various key points:

> In the summer of 1941 Admiral Kimmel, Commander in Chief of the American Pacific Fleet received many warnings from Washington about the possibility of war with Japan. [His men were not fully ready so he instituted a training programme, but he did not suspend peace-time shore leave. As a result,] at weekends there were sixty American warships anchored in Pearl Harbour and the airports on Hawaii contained lines of planes wing-tip to wing-tip . . .
>
> On 24 November he was warned by naval headquarters that a 'surprise aggressive movement in any direction including attack on Philippines or Guam is a possibility'. Despite a meeting with his staff he decided not to change his orders. One of [his] staff pointed out that Pearl Harbour had not been mentioned in the message from Washington and was therefore not at risk. Although this was clearly not implied by the message, which referred to an 'attack in any direction', the meeting came to the conclusion that there was no further need for action . . . If [Kimmel] thought the message was ambiguous, he should have asked Washington to clarify it. Moreover, he assumed, wrongly, that the army, which manned the anti-aircraft guns, was on full alert. He had only to pick up the telephone to check his assumption, but he failed to do so . . .
>
> Further warnings of war were received on 27 November and 3 December. The latter reported that American cryptographers had decoded a message from Japan ordering their embassies throughout the world to destroy 'most of their secret codes' . . . Kimmel and his staff seized on the word 'most': surely if Japan were going to war with America they would have instructed their embassies to destroy *all* secret codes.

On 6 December, the day before the battle of Pearl Harbour, there was more evidence of an impending attack. Kimmel was given orders to burn all confidential documents on outlying Pacific islands. Moreover, his chief intelligence officer reported that the location of Japan's aircraft carriers was unknown, since for several days it had been impossible to intercept their radio signals. This information convinced him that they were about to attack: the question was where . . . his staff officers reassured him, arguing that the Japanese had not sufficient strength left over from their operations in the Asiatic area to attack Pearl Harbour.

Five hours before the Japanese attack, two American mine sweepers saw a submarine which they assumed to be Japanese just outside Pearl Harbour. Because there was no full alert, this was not reported, but one hour before the attack, a Japanese submarine was sunk near the harbour entrance. The officer of the watch reported it to all the relevant naval officers he could contact and the message reached Admiral Kimmel. Instead of taking immediate action, he decided to wait for confirmation that the submarine really had been Japanese. The destruction of the American fleet followed. As for Admiral Kimmel, he was court-martialled and demoted. (Sutherland, 1992, pp. 131–3)

11.5 To summarise

The thinking involved in making decisions or in recommending a course of action deserves special attention. We often do this poorly because we jump to a decision and then rationalise it. If we are to make decisions well, we need to avoid the common weaknesses in thinking of this kind, so we need to be clear what the problem is, we need to consider a reasonable range of options and their possible consequences and so on *before* coming to a decision or recommendation.

In getting clear what the problem is this may necessitate formulating objectives, though not necessarily. In thinking of possible consequences we need to be as imaginative as possible, but we must then judge carefully *how likely* they are, and *how valuable,* to come to a rational decision. In doing this we may also need to undertake some investigations and take account of moral considerations. We may then be in a position to come to a well reasoned, overall decision.

These are simple ideas but they have proved their value over many years and are widely used. Charles Darwin says, in his *Autobiography* that he used the method of spelling out pros and cons in deciding whether to marry! I'm not sure how well the method applies in such a case but it **is** very useful in many decision-making situations.

Question 11.11

To conclude this chapter you should use the ideas you have studied here to help you answer two of the following:

11.11.1 Questions appendix, passage 46.
11.11.2 Questions appendix, passage 47.
11.11.3 Questions appendix, passage 48.
11.11.4 Questions appendix, passage 49.
11.11.5 Questions appendix, passage 50.

Further reading

Swartz and Parks (1993) and (1994); sections on decision-making.

Questions appendix

This appendix contains a large number of passages on which to practise your critical thinking skills. They are taken from various sources. The first 32 are stimulus passages in the multiple choice questions in Paper 1 of the new *Critical Thinking* examination at Advanced Subsidiary (AS) GCE level produced by the Oxford, Cambridge and RSA Examinations Board (OCR) in 1999 and 2000. The next eight are stimulus passages from the University of East Anglia *Test of Logical Reasoning* designed by Alec Fisher and Anne Thomson. American readers will immediately see that these passages are very like the stimulus passages to be found in the *Scholastic Aptitude Test*, the *Law Schools Admission Tests*, the *Graduate Record Examination* and similar North American Tests.

Following these first 40 passages are some further, mostly longer passages. Some of these come from Paper 2 of the new Critical Thinking Examination mentioned above (these are presented with their original question and their source is cited as *Critical Thinking* AS (date and paper number)). Other passages come from newspapers, magazines and so on. Again, many of these resemble stimulus passages to be found in some North American tests.

Notice that many of the questions which are to be found in the text could be tried at different stages of your progress through this course. For example, you might like to write an answer to one or more of the questions in 7.11 before studying chapters 6 and 7 on making credibility judgements, and then, when you have studied chapters 6 and 7 and without looking back at what you first wrote, you could write a second answer. You (or a teacher) could then compare the two answers to see if you wrote a really good answer first time or whether you improved as a result of studying this chapter (or wrote a worse answer!).

Notice also that answers to most of the questions in the text are to be found either in the text itself or in the Answers section which follows (p. 201).

All the passages used here are reproduced with the kind permission of the copyright holders.

Passages

The first sixteen passages are stimulus passages from the multiple choice section of Paper 1 of the Critical Thinking AS examination, 1999.

1 Being a driving instructor is a challenging and rewarding occupation. One has great freedom in working for oneself, and it is unnecessary to have passed any 'A' levels. Therefore, a suitable job for anyone without 'A' levels is that of driving instructor.

2 There is a growing number of organisations which have been set up to deal with bullying. The only possible reason for this is that bullying is on the increase.

3 If the world's climate was getting warmer, we would find that some of the ice at both the North and the South Pole was melting at an unusually high rate. If the ice was melting, we would see its effect in the raising of the level of the sea. There is evidence that this level is increasing, so the world's climate must be getting warmer.

4 The traditional British approach to food safety has been one where local health officials only intervene at the level of food retailing, for instance inspecting premises where food is prepared or sold. However, a much broader approach to the question is needed. Many of the dangers to our health resulting from the food we eat arise from the way it is produced in the first place, that is the modern intensive farming practices involved, rather than small-scale organic farming. A national food safety agency that fails to address the question of food production will therefore be unlikely to protect us effectively from damaging our health through the food we eat.

5 The decline in the number of small birds has numerous causes but the most significant is the growth in the population of their predators – mainly magpies. But ultimately it is human activity which has caused this decline. Magpies on the other hand have dramatically increased in numbers. This

increase is due to a ready diet of carcasses of wild animals killed by traffic. Traffic is a man-made phenomenon.

6 Opera companies have applied for grants from the National Lottery to improve their theatres. It seems unfair that lottery money should be used to subsidise activities which are of no interest to the typical buyer of a lottery ticket. The money should be used to benefit such things as sporting activities, which are enjoyed by a wide section of the population.

7 If people who claim to have been abducted by aliens really have been abducted, then we would need to take reports of UFO sightings very seriously. However, such claims are very suspect. There are many possible explanations for such apparent abductions, ranging from obvious untruthfulness on the part of those claiming abduction to hallucinations and temporary paralysis. Given that we can explain these apparent abductions in ways that do not involve aliens, we do not need to take reports of UFO sightings seriously.

8 Making a sport of killing animals is abhorrent to most people in this country. This alone does not establish a strong enough case for an outright ban. There needs to be a compelling reason – over and above public distaste – for legislation to be justified.

9 Every year the town of Bridgewater holds its traditional carnival consisting of 'floats' which members of the local 'Carnival Clubs' have spent several months constructing. They say they do this to raise money for charity. However the amount of money spent on constructing the floats exceeds the amount raised by the carnival.

10 Employment agencies say that employers are increasingly looking for temporary rather than permanent staff. Furthermore, the Department of Employment says that the traditional demand for temporary summer staff has almost disappeared, indicating that employers are using temporary staff all the year round as part of the work force. Thus it is clear that a fundamental change is taking place as employers, content with a higher ratio of temporary to permanent staff, alter the structure of their work force.

11 A group of European scientists has looked at a number of studies of the link between passive smoking and lung cancer. The scientists have said that these studies do not demonstrate that there is a significant risk of lung cancer for non-smokers who are exposed to environmental tobacco smoke at work or in the home, either from a smoking parent or spouse. But this analysis was commissioned by the tobacco industry. So findings of the analysis are likely to be incorrect.

12 The switchboards of some large companies and public organisations have systems by which incoming telephone calls are answered automatically and the callers put in a queue. When telephone callers are caught in one of these queues they are given no idea how long they will have to wait. Callers should be updated on the current length of the queue. This is quite within the capabilities of the technology which runs the queuing system. At least then there would be some information on how much the call will cost, giving the caller a rational choice of whether to ring off.

13 Since the majority of people are right handed, tennis players are more accustomed to playing against right handers than left handers. This gives left-handed players an advantage as their opponents often do not know what to expect. This is borne out by the fact that, among the world's top tennis players, there is a greater proportion of left handers than there is in the population as a whole. Players could increase their chances of success by learning to play with their left hands.

14 Recent evidence shows that modern cars vary in their ability to withstand impact. This might suggest that owners of those cars which did badly in impact tests should be anxious about their safety. However, anybody travelling in the type of cars tested can be reassured that they are adequately protected. The degree of force that was applied to the cars was far in excess of that experienced in a road accident. Whilst some cars did better than others, in absolute terms they were all able to reach a satisfactory standard of withstanding impact in the event of an accident.

15 Homeless people are frequently blamed for being homeless. They are regarded as being responsible for their own plight as

a result of managing their finances badly, refusing employment opportunities and being generally lazy and disorganised. Young homeless people are told they should not have left home so soon. These accusations may be true in a small minority of cases, but all too often they deflect attention from the shortage of available housing at affordable prices and the inadequacy of public policies designed to provide more, and suitable, homes. Many people are homeless through no fault of their own but are caught in circumstances that prevent them from obtaining a home of their own. There are just not enough affordable homes to go round.

16 Perhaps the most common response to the call for the elimination of animals from toxicity testing is the benefits argument. It runs thus: human beings and animals have benefited from toxicity tests on animals; therefore these tests are justified. But those who support this argument would have to establish that the benefits to animals outweighed the distress and indignity caused to them in the process, and if it did do we might be on our way to receiving an interesting defence of toxicity testing. Unfortunately for those who countenance these tests, however, the benefit to animals cannot be established and, therefore, the benefits argument fails.

The following sixteen passages are stimulus passages from the multiple choice section of Paper 1 of the Critical Thinking AS examination, 2000. Passage 17 is the stimulus passage to question 1, passage 18 is for question 2 and so on.

17 The outstanding success of Ted's company, which was launched against the advice, and without the support, of bankers, business consultants and financiers, just goes to show that one person's vision can prove all the experts in the world wrong. Anyone thinking of setting up a business, therefore, should trust their own judgement, and not be influenced by the advice of others.

18 Recent research suggests that our understanding of how clouds interact with sunlight might be wrong: new measurements suggest that clouds absorb four times as much energy as previously thought. Since existing models of how the climate functions are based on the original measurements, if the new measurements are shown to be accurate, models of

how the climate works will need to be completely overhauled. Climate models are used in our attempts to measure global warming so, if these climate models are shown to be inaccurate, we will have to revise completely our understanding of global warming.

19 One in 1,000 people in Britain is estimated to be a carrier of the potentially fatal liver disease hepatitis B, although this estimate is likely to be far too low. There should be a mass vaccination programme to eradicate this disease. Seventy five countries carry out such a programme, and including hepatitis B in Britain's existing vaccination programme would be a simple matter. The main problem has been given as that of cost. Each shot of the vaccine costs at present £5 and the total cost of a mass campaign at this price would be more than £20 million. However, this cost would be substantially reduced if a mass campaign was introduced because the manufacturers would supply the vaccine at a much lower price for bulk purchase.

20 According to a recent survey, many people believe that about a quarter of the population will become victims of violent crime in the next year, whereas crime statistics show that it is only about 1 per cent. Furthermore, those with the greatest fear of crime, namely the elderly, are the least likely to be affected (since most victims are young men). The increasing number of television programmes which show re-enactments of crimes add to people's fears about violent crime by making it seem more common than it is. It is time that we stopped making such programmes.

21 The history of the world is full of many examples of the extinction of species, and we should not regard such extinction as a serious environmental problem. 245 million years ago, 90 per cent of all species vanished; 65 million years ago, 50 per cent of all living things died out, including the dinosaurs. Much more recently, the influence of humans has led to many species becoming extinct: in Hawaii, for example, this influence led to huge losses of species of plants, insects, and animals. But in each example of extinction we have seen the lost species replaced by new ones (for instance, mammals replaced dinosaurs).

22 Charging skiers around £12 extra for carrying their skis or snowboards on charter flights is unjustifiable in economic terms, though many tour operators now do it. Their sole ground is that carrying skis and boards raises costs because they incur extra handling charges and add to the weight of the plane and, therefore, to fuel consumption; and they believe that it is right to charge only those passengers who choose to bring their ski-gear. But when a tour operator runs a charter flight it hires the plane at a fixed price, estimated in advance, which includes all fuel and handling charges. The cost of the plane would be just the same even if none of the passengers brought skis or snowboards.

23 Every motorist pays the same amount for road tax, regardless of how much they use the roads: someone who covers only 1,000 miles a year pays the same as someone who covers 20,000. This is surely unfair. The justification for having a road tax system is that it brings in revenue for the Government, revenue which should be used to improve the road system and to help reduce levels of pollution. But even more revenue could be brought in by scrapping the system and replacing it with an increase in the amount of tax on fuel. This must be not only a better way of raising revenue but also a much fairer system. It is a change which therefore should be made.

24 Over the past ten years, there has been a four-fold increase in the number of people killed in road accidents who are found to have illegal drugs in their bodies. The rate of increase is much greater than the corresponding figure for those people killed in accidents who were found with alcohol in their blood. This shows that the campaign against drink-driving has succeeded. Consequently, the Government ought now to concentrate on targeting those people who drive whilst under the influence of illegal drugs.

25 The Government is proposing to allow 14-year-olds to spend half of their school year at work, if they want to. This is because many in this age group are seen as being uninterested in what the schools are teaching. But what about those children who have been getting on with their school work and attending regularly? These children will have to watch

their less conscientious classmates being allowed to get frequent breaks from the discipline and demands of school work. The effect will be to create a lot of unrest in the children left behind, an unrest which will turn into a lack of interest in school work. The Government proposal will have the opposite effect to that intended: it will turn more children off what schools have to offer.

26 There is evidence that birds of prey such as kestrels, buzzards and black kites prefer to hunt for their prey near roads than in the open countryside. Furthermore, they prefer to hunt near busy rather than quiet roads. The evidence can be explained in a number of ways. For one thing, a busy road like a motorway provides a steady stream of fast-moving traffic which the birds can adjust to more easily than the sight and sound of an occasional vehicle on quiet roads. For another, motorways have verges which provide open areas for hunting, and shrubs of useful perching height. The evidence shows that plans to expand our road-building programme are good news for wildlife.

27 There has been a decline in the rate of many illnesses of old age. For example, arthritis, dementia, and strokes are all declining year by year. The causes of this decline include such medical advances as beta-blockers to control high blood pressure and the fitting of hip replacements. There is, however, another factor. The present generation of sixty and seventy-year-olds had much better nutrition as children than did their parents. Good nutrition in childhood is important in laying the foundations of good health in adulthood. Since improvements in nutrition have continued over the past sixty years, we can expect that many of the illnesses of old age will continue to decline.

28 The Government has announced that it wants to reduce the level of ill-health due to stress. A recent study of 8,000 white-collar workers in America found that men who had considerable control over the way they carried out their jobs had a low rate of heart disease, a stress-related illness. Thus the most stressful jobs are those in which employees have little control over the pace of their work and how it is organised. If the Government is serious about wanting to reduce the level

of stress-related illness, then it needs to encourage employers to give their workers high levels of control over their work.

29 Random drug-testing of prisoners was introduced in 1995 in order to solve the many problems associated with prisoners taking drugs. Since cannabis can be detected in the body up to a month after having been smoked, prisoners are tempted to switch to heroin, which stays in the system for only 48 hours. As a result, since drug-testing was introduced, cannabis use has declined by a fifth, whereas heroin use has doubled. Heroin is not only a much more damaging drug than cannabis, but it is also extremely addictive. There is evidence that heroin addiction encourages prisoners to intimidate others in order to pay for the drug.

30 Since the imposition of much higher charges for dental treatment, there has been a significant reduction in the number of people who visit the dentist on a regular basis. In a recent survey, almost half of those who had not visited their dentist for at least eighteen months said that the level of the charges had been the reason for their staying away. Clearly, if we are to improve the dental health of the population, we must reduce the level of charges.

31 One group of theories about the origin of human language suggests that the first words were imitative of sounds in the natural world. The apparent survival of such words in modern languages is offered as evidence for this explanation. For instance, a Welsh term for owl, *gwydihw*, pronounced 'goody-hoo', seems to mimic the sound an owl makes. But if some words really did resemble natural sounds, you would expect them to be the same or similar in every language. Interestingly enough, they are not. Dogs go *oua-oua* in France, *bu-bu* in Italy, *mung-mung* in Korea. A purring cat goes *ron-ron* in France, *schnurr* in Germany – and so on. These so-called imitative words are no more alike than any other synonymous words from different languages.

32 Young drivers (those between the ages of seventeen and twenty one) have to pay higher insurance premiums than older drivers because they are seen as a much higher risk. There is certainly evidence that they have an accident rate

which is greater than that for other age groups. Drivers aged between seventeen and twenty one represent 10 per cent of licence holders and, even though they do less than average mileage, they are involved in 20 per cent of all accidents. It has been proposed that, if they agree to have extra tuition after they have passed their driving test, their insurance premiums could be lowered. Therefore, in both their interests and every-one else's, they should be required to have such extra lessons.

The next eight passages are stimulus passages (numbers 4, 5, 11, 15, 16, 25, 27 and 28) taken from Testing Reasoning Ability, Centre for Research in Critical Thinking, University of East Anglia, 1993. Question 33 is number 4 and so on.

33 The number of crimes committed by people under the age of seventeen has almost doubled in the last seven years. The Criminal Justice Act which becomes law this year should have the effect of reversing this trend. Children who commit crimes know that the penalties are minimal. But the new Act will make it possible for parents to be made liable for fines and compensation, and for them to be compelled to appear in court alongside offspring who are under seventeen years of age. The level of fines will be related to parental income, and wealthy parents may have to pay up to £5,000 for their chil-dren's crimes.

34 The idea that we should cease to aim for economic growth is crazy. When should growth have stopped? Presumably the Stone Age – surely the most 'environmentally friendly' period ever. Think of all the wildlife and the rain forests. Or perhaps the Victorian Age? But in those days, before the availability of affordable transport, you could travel to beauty spots only if you were rich. Now all those who wish to see these places can do so. How can this be bad? One can still find such beautiful places – all the more so as economic growth takes us away from the 1950s and pesticides. It would have been a tragedy if our worries about pollution had made us stop economic growth in that decade.

35 Despite the appalling mortality rate from polio in the past, some parents choose not to have their children vaccinated against it, because they think there is now only a low risk that

their children will become infected with the disease. Moreover, some believe that there is a more than negligible risk that the vaccine will have harmful side effects. In their eyes, a decision to avoid vaccination may appear entirely rational. But what they do not realise is that if a substantial percentage of a population is not vaccinated against polio, there will be regular outbreaks of the disease every few years as the number of non-immune people increases.

36 The police force should ban their officers from driving at high speed in pursuit of young joyriders who steal cars. Many deaths, both of joyriders and of innocent bystanders, have occurred as a result of such chases. The police say that they have policies which are aimed at preventing danger to the public during car chases, by requiring police drivers to abandon the chase when speeds become too high for safety. But the excitement of the chase inevitably makes the police drivers forget the policy, and disregard public safety. No stolen car is worth a human life.

37 If you don't vote, it won't make any difference to the election result. But if everyone like you doesn't vote, it will make a difference to the election result. So you should vote.

38 For many A-levels, students do most of their work in class, and they have to accept and learn what their teachers say if they are to obtain the high grades required for university entry. Thus it is often the most docile and teacher-dependent students who succeed. It is hardly surprising that such students have difficulty in motivating themselves and organising their time when they go to university, where they are suddenly expected to do most of their learning by themselves. Nor is it surprising that they expect the whole of the required syllabus to be delivered to them through the medium of lectures and tutorials. Until A-levels are reformed, good teaching in universities is not enough. It is necessary to inculcate the skill of learning for oneself.

39 When prisoners under sentence of death are given the choice between life in prison and execution, 99 per cent of them choose life imprisonment. This shows that they fear death more than they fear life imprisonment. Since one is most

deterred by what one most fears, it is evident that the threat of the death penalty is more likely to deter most potential murderers than is the threat of life imprisonment.

40 There should be an international criminal court of justice which would take the process of prosecution for war crimes out of the hands of victors. At present, punishment for war crimes is bound to *appear* unfair, because the winning side will be seen as imposing its own values, and ignoring the point of view of the losing side. An even more serious reason is that the present system of punishment is bound to *be* unfair, in that some guilty people will escape punishment. People are likely to be brought before a court for war crimes only if the state they served has been defeated in war.

The following passages come from various sources, which are acknowledged in each case. Sometimes these passages come from the OCR Advanced Level Critical Thinking examinations of 1999 and 2000 and in these cases they are presented here with their original question. Other passages have associated questions in the body of the foregoing text.

41 The forensic experts who were sent to Kosovo after NATO's bombing campaign have been coming to some surprising conclusions. They were sent to unearth the evidence of genocide by the Serbs which had precipitated NATO's action. During the war the US Defence Secretary said that up to 100,000 Albanians had been killed by the Yugoslav military. The British Minister of State at the Foreign Office said 10,000 had been killed. President Clinton said tens of thousands had been killed on President Milosevic's orders. The UN told experts from fifteen countries to expect 44,000 deaths. However, Emilio Perez Pujol, head of a Spanish team which went home in disgust last month after finding just 187 bodies, said there may be far fewer dead than previous estimates; several sites publicised by NATO as possible mass graves turned out to be empty. Stratfor, an analytical group examining data from Kosovo, suggests that the final toll might be as low as a few hundred. (Adapted from *The Times* leader, 2 November 1999)

42 In the following passage you are given some information about a situation in which there is a dispute as to what happened. Using this information, write out a reasoned case for judging who

was to blame for the accident. In your answer you should make clear what assumptions you are making about what the participants could have seen, what motives they might have for saying what they do, what expertise they have and any other relevant factors.

One of the employees at Dovetail Joinery has had an accident with a circular saw. Whilst pushing a large piece of wood through the saw, his hand was seriously injured by the blade. A dispute has now arisen over who was to blame for the accident.

The injured employee, Ashworth (A), claims that he followed all the company's safety procedures but that the owner of the company, Bell (B), had not ensured that the machine was as safe as possible. (B) is adamant that the machine was in a perfectly safe condition. If it had not been, he argues, he would have been told by the foreman (F).

(F) also insists that the machine was always maintained satisfactorily and, to emphasise his point, he has given the written maintenance record to the tribunal. In addition, (F) claims that, just before the accident, he saw (A) 'laughing and joking and messing about with his workmates'.

One of these workmates, Chandra (C), agrees with (A) that, despite its regular maintenance, the saw was not as safe as it should have been because its safety guard was poorly designed and did not function well. Furthermore, they had told (F) about it.

A health and safety inspection (I), who has inspected the machine, reports that the safety guard is poorly designed to protect operators in a number of circumstances which are familiar to operators of circular saws. (*This question comes from the AS Level Critical Thinking examination, Paper 2, 27 May 1999. Answer time: about 30 minutes.*)

43 As the warden of Larkfield Park, you have been called to investigate an incident involving a fight between two dogs. The fight took place in the park fifteen minutes ago. Using the information given in the following passage, write out a reasoned case for judging which dog (and therefore which owner), if either, was to blame. In your answer you should make clear what assumptions you are making about what the participants could have seen, what motives they might have for saying what they do, what expertise they have and any other relevant factors:

The owner of the first dog (A) claims that the second dog attacked hers 'viciously and without warning'. The owner of the second dog (B) denies this, pointing to the injuries on her dog as evidence that it was (A)'s dog which attacked viciously. (You can see that (B)'s dog is indeed more injured than (A)'s.)

The owner of a third dog (C) says that, about half an hour ago, her dog had been involved in a fight with (B)'s dog, a fight that was started, without any provocation, by (B)'s dog. In addition, she insists on making the point that (A)'s dog 'always gets on well with hers'.

A jogger (J) tells you that, from a distance, he had seen both incidents in which (B)'s dog is alleged to have been involved. In both cases, he says, (B)'s dog did seem to be the one that was chasing the other dog and making the most noise.

Another dog owner (D), who has just come into the park, says that he has often walked with (A) and her dog; he finds it impossible to believe that (A)'s dog could be vicious. (*This question comes from the AS Level Critical Thinking examination, Paper 2, 27 May 1999. Answer time: about 30 minutes.*)

44 In the following passage you are given some information about a situation in which there is a dispute as to what happened. Using this information, write a reasoned case in which you come to a judgement as to what did happen. In your answer you should make clear what assumptions you are making about what the participants could have seen, what motives they might have for saying what they do, what expertise they have and any other relevant factors.

The appointment of a new ambassador from a South American country provoked considerable controversy because the ambassador had been accused by many human rights groups of having been personally involved in the torture of political opponents some years before. A demonstration against his appointment had been organised by the Anti-Fascist Alliance (AFA). However, this had provoked the group Rebirth-1933 (known otherwise as R33) to organise a counter-demonstration, welcoming the ambassador as 'a fighter against moral decline'.

The police had decided to let both demonstrations go ahead, but provided a very heavy presence in order to keep the two sides apart. Unfortunately, the number of demonstrators on both sides was greater than had been expected, and it became difficult to prevent violence breaking out. One of those hurt was the leader of the AFA, Fran Lee (F), who suffered serious head injuries, and had to be taken to the nearest hospital, where she remains in a coma.

The situation surrounding (F)'s injuries remains unclear. At the time that she was injured, she was being restrained by a policeman (P) who claims she was hit by a 'rock' which also struck his helmet and which was thrown from a group of R33 demonstrators. Furthermore, (P) insists that he was one of a group of police who were trying to ensure that she did not get attacked by some R33 members who had got very close to her. On the other hand, a well-known lawyer and human-rights activist (A), who was with her at the time, claims that (F) was injured by the police, especially (P), using their batons with unreasonable force against her and other AFA members. A TV news crew (N), whose camera was damaged in the melee, said that they had filmed several police using their batons heavily on (F) and other AFA members just before she was grabbed by (P). Though R33 leaders deny that she was hit by something thrown by one of their supporters, an R33 member (M), who refused to be identified, boasted in an interview to the *BBC* of having 'split Lee's head with a brick'. Another witness, a Dutch tourist (D), who had taken shelter from the violence in a doorway, says she certainly saw police using their batons strongly to try to separate people, but she did not see any missiles being thrown. A hospital spokesperson (H) said, 'Frances Lee sustained a fractured skull which appears to have been caused by at least one very severe blow to the head.' (*This question comes from the AS Level Critical Thinking examination, Paper 2, 24 May 2000. Answer time: about 30 minutes.*)

45 The following is a difficult piece of reasoning about credibility considerations – and miracles:

. . . there is no species of reasoning more common, more useful, and even necessary to human life, than that which is derived from the testimony of men, and the reports of eye-witnesses and spectators . . . [But]
    Suppose . . . that the fact, which the testimony endeavours to establish, partakes of the extraordinary and the marvellous; in that case, the evidence, resulting from the testimony, admits of a diminution, greater or less, in proportion as the fact is more or less unusual . . .
    [Now] suppose that the fact which [witnesses] affirm, instead of being only marvellous, is really miraculous . . .
    Nothing is esteemed a miracle, if it ever happens in the common course of nature. It is no miracle that a man, seemingly in good health, should die on a sudden: because such a kind of death, though more unusual than any other, yet has been frequently observed to happen. But it is a miracle, that a dead man should come to life; because that has never been observed in any age or country . . .

The plain consequence is . . . 'That no testimony is sufficient to estab-lish a miracle, unless the testimony be of such a kind, that its falsehood would be more miraculous, than the fact, which it endeavours to estab-lish' . . . When anyone tells me, that he saw a dead man restored to life, I immediately consider with myself, whether it be more probable, that this person should either deceive or be deceived, or that the fact, which he relates, should really have happened. I weigh the one miracle against the other; and according to the superiority, which I discover, I pronounce my decision, and always reject the greater miracle. If the falsehood of his testimony would be the more miraculous, than the event which he relates; then, and not till then, can he pretend to com-mand my belief or opinion. (David Hume, *Enquiries Concerning Human Understanding*, Section X, Part 1, para. 91)

46 Write a critical evaluation of the argument which is presented below, introducing any further arguments you judge to be relevant. Your evaluation should show that you are clear about the structure of the argument (for example, which claims are reasons, conclu-sions and assumptions) but no credit will be given for merely paraphrasing the argument.

Children

It is widely assumed that education is a crucial part of children's development but it needs to be remembered that three-quarters of their waking hours are spent outside school. This time out of school is full of potentially useful experiences.

Unfortunately, however, access to these experiences has been increasingly diminished because parents want to protect their children from harm, whether from traffic or from molesting strangers. For example, although most children own a bicycle, few are allowed to use it as a means of transport, in spite of the fact that it is an ideal way of making children fit. Thus, in twenty or thirty years, the incidence of heart disease might rise sharply owing to children of today having had insufficient exercise during the critical early years.

In the early 1970s, only 14 per cent of junior school children were driven to school; now, it is 64 per cent. Parents obviously had their concerns more in perspective twenty five years ago. This huge percent-age increase represents thousands of isolated children, stuck inside cars. Such isolation, it has been claimed, could lead to various behav-ioural problems.

The number of crimes committed against children is actually very low. Parents should acknowledge this and then they would see that the increasing control of children's lives is very damaging by denying opportunities for them to take risks, make mistakes, and suffer the consequences.

Children always used to play on the streets; children always used to walk or cycle to school or to see their friends. They should be allowed to do so again. (*This question comes from the AS Level Critical Thinking examination, Paper 2, 27 May 1999. Answer time: about 30 minutes.*)

47 Write a critical evaluation of the argument which is presented below, introducing any further arguments you judge to be relevant. Your evaluation should show that you are clear about the structure of the argument (for example, which claims are reasons, conclusions and assumptions) but no credit will be given for merely paraphrasing the argument.

Free Willy

The film *Free Willy* was a very effective way of highlighting the plight of a captive killer whale (or orca). People were rightly concerned that such creatures should not be kept in captivity, and this concern became reality when £7.5 million was raised from the public in order to release the orca star of the film, Keiko, back into the Atlantic.

It makes a lovely story, of course. But, just think of it: £7.5 million to return one animal into the wild. The animal lovers who sent their money could have used it to far greater effect. For example, it could have secured for ever the turtles and seabirds of a marine reserve in Tanzania, or it could have stopped the decline of the bullfinch in this country.

Even if they just wanted to use the money for whales, it could have helped the campaign to restrict (or even stop) commercial whaling. Would those who sent their money for Keiko's release be happy if he swam free but alone in the vastness of the Atlantic?

But there are causes beyond that of animal welfare. A very good example is the campaign to save the sight of people in the developing world by funding simple operations. £7.5 million would have helped thousands of such people.

The sentimentality that leads people to spend £7.5 million on saving a single animal is misplaced.

It is obvious that future projects which raise this sort of money should be spent in ways that improve the welfare of as many animals (or people) as possible. (*This question comes from the AS Level Critical Thinking examination, Paper 2, 27 May 1999. Answer time: about 30 minutes.*)

48 Write a critical evaluation of the argument which is presented below, introducing any further arguments you judge to be relevant. Your evaluation should show that you are clear about the structure of the argument (for example, which claims are reasons, conclusions and assumptions) but no credit will be given for paraphrasing the argument.

Divorce

Although not all single-parent families are the result of divorce, in this country almost a quarter of families with dependent children are headed by a single parent. This compares with an average figure of only 14 per cent in the rest of the European Union. These figures show that divorce has been made far too easy in this country.

The significance of these figures is emphasised by the fact that there are almost three million children in single-parent families. When couples split up, this will commonly cause distress and confusion for the children, and seven out of every ten divorcing couples have children. Such distress and confusion could easily lead to psychological disturbance in these children's later life.

Divorce is not just a personal tragedy for the individuals involved; it is also a huge cost to the nation. The marriage guidance organisation Relate estimates that divorce costs the country at least £2 billion a year. One major item in this cost is the hundreds of millions of pounds spent on legal aid. (And why should we pay for this? If people are prepared to spend an average of £8,000 on a wedding, they should pay for their own divorce.) Another large item is the cost to the National Health Service, which has to treat those suffering from a wide range of stress-related disorders.

When a couple works hard at their marriage, they are very unlikely to find themselves in the divorce court. A low rate of divorce in a country will therefore indicate couples taking their marriage seriously, both for themselves and for their children. A low rate of divorce is more easily achieved when divorce is made more difficult. Therefore the Government should change the law accordingly. (*This question comes from the AS Level Critical Thinking examination, Paper 2, 27 May 1999. Answer time: about 30 minutes.*)

49 Write a critical evaluation of the argument which is presented below, introducing any further arguments you judge to be relevant. Your evaluation should show that you are clear about the structure of the argument (for example, which claims are reasons, conclusions and assumptions) but no credit will be given for merely paraphrasing the argument.

A recent offer by a tobacco company to fund a chair of international relations at a university provoked considerable opposition. Such opposition, however, was unjustifiable.

It is accepted by most people that tobacco, being both dangerous and addictive, is responsible for much illness and many deaths worldwide. But cars are probably more dangerous when we look at the deaths, disability, and illness they cause from both accidents and pollution. It could be argued that skis and parachutes are just as dangerous to their users as tobacco is to its. And what about the health problems associated with dairy products like butter?

If we are to refuse to have any dealings with tobacco companies, what about companies such as British Aerospace and Rolls-Royce which make armaments? After all, smokers have a choice as to whether or not to smoke, whereas civilians killed or injured by armaments have no choice over their involvement with the product. Just because a company makes a dangerous product is not a reason to refuse to associate with it.

Those who are opposed to the tobacco company's offer have to face the fact that, since tobacco products are legally produced, sold, and bought in this country, the company is doing nothing wrong. Furthermore, by offering to give money to a university, it was doing something beneficial to possibly thousands of people.

Those opposed to the offer have an additional problem. Unless they argue that tobacco should not be taxed, they are inconsistent in accepting government money (raised from smoking) to pay for universities, whilst refusing money direct from the company. What is the difference?

Tobacco companies should be treated like any other companies. In consequence, offers of funding from them, like that from any other companies, should always be gratefully accepted. (*This question comes from the AS Level Critical Thinking examination, Paper 2, 24 May 2000. Answer time: about 30 minutes.*)

50 Write a critical evaluation of the argument which is presented below, introducing any further arguments you judge to be relevant. Your evaluation should show that you are clear about the structure of the argument (for example, which claims are reasons, conclusions and assumptions) but no credit will be given for merely paraphrasing the argument.

It has been argued recently that we ought to have a right of access to most of the countryside. But there are many problems associated with this proposed 'right to roam'.

Firstly, a MORI poll has shown that 92% of people in this country say that, to protect wildlife, they would support restrictions on the right to roam. This evidence shows that very few people in this country want unrestricted rights of access. Furthermore, there is already access to thousands of miles of footpaths. Why would people need even more?

Another problem is that crime in the countryside is increasing. According to a Norfolk farmer, the cost of reported theft, vandalism and livestock rustling has increased by over 200 per cent over the past ten years. The true cost of rural crime must be much higher because a lot of theft will go unreported. Indeed, the problem of rural crime will get worse. With the widespread introduction of CCTV cameras, thieves and vandals will find operating in towns and cities more difficult, and thus head to the countryside to commit their crimes.

The problem of access is emphasised by the growing trend towards free-range methods of farming animals. The urban population can't have it both ways: if they want animals to be reared using free-range methods, they can't also demand a right to roam amongst them.

In support of their case, the right to roam campaigners use the evidence of European countries such as Germany, Switzerland, and Norway which have considerable rights of rural access. But the evidence of African countries such as Kenya, which have some of the finest game reserves in the world, points the other way. In these reserves access by visitors is strictly controlled.

Given all the problems, it is clear that an unrestricted 'right to roam' cannot therefore be justified. (*This question comes from the AS Level Critical Thinking examination, Paper 2, 24 May 2000. Answer time: about 30 minutes.*)

51 Suppose (as Aristotle believed) that the heavier a body is, the faster it falls to the ground and suppose that we have two bodies, a heavy one called M and a light one called m. Under our initial assumption M will fall faster than m. Now suppose that M and m are joined together thus $M + m$. Now what happens? Well, $M + m$ is heavier than M so by our initial assumption it should fall *faster* than M alone. But in the joined body $M + m$, m and M will each tend to fall just as fast as before they were joined, so m will act as a 'brake' on M and $M + m$ will fall *slower* than M alone. Hence it follows from our initial assumption that $M + m$ will fall both *faster* and *slower* than M alone. Since this is absurd our initial assumption must be false. (From Galileo's *Dialogues Concerning Two New Sciences*)

52 James Lovelock, author of the Gaia hypothesis (that the Earth is a self-regulating biosphere geared to preserving life) has recently argued that the way to power economies without the damage being done to the biosphere by polluting greenhouse gases is to adopt nuclear power.

'The real dangers to humanity and the ecosystems of the earth from nuclear power are almost negligible. You get things like Chernobyl but what happens? Thirty-odd brave firemen died who needn't have died but its general effect on the world population is almost negligible.

What has it done to wildlife? All around Chernobyl, where people are not allowed to go because the ground is too radioactive, well, the wildlife doesn't care about radiation. It has come flooding in. It is one of the richest ecosystems in the region. And then they say: 'what shall we do with nuclear waste?' Lovelock has an answer for that, too. Stick it in some precious wilderness, he says. If you wanted to preserve the biodiversity of the rain forest, drop pockets of nuclear waste deep into it to keep the developers out. The lifespans of the wild things might be shortened a bit, but the animals wouldn't know, or care. Natural selection would take care of the mutations. Life would go on.

'I have told [British Nuclear Fuels] that I would happily take the full output of one of their big power stations. I think the high-level waste is a stainless steel cube of about a metre in size and I would be very happy to have concrete pit . . . that they would put it in.' He says he would use the waste for two purposes. 'One would be home heating. You would get free home heat from it. And the other would be to sterilise the stuff from the supermarket, the chicken and whatnot, full of salmonella . . . Just drop it down through a hole. [And] they would be welcome to take pictures of my grandchildren sitting on top of it'.
(*The Guardian*: *Saturday Review*, 16 September 2000, p. 1)

53 ACUPUNCTURE
What's the answer?
Despite this wealth of problems, there is hope. Good RCT's [randomised controlled trials] can be done on acupuncture. But the sort that are needed are 'pragmatic trials', which reflect everyday practice. A few hundred migraine patients, for example, could be allocated at random to different types of treatment, one of which would be acupuncture. This would let practitioners tailor the treatment to suit each patient and to assess its long-term effectiveness. This leaves the problem of how to take the patients' experiences into account. Many trials focus on measuring changes in physiology, such as blood pressure

– 'hard data' that can be measured objectively. 'Soft' data, like the sense of pain or 'feeling better', is subjective, and harder to define. Yet this is what really matters to patients.

Room for hope

Trials should therefore include patients' experiences of how effective treatment is. In fact, patients are the bridge between acupuncture and orthodox medicine. Just as acupuncture needs to be subjected to good trials, so Western methods of research should be adapted to the needs of good acupuncture – and of patients. If acupuncturists can prove themselves to sceptical doctors and NHS managers, we might all benefit. This would clear the way for Eastern and Western medicine to join forces, and a much wider range of NHS treatment could become available. ('Acupuncture', *Health Which*, June 1996)

54 Leonardo da Vinci

[I have engaged in practical] research, covering some thirty years, into Leonardo da Vinci's painting methods. By successfully attempting to recreate the distinctive effects that Leonardo achieved in the *Mona Lisa*, I have come to realise that when depicting flesh areas, he departed from the specific rules then laid down for producing resistant oil paint films. In these zones, his method was more akin to the techniques of the watercolourist than to those of the painter in oils. It consisted of a very gradual, deliberate build-up of successive layers of ultra-thin, overdiluted glazes. (I call this technique 'micro-divisionism'.)

For these reasons, the glazes in areas of paint where Leonardo was depicting flesh are extremely thin and, in all probability, porous, friable and powdery. Therefore, the varnish lying on these areas acts as a useful reinforcement. Any attempt to remove this integrated varnish by solvents and scalpels could seriously endanger Leonardo's own work. Since the last stages of artistic 'finessing' form the upper layer, the most crucial effects are also the most vulnerable ones.

In 1994, the Louvre in Paris considered cleaning Leonardo's *The Virgin and Child with St Anne*. As a consultant to the museum, I was able to point out in advance these physical and aesthetic vulnerabilities. My testimony was listened to and accepted by the Louvre's committee for restoration. Happily, the project was dropped, but other experts challenged my views – in particular David Bull, head of painting conservation at the National Gallery of Art, in Washington.

Although Bull agreed that the surfaces produced by Leonardo are 'paper-thin' and finely manipulated, he doubted that they would be fragile structurally. He recommended that the varnish be removed. Bull contends that Leonardo achieved his impalpably vaporous effects not by delicate brush-work, but much more robustly by spreading paint with his fingertips and, even, with the palm of his hand. I reject this hypothesis. It might, at first glance, seem to rest on hard physical evidence – namely the traces of fingerprints found on certain of Leonardo's paintings. In reality, it reveals a misreading of evidence and a misconstruing of technical practice.

I am familiar with the method of work that Bull suggests, and in my attempts to 'reconstruct' Leonardo's art I have experimented with it over several years. It is a process which I abandoned when I realised that no matter how skilled or practised the hand, the master's famous sfumato effects, characterised by an extremely gradual transition between areas of different colour or shade, could not be so obtained. It might be argued that the failure was my own. But, having tried to create the effects with both brush and hand, and comparing them at length, I can justifiably claim sufficient expertise on the issue.

Those who continue to champion 'fingerwork' have yet to demonstrate the practice. My 'practical' position is widely supported by historical evidence and scientific pointers, but nowhere in Leonardo's extensive theoretical writings on painting does he mention anything like the method which Bull adduced.

In fact, the fingerprints are only encountered in unfinished sections – which is to say those that have not received the delicate multilayered treatment described above. The 'fingerwork', self-evidently, served as a quick method of laying down an intermediate stage, and not as a final effect. The more fragile of these two distinct types of work is the more complex and subtle one (that is to say, 'micro-divisionism'), which means that restoration must be equally delicate and cautious. (Extracted from 'Let's keep the Mona Lisa smiling', *New Scientist*, 11 May 1996, p. 48, by Jacques Franck, an art historian specialising in the techniques of old masters, in Suc-en-Brie, France)

55 It is important to note, however, that thinking is always thinking *about* something. To think about nothing is a conceptual impossibility. The importance of this simple point is that it raises serious questions about the meaning of such commonly heard claims as 'I teach thinking', or 'I teach students to think.' One may well ask 'About what?' Nor would the claim that one taught 'thinking in general' or

'thinking about everything' be any more helpful. For to think about nothing in particular is equivalent to not thinking at all. And to think of 'everything in general' is incoherent.

. . . it is a matter of conceptual truth that thinking is always *thinking about* X, and that X can never be 'everything in general' but must always be something in particular. Thus the claim 'I teach my students to think' is at worst false and at best misleading.

Thinking, then is logically connected to an X. Since this fundamental point is reasonably easy to grasp, it is surprising that critical thinking should have become reified into a curriculum subject and the teaching of it an area of expertise on its own . . .

In isolation from a particular subject, the phrase 'critical thinking' neither refers to nor denotes any particular skill. It follows from this that it makes no sense to talk about critical thinking as a distinct subject and that it therefore cannot be profitably taught as such. To the extent that critical thinking is not about a specific subject X, it is both conceptually and practically empty. The statement 'I teach critical thinking', *simpliciter*, is vacuous because there is no generalised skill properly called critical thinking. (McPeck, 1981, pp. 3, 4)

56 **Pascal's Wager**

Either there is a Christian God or there isn't. If you believe in Him and live a Christian life, then if He exists you will enjoy eternal bliss and if He doesn't exist you will lose very little. On the other hand, if you don't believe in Him and don't live a Christian life, then if He doesn't exist you will lose nothing, but if He does exist, you will suffer eternal damnation! So it is rational to believe in God's existence and live a Christian life.

57 Richard Dawkins, 'The more you understand evolution, the more you move towards atheism. (This is an edited version of Dr Dawkins' speech at the Edinburgh International Science Festival on 15 April 1992. Reprinted from the *Independent* with the permission of Dr Dawkins.)

As a Darwinian, something strikes me when I look at religion. Religion shows a pattern of heredity which I think is similar to genetic heredity. The vast majority of people have an allegiance to one particular religion. There are hundreds of different religious sects, and every religious person is loyal to just one of these.

Out of all the sects in the world, we notice an uncanny coincidence: the overwhelming majority just happen to choose the one their parents belonged to. Not the sect that has the best evidence in its favour, the best miracles, the best moral code, the best cathedral, the best stained-glass, the best music: when it comes to choosing from the smorgasbord of available religions, their potential virtues seem to count for nothing compared to the matter of heredity.

This is an unmistakeable fact; nobody could seriously deny it. Yet people with full knowledge of the arbitrary nature of this heredity, somehow manage to go on believing in their religion, often with such fanaticism that they are prepared to murder people who follow a different one.

Truths about the cosmos are true all around the universe. They don't differ in Pakistan, Afghanistan, Poland or Norway. Yet we are apparently prepared to accept that the religion we adopt is a matter of an accident of geography.

If you ask people why they are convinced of the truth of their religion, they don't appeal to heredity. Put like that it sounds too obviously stupid. Nor do they appeal to evidence. There isn't any, and nowadays the better educated admit it. No, they appeal to faith. Faith is the great cop-out, the great excuse to evade the need to think and evaluate evidence. Faith is belief in spite of, even perhaps because of, the lack of evidence. The worst thing is that the rest of us are supposed to respect it: to treat it with kid gloves.

If a slaughterman doesn't comply with the law in respect of cruelty to animals, he is rightly prosecuted and punished. But if he complains that his cruel practices are necessitated by religious faith, we back off apologetically and allow him to get on with it. Any other position that someone takes up can expect to be defended with reasoned argument. But faith is immune. Faith is allowed not to justify itself by argument. Faith must be respected: and if you don't respect it, you are accused of violating basic human rights.

Even those with no faith have been brainwashed into respecting the faith of others. When so-called Muslim community leaders go on the radio and advocate the killing of Salman Rushdie, they are clearly committing incitement to murder – a crime for which they would ordinarily be prosecuted and possibly imprisoned. But are they arrested? They are not, because our secular society respects their faith, and sympathizes with the deep hurt and insult to it.

Well I don't. I will respect your views if you can justify them. But if you justify your views only by saying you have faith in them, I shall not respect them.

I want to end by returning to science. It is often said . . . that although there is no positive evidence for the existence of a God, nor is there evidence against His existence. So it is best to keep an open mind and be agnostic.

At first sight that seems an unassailable position, at least in the weak sense of Pascal's wager. But on second thoughts it seems a cop-out, because the same could be said of Father Christmas and tooth fairies. There may be fairies at the bottom of the garden. There is no evidence of it, but you can't *prove* that there aren't any, so shouldn't we be agnostic with respect to fairies?

The trouble with the agnostic argument is that it can be applied to anything. There is an infinite number of hypothetical beliefs we could hold which we can't positively disprove. On the whole, people don't believe in most of them, such as fairies, unicorns, dragons, Father Christmas, and so on. But on the whole they do believe in a creator God, together with whatever particular baggage goes with the religion of their parents.

I suspect the reason is that most people . . . nevertheless have a residue of feeling that Darwinian evolution isn't quite big enough to explain everything about life. All I can say as a biologist is that the feeling disappears progressively the more you read about and study what is known about life and evolution.

I want to add one thing more. The more you understand the significance of evolution, the more you are pushed away from the agnostic position and towards atheism. Complex, statistically improbable things are by their nature more difficult to explain than simple, statistically probable things.

The great beauty of Darwin's theory of evolution is that it explains how complex, difficult to understand things could have arisen step by plausible step, from simple, easy to understand beginnings. We start our explanation from almost infinitely simple beginnings: pure hydrogen and a huge amount of energy. Our scientific, Darwinian explanations carry us through a series of well-understood gradual steps to all the spectacular beauty and complexity of life.

The alternative hypothesis, that it was all started by a supernatural creator, is not only superfluous; it is also highly improbable. It falls foul of the very argument that was originally put forward in its favour. This is because any god worthy of the name must have been a being of colossal intelligence, a supermind, an entity of enormous sophistication and complexity. In other words, an entity of extremely low statistical probability – a very improbable being.

Even if the postulation of such an entity explained anything (and we don't need it to), it still wouldn't help because it raises a bigger mystery than it solves.

Science offers us an explanation of how complexity (the difficult) arose out of simplicity (the easy). The hypothesis of God offers no worthwhile explanation for anything, for it simply postulates the difficult to explain and leaves it at that. We cannot prove that there is no God, but we can safely conclude that He is very, very improbable indeed.

58 The all-party Parliamentary Pro-Life Group's report which claims that foetuses may feel pain from the 10th week of development is the latest in a number of attempts by those who oppose abortion to claim that foetuses suffer.

'Foetal pain' is an issue with an agenda. Despite the claims of the Pro-Life group, there is no 'new science' to show that foetuses suffer pain during abortion. In fact, the weight of evidence is rather that they are incapable of suffering – at least in the earlier stages of pregnancy during which the overwhelming majority of abortions occur.

No one can doubt that foetuses, from early on in their development, respond to physical stimuli. Experts know that when blood samples are taken from a foetus in late gestation, the procedure causes a rise in stress hormones associated with pain. But writing in *The Lancet*, the authors of a recent paper discussing this phenomenon were careful to stress that 'a hormonal response cannot be equated with the perception of pain'.

When, at the request of the Department of Health, Professor Maria Fitzgerald reviewed current scientific knowledge on foetal pain, she confirmed that the development of the brain and the nervous system rules out foetal perceptions of pain, at least prior to 26 weeks' gestation. True pain experience, she suggested, could develop only 'postnatally, along with memory, anxiety and other brain functions'.

Fitzgerald is professor of neurobiology in the Department of Anatomy and Development Biology at University College, London, so you would have thought her paper would have resolved it. But no. Those who wish to make a case that the foetus does feel pain, in particular during abortion, scrabbled to find counter argument. And so the discussion goes on.

It is worth asking: why has it become such an issue? Members of the Pro-Life group are opposed to all abortions, whether or not they cause pain to the foetus. Even if it could be demonstrated beyond all doubt that foetuses do not feel pain, they would still object to an abortion. For them, the issue is that abortion is wrong, however and whenever it is done. They are against it in principle. So why not oppose it in principle? Why focus on such an esoteric issue as foetal pain?

Increasingly, the anti-choice movement tries to shift public discussion from *why* women end pregnancies to *how* they are ended. Those who oppose abortion stress the consequence of the procedure for the foetus, never the consequence of the pregnancy for the woman. The anti-choice lobby know that most women are touched by images of baby-like foetuses floating serenely in amniotic fluid and spelling out in graphic detail how an abortion is performed is far more likely to win them support than a graphic description of the reasons why a woman feels she needs to end her pregnancy.

By raising the issue of foetal pain, those who oppose abortion in principle are trying to reset its agenda. They turn attention to the *possible* suffering of foetuses to shift attention from the *actual* suffering of women seeking abortion. In the abstract debate about foetal pain, it is important that the undeniable, manifest pain of women is never forgotten (Ann Furedi, Director of the Birth Control Trust, *The Guardian*, 22 July 1996.).

59 The following passage was written by Sidney Smith as a kind of summary review of Jeremy Bentham's, *The Handbook of Political Fallacies*. The text is an imaginary speech by a Member of Parliament (the Noodle) which commits a large number of the fallacies Bentham discussed in his book. The exercise for you is to find all the mistaken lines of argument you can. This will require some interpretation of the text because its language is rather antiquated but express the fallacies in modern language – you will then see how common they are today!

THE NOODLE'S ORATION

What would our ancestors say to this, Sir? How does this measure tally with their institutions? How does it agree with their experience? Are we to put the wisdom of yesterday in competition with the wisdom of centuries? (*Hear, hear.*) Is beardless youth to show no respect for the decisions of mature age? (Loud cries of *Hear! hear!*) If this measure is right, would it have escaped the wisdom of those Saxon progenitors to whom we are indebted for so many of our best political institutions? Would the Dane have passed it over? Would the Norman have rejected it? Would such a notable discovery have been reserved for these modern and degenerate times?

Besides, Sir, if the measure is good, I ask the honourable gentleman if this is the time for carrying it into execution – whether, in fact, a more unfortunate period could have been selected than that which he has chosen? If this were an ordinary measure, I should not oppose it with so much vehemence; but, Sir, it calls in question the wisdom of an irrevocable law – of a law passed at the memorable period of the Revolution. What right have we, Sir, to break down this firm column, on which the great men of that day stamped a character of eternity? Are not all authorities against this measure: Pitt, Fox, Cicero, and the Attorney- and Solicitor-General?

The proposition is new, Sir; it is the first time it was ever heard in this house. I am not prepared, Sir – this house is not prepared, to receive it. The measure implies a distrust of His Majesty's government; their disapproval is sufficient to warrant opposition. Precaution only is requisite where danger is apprehended. Here the high character of the individuals in question is a sufficient guarantee against any ground of alarm.

Give not then your sanction to this measure; for, whatever be its character, if you do give your sanction to it, the same man by whom this is proposed, will propose to you others to which it will be impossible to give your consent. I care very little, Sir, for the ostensible measure; but what is there behind it? What are the honourable gentleman's future schemes? If we pass this bill, what fresh concessions may he not require? What further degradation is he planning for his country?

Talk of evil and inconvenience, Sir! Look to other countries – study other aggregations and societies of men, and then see whether the laws of this country demand a remedy, or deserve a panegyric. Was the honourable gentleman (let me ask him) always of this way of thinking? Do I not remember when he was the advocate in this house of very opposite opinions? I not only quarrel with his present sentiments, Sir, but I declare very frankly, I do not like the party with which he acts. If his own motives were as pure as possible, they cannot but suffer contamination from those with whom he is politically associated. This measure may be a boon to the constitution, but I will accept no favour to the constitution from such hands. (Loud cries of *Hear! hear!*)

I profess myself, Sir, an honest and upright member of the British Parliament, and I am not afraid to profess myself an enemy to all change, and all innovation, I am satisfied with things as they are; and it will be my pride and pleasure to hand down this country to my children as I received it from those who preceded us.

The honourable gentleman pretends to justify the severity with which he has attacked the noble Lord who presides in the Court of Chancery. But I say such attacks are pregnant with mischief to government itself. Oppose ministers, you oppose government; disgrace ministers, you disgrace government; bring ministers into contempt, you bring government into contempt; and anarchy and civil war are the consequences.

Besides, Sir, the measure is unnecessary. Nobody complains of disorder in that shape in which it is the aim of your measure to propose a remedy to it. The business is one of the greatest importance; there is need of the greatest caution and circumspection. Do not let us be precipitate, Sir; it is impossible to foresee all the consequences. Everything should be gradual; the example of a neighbouring nation should fill us with alarm!

The honourable gentleman has taxed me with illiberality, Sir. I defy the charge. I hate innovation, but I love improvement. I am an enemy to the corruption of government, but I defend its influence. I dread reform, but I dread it only when it is intemperate. I consider the liberty of the press as the great palladium of the constitution; but, at the same time, I hold the licentiousness of the press in the greatest abhorrence. Nobody is more conscious than I am of the splendid abilities of the honourable mover, but I tell him at once, his scheme is too good to be practicable. It savours of utopia. It looks well in theory, but it won't do in practice. It will not do, I repeat, Sir, in practice; and so the advocates of the measure will find, if unfortunately, it should find its way through Parliament. (*Cheers.*)

The source of that corruption to which the honourable member alludes is in the minds of the people; so rank and extensive is that corruption, Sir, that no political reform can have any effect in removing it. Instead of reforming others, instead of reforming the state, the constitution, and everything that is most excellent, let each man reform himself! Let him look at home, he will find there enough to do, without looking abroad, and aiming at what is out of his power: (*Loud cheers.*) And now, Sir, as it is frequently the custom in this house to end with a quotation, and since the gentleman who preceded me in the debate has anticipated me in my favourite quotation of the 'Strong pull and the long pull', I shall end with the memorable words of the assembled barons – '*Nolumus leges Angliae muturi.*'

Answers to questions

Chapter 1

1.1   This is entirely your own answer.

1.2   On Dewey's account critical thinking requires 'active, persistent and careful consideration (etc.)' and it is clear this passage displays these qualities, whether you agree with its claims or not.

1.3   Your new definition should pick up on all or most of the points made so far, that critical thinking (i) is 'active' (you construct your own answers, you do not just accept what others tell you), (ii) is 'persistent' (you weigh alternatives and take time to consider the issues, you do not just decide quickly without thinking), (iii) centrally involves giving and evaluating reasons, (iv) concerns both what we believe and what we do and (v) involves dispositions as well as skills.

1.4   'Great. Now we'll play basket ball again, but this time, guard your opponents well and when you get a chance to pass, try to do it in the way you just practised – and if you get a chance to shoot, don't forget what we practised there too.'

1.5.1   You reflect on your current way of doing something; watch while a good model is shown; then practise doing it yourself, trying to do it in the way shown in the good model. The fourth stage is when you deploy the skill in real situations, monitoring what you are doing and trying to do it well.

1.5.2   This is for you to say.

1.6.1   This depends roughly on whether you have to work things out or just let it 'wash over you'.

1.6.2   Even if you are reasoning your way through to a conclusion, if this is a 'mechanical' process requiring little judgement, interpretation and so on, it involves very little critical thinking.

1.6.3   This depends on how much 'figuring out' he is doing, trying to work out what his opponents will do and how to outwit them; this could involve a lot of critical thinking.

1.6.4   Provided you do not just make a snap decision, but investigate the alternatives, get the information you need to judge which will suit you best and so on, this could involve a great deal of critical thinking (see chapter 11).

1.6.5   If you have to 'figure things out' from the guidance you are given this might involve a lot of critical thinking, but if you are just blindly following the instructions it does not.

1.7.1   The differences between the two imagined cases are that in one case Andy questions evidence from a source which has a vested interest, looks for relevant evidence from independent sources and weighs the pros and cons reasonably skilfully (allowing for the costs of doing this and the time available); in Case 2 Andy displays 'reflective thinking' before buying his car, but not in Case 1.

1.7.2   'Yes' to all of parts of this question.

1.7.3   Only in Case 2.

1.8.1   In this case, the issue is how to interpret a TV news report (about the reported accuracy of certain US weapons). On the face of it, Bertha is simply swallowing what is presented to her, and does not even want to question it when her friend raises doubts. The question then is whether Cheryl has reasonable grounds for being sceptical and the evidence is that she has if what she says is true. In this case, Bertha is not thinking critically, but Cheryl is.

1.8.2   Broadly 'yes' for Cheryl, but broadly 'no' for Bertha.

1.8.3   Same as 1.8.2.

Chapter 2

2.1.1   This is simply a descriptive passage. It does not give reasons for a conclusion (though we naturally make various inferences as we read it).

2.1.2   This passage does give reasons for a conclusion; it gives reasons for thinking we may have to revise completely our understanding of global warming.

2.1.3 This does not give reasons for a conclusion. It describes a possible 'solution' to a problem but there is no reasoning.

2.1.4 This passage gives reasons for the conclusion that certain problems can only be addressed by international action.

2.1.5 This passage is largely just descriptive though it does report Gall's basic reason for his basic conclusion.

2.1.6 This passage gives reasons for the conclusion that the only way to deliver 'thinking schools' is to assess thinking skills and dispositions directly.

2.1.7 This passage does not contain reasoning to a conclusion. As the sketch goes on to say, this exchange is not an argument but is simply abuse!

2.2 Answered in the text immediately following the question.

2.3 Answered in the text immediately following the question.

2.4 Answered in section 2.4, but give your own answer before reading that answer.

2.5 We mark the argument indicators in bold. To show which sentences are reasons and which are conclusions, let us use the notation R1<....>, R2<....>, and C1[...], C2[...], etc., (and notice that a sentence can be both a reason and a conclusion). Given this, a natural way (though not the only possible way) to construe the reasoning presented for the various conclusions is as follows:

2.5.1 R1<During the football game he committed a serious foul> **so** C1[he deserved to be sent off.]

2.5.2 R1<Women's brains are on average smaller than men's> **therefore** C1[women are less intelligent than men].

2.5.3 R1<The butler was in the pantry>. R2<In that case he couldn't have shot the master, who was in his study>. **Hence** C1[the butler couldn't have done it!].

2.5.4 C1[The sovereignty of Parliament is open to abuse by any Government] **as** R1<power in Britain is too centralised>.

2.5.5 C1[The Green Movement is mistaken in thinking we should recycle materials like paper and glass] **because** R1<paper comes from trees, an easily renewable resource, and glass is made from sand, which is plentiful and cheap>. **Furthermore**, R2<in some American cities recycling schemes have been abandoned because they are too expensive>.

Note that R2 is an explanation (see section 3.7) and it is plausible to say that both R1 and R2 are being presented as reasons for C1.

2.5.6   R1<The traditional British approach to food safety has been one where local health officials only intervene at the level of food retailing, for instance inspecting premises where food is prepared or sold>. However, C2[a much broader approach to the question is needed]. R2<Many of the dangers to our health resulting from the food we eat arise from the way it is produced in the first place, i.e. the modern intensive farming practices involved, rather than small-scale organic farming>. C1[A national food safety agency that fails to address the question of food production will **therefore** be unlikely to protect us effectively from damaging our health through the food we eat]. (You might find this easier to see after reading section 2.4 and doing question 2.7.1.)

2.5.7   R1<The outstanding success of Ted's company, which was launched against the advice, and without the support, of bankers, business consultants and financiers>, **just goes to show that** C1[one person's vision can prove all the experts in the world wrong]. C2[Anyone thinking of setting up a business, **therefore**, should trust their own judgement, and not be influenced by the advice of others].

2.5.8   R1<There has been a decline in the rate of many illnesses of old age. For example, arthritis, dementia, and strokes are all declining year by year>. R2<The causes of this decline include such medical advances as beta-blockers to control high blood pressure and the fitting of hip replacements>. R3<There is, however, another factor. The present generation of sixty- and seventy-year-olds had much better nutrition as children than did their parents>. R4<Good nutrition in childhood is important in laying the foundations of good health in adulthood>. **Since** R5<improvements in nutrition have continued over the past sixty years>, C1[we can expect that many of the illnesses of old age will continue to decline].

2.6   Again, using the notation introduced in the answer to question 2.5, a natural way (though not the only possible way) to construe the reasoning presented for the various conclusions is as follows:

(a) R1<Most parents want their children to have successful careers> **and** R2<education is essential to success>, **so** C1[it

is the duty of parents to give children the best possible
education.]

(b) R3<it is the duty of parents to give children the best possible education> **and** R4<it is also in the country's economic
interest to have a highly educated population> **so** C2[the
Government should help parents to provide for their children's
education].

(c) R5<the Government should help parents to provide for
their children's education> **therefore** C3[all parents should
receive financial help towards the cost of their children's
education],

(d) R6<all parents should receive financial help towards the
cost of their children's education> **so** C4[the low paid should
receive tax credits and those who are better off should receive
tax relief].

2.7.1   R1<The traditional British approach to food safety has been
one where local health officials only intervene at the level of
food retailing, for instance inspecting premises where food is
prepared or sold>. However, R2<many of the dangers to our
health resulting from the food we eat arise from the way it is
produced in the first place, i.e. the modern intensive farming
practices involved, rather than small-scale organic farming>.
Therefore C1[a national food safety agency that fails to
address the question of food production will be unlikely to
protect us effectively from damaging our health through the
food we eat] **so** C2[a much broader approach to the question is
needed].

2.7.2   R1<The decline in the number of small birds has numerous
causes but the most significant is the growth in the population
of their predators – mainly magpies>. R2<Magpies have dramatically increased in numbers due to a ready diet of carcasses
of wild animals killed by traffic>. But R3<Traffic is a
man-made phenomenon> **therefore** C1[ultimately it is
human activity which has caused this decline in the number of
small birds].

2.7.3   R1<Recent evidence shows that modern cars vary in their ability to withstand impact>. However, R2<The degree of force
that was applied to the cars was far in excess of that experienced in a road accident>. **Therefore** C1[Whilst some cars did
better than others, in absolute terms they were all able to reach
a satisfactory standard of withstanding impact in the event of

an accident]. **So** C2[anybody travelling in the type of cars tested can be reassured that they are adequately protected] and C3[owners of those cars which did badly in impact tests should *not* be anxious about their safety].

2.7.4   R1<Homeless people are frequently blamed for being homeless. They are regarded as being responsible for their own plight as a result of managing their finances badly, refusing employment opportunities and being generally lazy and disorganised. Young homeless people are told they should not have left home so soon. These accusations may be true in a small minority of cases, but all too often they deflect attention from the shortage of available housing at affordable prices and the inadequacy of public policies designed to provide more, and suitable, homes>. R2<There are just not enough affordable homes to go round>. **Therefore** C2[Many people are homeless through no fault of their own but are caught in circumstances that prevent them from obtaining a home of their own].

2.7.5   R1<245 million years ago, 90 per cent of all species vanished; 65 million years ago, 50 per cent of all living things died out, including the dinosaurs>. R2<Much more recently, the influence of humans has led to many species becoming extinct: in Hawaii, for example, this influence led to huge losses of species of plants, insects, and animals>. R3<But in each example of extinction we have seen the lost species replaced by new ones (for instance, mammals replaced dinosaurs)>. **Therefore** C1[the history of the world is full of many examples of the extinction of species, and we should not regard such extinction as a serious environmental problem].

2.8.1   'Thus' is simply a conclusion indicator. 'Indicating' suggests a rather tentative inference in this context.

2.8.2   'Since' and 'so' are straightforward argument indicators; 'suggests' is tentative.

2.8.3   'This is an unmistakeable fact; nobody could seriously deny it' shows that Dawkins is very confident of his claim.

2.8.4   Numerous argument indicator words, 'because', 'so' etc., are used straightforwardly. 'At first sight this seems an unassailable position . . . But on second thoughts it seems a cop-out' shows a considerable measure of confidence in his position.

2.9   These are for you to do.

Chapter 3

3.1.1   Questions appendix, passage 3 is side-by-side reasoning.

3.1.2   Questions appendix, passage 11 is side-by-side reasoning.

3.1.3   Questions appendix, passage 17 has a chain structure.

3.1.4   Questions appendix, passage 30 is side-by-side reasoning.

3.1.5   This argument has a chain structure.

3.2.1   Questions appendix, passage 21 is side-by-side reasoning.

3.2.2   Questions appendix, passage 28 has a chain structure.

3.2.3   Questions appendix, passage 36 is side-by-side reasoning.

3.2.4   Questions appendix, passage 38 has a mainly chain structure.

3.3.1   Joint.

3.3.2   Not joint.

3.3.3   Joint.

3.4.1   (a) R1<Recent research suggests that our understanding of how clouds interact with sunlight might be wrong: new measurements suggest that clouds absorb four times as much energy as previously thought> and R2<existing models of how the climate functions are based on the original measurements>, **therefore** C1[if the new measurements are shown to be accurate, models of how the climate works will need to be completely overhauled].

       (b) C1 = R3<if the new measurements are shown to be accurate, models of how the climate works will need to be completely overhauled] and R4<Climate models are used in our attempts to measure global warming> **so**, C2[if these climate models are shown to be inaccurate, we will have to completely revise our understanding of global warming].

3.4.2   (a) R1<One in 1,000 people in Britain is estimated to be a carrier of the potentially fatal liver disease hepatitis B, although this estimate is likely to be far too low> and R2<Seventy five countries carry out {a mass vaccination} programme, and including hepatitis B in Britain's existing vaccination programme would be a simple matter>. R3<The main problem has been given as that of cost>. However, R4<this cost would be substantially reduced if a mass campaign was introduced> **therefore** C1[There should be a mass vaccination programme to eradicate this disease].

       (b) R5<Each shot of the vaccine costs at present £5 and the total cost of a mass campaign at this price would be more than

£20 million> **so** C2 = R3 [The main problem has been given as that of cost].

(c) C3 = R4 [this cost would be substantially reduced if a mass campaign was introduced] **because** R6<the manufacturers would supply the vaccine at a much lower price for bulk purchase>.

3.4.3   (a) R1<Over the past ten years, there has been a four-fold increase in the number of people killed in road accidents who are found to have illegal drugs in their bodies> and R2<The rate of increase is much greater than the corresponding figure for those people killed in accidents who were found with alcohol in their blood>. **This shows that** C1[the campaign against drink-driving has succeeded]. **Consequently,** C2[the Government ought now to concentrate on targeting those people who drive whilst under the influence of illegal drugs].

(b) R3 = C1<the campaign against drink-driving has succeeded> **consequently,** C2[the Government ought now to concentrate on targeting those people who drive whilst under the influence of illegal drugs].

3.4.4   (a) R1<When prisoners under sentence of death are given the choice between life in prison and execution, 99 per cent of them choose life imprisonment>. **This shows that** C1[they fear death more than they fear life imprisonment].

(b) R2 = C1<{prisoners under sentence of death} fear death more than they fear life imprisonment> and R3<one is most deterred by what one most fears>, **therefore** C2[it is evident that the threat of the death penalty is more likely to deter most potential murderers than is the threat of life imprisonment].

3.5.1   (a) R1<Radioactive elements disintegrate and eventually turn into lead> **therefore** C1[If matter has always existed there should be no radioactive elements left].

(b) R2 = C1<If matter has always existed there should be no radioactive elements left> but R3<there are still uranium and other radioactive elements around> **therefore this is scientific proof that** C2[matter has not always existed].

3.5.2   R1<If the civil population cannot be defended in the event of nuclear war, we do not need a civil defence policy>. But R2<we do need a civil defence policy if 'deterrence' is to be a convincing strategy>. **Therefore** C1[deterrence is not a convincing strategy].

3.5.3   Left to you.

3.5.4   Left to you.

3.6.1   The councillor is presumably arguing for the conclusion, 'we should get new, bright high-level sodium lights'. It is not clear quite whether 'Because our street lights are too dim, we have more accidents and more crime than we should' is an explanation or an argument; if it is accepted that 'our street lights are too dim' it is an argument. If it is accepted that 'we have more accidents and more crime than we should' then it is probably an explanation. Similarly with 'they are so low that they are easily and often damaged by vandals'.

3.6.2   Explanation.

3.6.3   Explanation.

3.6.4   Explanation.

3.6.5   Argument (but you could read it as an explanation).

3.6.6   The seismologist is *explaining* the 1906 San Francisco earthquake and *arguing* that another is due soon.

3.7.1   (i) They can't really do it to raise money for charity. (ii) They can't give much to charity. Perhaps others too.

3.7.2   (i) If enough parents refuse vaccination they will put their children at real risk of contracting polio. (ii) The medical authorities should publicise these risks and urge parents to have their children vaccinated.

Chapter 4

4.1.1   The (or 'the most plausible') explanation for the rise in sea level is that the world's climate is getting warmer.

4.1.2   A typical buyer of a lottery ticket is not interested in opera.

4.1.3   Regular visits to the dentist are necessary for improvements in dental health.

4.1.4   Lower insurance premiums will encourage young people to drive safely.

4.1.5   Some parents will be able to prevent their children from committing crimes.

4.2.1   Yale is a very prestigious university in the US so most people would assume its report was reliable. The American Federal Drugs Administration has a reasonably good reputation in the US for being careful about the safety of drugs, so Americans will tend to assume the FDA's judgement is sound. (There is no comparable Government agency, with a comparable reputation, in the UK, where BSE and other scares have given rise to quite different assumptions about food and drug safety.) One would need to investigate these matters – and perhaps the 'culture of litigation' which exists in the US –   to know what other assumptions could be attributed in virtue of context.

4.2.2   This argument was published at a time when Railtrack, the company responsible for the railway track in the UK, imposed draconian speed restrictions on much of the British railway system following a serious rail accident. They did this because, as they admitted, much of the track was unsafe and needed to be replaced. Because many rail journeys took much longer, many people travelled by car instead, causing more congestion and road accidents than usual. Kalentsky is assuming that it would be a good thing to reduce the extra toll on the roads even if there was slightly higher risk of accident on the railways, that the Government had the power to lift the speed restrictions, and that people would understand that this was a rational thing to do to reduce the overall level of injury and death. (Kalentsky is a very interesting writer who often argues very clearly for unusual views.)

4.2.3   Investigation will show you that this argument was much influenced by Charles Darwin's *Origin of Species* and was written not long after the French Revolution, when many 'upper class' and wealthy people in Europe were afraid revolution might come to them. It assumes that what happens in the plant and animal worlds also happens with human beings, that there is not much scope for science and technology to increase food production etc., that redistributive policies could not work and that birth control could not have a significant impact on population growth (see Fisher, 1988, chapter 3).

4.3   The reasons are plausible in the UK context and the argument seems reasonable. Attitudes to cars and railways are very different in the US. Investigation would probably show that nearly everyone in America expects to have a car and to travel freely by road, that the Mid-West is not very crowded and its roads are not generally crowded, so the reasons do not apply there and the argument will probably seem irrelevant.

4.4.1   Mostly left to you, but this argument surely assumes that at least some parents will be able to influence their children against committing crimes they would otherwise have committed. Presumably many children who get into crime have bad relationships with their parents, so this Act will be ineffective with them.

4.4.2 Left to you.

4.4.3 Left to you.

4.4.4 This argument clearly assumes that there are no compensating benefits to the paintings – such as earning extra revenue which can enable their owners to provide better for their care and normal keeping. Nothing is said about that possibility, but we really need to quantify the risks and benefits to decide this issue. It is a weak argument at present.

4.5 Left to you.

Chapter 5

5.1.1–5.1.3

Left to you. Try your answers on fellow students.
Discussed in section 5.1.

5.2.1 In this case the problem is to explain a term which has a **precise** mathematical meaning to a child. If you do not know what a 'polygon' is, you could look in a dictionary or a mathematics book or ask someone you would expect to know (like a mathematics teacher). If you do know, the best way to explain this idea to a child would probably be to say something like, 'It is a figure which has many straight sides ("poly" means "many" and "gon" means "angle") like these' and then draw a pentagon (a five-sided figure), a hexagon (a six-sided figure) and so on, and explain that the word 'polygon' enables us to talk about lots of different figures, with different numbers of sides. More or less help might be needed depending on the ease with which the child grasped the idea.

5.2.2 A natural resource like coal or oil is used up and does not get renewed, the water that flows in a river gets renewed. Curiously I find that people in different parts of the world view this example differently; those with plentiful supplies of water (like the UK) think it is different from other natural resources, whereas those with limited water supplies (like Singapore) think it is very similar.

5.3.1 Someone who had never heard the phrase; the members of a jury; a university law seminar discussing recent decisions in some criminal cases. The rest is left to you.

5.3.2   Left to you.

5.4   My *Shorter Oxford English Dictionary* tells me that circumstantial evidence 'tends to establish a conclusion by inference from known facts which are otherwise hard to explain'. So the circumstantial evidence would suggest Jones stole the paintings if we discover that Jones is not a wealthy man, that many of the paintings were reported stolen years ago, that Jones has no proof of purchase, that his friends did not know he had these paintings and that his explanations of how he came by them are vague, uncheckable or provide no proof that he got them legitimately. This would probably suffice for everyday purposes though, of course, in a court of law greater precision would be needed.

5.5.1   To say that the conclusion of an argument **necessarily follows** from its reasons, means that if the reasons are **true** then the conclusion **must** also be true; or, to put it another way, it is **impossible** for the reasons to be true and the conclusion false. For example, if someone argues as follows: 'All students work hard and all those who work hard deserve to succeed, therefore all students deserve to succeed' the conclusion **necessarily follows** from the reasons; this claim says nothing about whether the reasons **are** true (do all students work hard?); it simply says **if** they are true then the conclusion **must be**. As such the argument may fail to convince you of its conclusion even though it necessarily follows from its reasons.

To say that a conclusion does **not necessarily follow** from its reasons means that the reasons could be true and the conclusion false; or, to put it another way, it is possible for the reasons to be true and the conclusion false. For example, if someone argues, 'The weapon which killed Smith was found in Jones's house and had his fingerprints on it; Jones hated Smith and cannot provide an alibi for the time of the murder; therefore he must have killed Smith', the conclusion does **not** necessarily follow (it may be a very compelling argument but it does not necessarily follow).

5.5.2   A dictionary or encyclopaedia will give you a phrase like, 'Democracy is government **of** the people, **by** the people, **for** the people. The essential thing is that the government is **elected** by the people and can be replaced by others if the people are dissatisfied.' This simply reports common usage (it is a reported definition); it may still be too vague to make it easy to decide if certain countries are democracies though some examples might help. Presumably, if any country is a 'democracy', the United States is, as are various western European countries; certainly Hitler's Germany was not, Franco's Spain was not, and modern Saudi Arabia is not. A politics text would no doubt give you much more detail.

5.6.1   Left to you.

5.6.2   In a famous study of poverty in the United Kingdom, Peter Towsend gave the following definition, 'Individuals, families and groups in the population can be said to be in poverty when they lack the resources to obtain the types of diet, participate in the activities and have the living conditions and amenities which are customary, or at least widely encouraged or approved, in the societies to which they belong' (*Poverty in the United Kingdom*, 1979, p. 31). This criterion was defended in terms of general usage, but also as usable for empirical research and has been widely acknowledged for its usefulness. No doubt there is a history of other usages before and since which could help you.

5.6.3   Left to you.

5.7.1   This may seem plausible at first, but the student evaluation form may be measuring how much the students *like* the teacher and surely someone could be a good teacher without being greatly liked or could be liked without being a good teacher. They might be popular, friendly and give high grades but might be relatively ineffective at getting students to learn what the course is about; surely we should not count such a person a good teacher. Thus, in the terminology favoured by philosophers, a good score is neither a *necessary condition* for being a good teacher nor a *sufficient condition* either (for an instructive discussion of this example see Scriven, 1976, p. 127).

5.7.2   Left to you.

5.7.3   It seems necessary to be human, male, unmarried and of marriageable age to be a bachelor. But are these sufficient? Left to you.

5.8   Here is a possible response:

It is easy to see what is being argued here, but what do 'sensitive' and 'fully developed human being' mean? Most of us probably feel we could describe situations in which individuals were sensitive or insensitive, human or inhuman. The dictionary tells me that 'being sensitive' means 'being aware of and responsive to other people's feelings'. This is obviously a matter of degree and even though it may be true that many men have difficulty in being sensitive to others, many are reasonably sensitive. Whatever the author means by 'fully developed human being' this would probably include a reasonable degree of sensitivity to others (if someone was utterly insensitive this would surely make them less than fully human) but you do not need to be enormously sensitive to be human. For example, is the employer who makes employees redundant being 'insensitive' or failing as a 'fully developed human being'? And how sensitive do you want your soldiers to be? Are tough, thick-skinned political leaders less than fully developed human beings? Perhaps women do generally find it easier to be sensitive to others but surely the responsibility for being sensitive must be placed squarely on the person concerned. Yes, perhaps others can help but the inference that women have a special responsibility to help men is very weak. I am assuming that this whole argument relates to Britain at the present time, where there is much debate about the relationship between men and women, including their respective rights and responsibilities; perhaps it has more force in other societies.

5.9   Left to you.

5.10   Left to you.

5.11.1 People should pay for road use according to the mileage they cover.

5.11.2 Technically, it means that, of all those who die from mesothelioma, half will die within eight months of diagnosis and the other half will die after that. The next thing Gould wanted to know was 'What are my chances of being in the half of people who live longer than eight months?' At the time of writing, he is still alive.

5.11.3– 5.11.6

Left to you.

Chapter 6

6.1 Discussed in the text immediately following the question.

6.2 Discussed in a later chapter but do not look ahead yet.

6.3 Discussed in the text immediately following the question.

6.4 It is difficult to say what evidence would show that 'TV violence affects behaviour' because so many factors come into play. However, if the claim is that watching TV violence makes more people more violent than they would otherwise be, it might be possible to measure levels of violence in otherwise similar groups who have very different TV habits (with some groups tending to watch more violence than others). It might also be relevant to find people who say they are influenced by what they saw on TV, some being made more violent and some being put off violence. One only has to suggest these possibilities to think of complications, so perhaps this claim cannot really be shown to be true or false!
'TV advertising works' is left to you.

6.5 'People should be free to watch what they please.' We live in a society which puts a high value on allowing people to make their own choices about how to live their lives – provided they do not harm others – so this principle will give strong support to the claim made here. However, by that same principle, if we could show that watching certain kinds of TV programmes had undesirable effects – inclining some people to harm others – this would tell against this claim. But we just saw that this could be very difficult.

6.6 Factual claim: 'Many trials focus on measuring changes in physiology, such as blood pressure.' Easily verified by checking trial reports.
Recommendation: 'Trials should include patients' experiences of how effective treatment is.' To evaluate this we need to check whether it is possible and whether it could produce useful results in this context.
Definition: 'hard data' equals data which can be measured objectively, like blood pressure; contrasted with 'soft data', like the sense of pain or feeling better. It marks a reasonably clear distinction to the layman; we could check with doctors whether this distinction works reasonably well.

6.7.1   Dawkins is claiming with great certainty that 'religion shows a pattern of heredity which . . . is similar to genetic heredity'. He made his claim originally in a great public lecture which was subsequently published in *The Independent*. It does seem true that most people remain in the faith in which they are brought up, at least in broad terms of remaining Christian, Moslem, Hindu, Buddhist and so on. Perhaps people change sects more within their broad religious category, say changing from Church of England to Roman Catholic, but the broad claim seems true within my experience of people's religious beliefs and seems to fit well with everything else I know. The rough analogy with heredity also captures something of the unreflective nature of most people's religious commitment in my experience. So, for these reasons, I regard it as acceptable for the purpose of this argument.

6.7.2   This piece claims that 'good randomised controlled trials can be done on acupuncture'. It then explains how this could be done, with 'pragmatic trials', and concludes that positive results could benefit us all. It makes these claims fairly cautiously, but *Health Which* is reasonably reputable, so this counts in favour of what is claimed. However, I cannot quite see how 'pragmatic trials' could distinguish real effects from imagined ones; maybe this would be a problem; this really needs expertise (in designing medical trials) to decide whether they could work. So the jury is out for me and I do not accept the claims made here about pragmatic trials.

6.7.3   This report was in the *New Scientist* so that lends it credibility. The marine scientists who reviewed the plan are likely to have the relevant expertise and were probably independent, so that lends credibility to their views. So I accept that Norsk Hydro's plan was probably flawed. This exercise is really all about credibility – with which we are about to deal.

6.8   Discussed in the text immediately following the question.

6.9   Left to you.

Chapter 7

7.1   (C) She is very likely to have the relevant expertise to be highly credible.

(D) The reporter will probably have the expertise to pass on what was presented. This may depend on the TV channel.

7.2 Partly answered in the text immediately following the question, but you may have your own questions.

7.3 Most people say at this point that the red and white car drivers can not be given much credence because they have too much to lose or gain (even though they can see well, etc.). The policeman and mother seem to be credible witnesses at this stage (though we may need to know a bit more) and the child is not.

7.4 Left to you.

7.5 Rufus probably has much to lose if he is convicted, so (although he **may** be telling the truth) we generally treat such testimony rather sceptically in the absence of other evidence – because he has a vested interest. The doctor presumably has nothing to lose from reporting accurately what she found – she has nothing to gain or lose, no vested interest – in giving evidence one way rather than another. She also has the relevant expertise and the court context adds weight, so her evidence is highly credible. Rufus is in trouble!

7.6 Left to you.

7.7 Direct evidence would come from someone saying, for example, that they had seen little green men walking out of a spaceship on to the lawn in their garden. Circumstantial evidence for the same claim might be indentations and scorch marks where the spaceship was alleged to have landed and taken off, what looked like footprints of small men on the lawn surface and forensic evidence from the grass that unusual chemical compounds had come into contact with it. Perhaps you can think of more.

7.8 The mother might say, 'I wanted to cross the road safely with my child so, although he was having a tantrum, I was holding his hand tightly and attending carefully to the traffic and the traffic lights. I have good eyesight, visibility was excellent, I drive myself so I know what to look for and I don't know the two drivers or the policeman.' The policeman might say, 'I was on duty. I was attending to the junction; I have good eyesight

and visibility was excellent. I have also received extensive training in how to observe and report accurately what I observe and
on my responsibilities when giving evidence in court.'

7.9   'The Sun crosses the sky from east to west' versus 'The Sun
       orbits the Earth', or 'The gate is open and the sheep are on the
       road' versus 'The sheep have escaped from their field.'

7.10   I assume everyone had good visibility, was not under the influ-
       ence of drugs of any kind and was attending to what happened,
       except the child, who was having a tantrum. I also assume that
       none of the witnesses knew any of the other witnesses (except
       of course the mother and child). I also assume that the traffic
       lights were working correctly and normally.
          We cannot attach much credibility to either of the drivers
       because they have a vested interest. Nor can we attach any
       weight to what the child says (he was not attending to what
       happened). I assume the mother was a driver and knew what
       to look for; given everything else we assumed about her, her
       evidence is highly credible. I assume the policeman was under
       no particular pressure to get convictions. Then, given his
       expertise and everything else we have assumed, his evidence is
       highly credible too. Furthermore, we have two independent
       witnesses saying the same thing so their evidence corroborates
       each other's. This makes a very strong case for believing that
       the red car **did** jump the red light.

7.11.1 Left to you.
7.11.2 The tobacco industry stands to gain from such results, so we
        need to know how independent the scientists were. If they were
        reputable, independent scientists who were free to publish
        whatever they found and were under no pressure to find results
        helpful to the tobacco industry, their results are credible. If they
        were tobacco industry scientists or scientists who had some
        other kind of vested interest, their results deserve less credence.
7.11.3 Left to you.
7.11.4 Here is a possible answer – based on particular assumptions:
        The owner of the company (B) probably has much to lose (he
        may have to pay compensation or suffer in other ways) if he is
        held to be responsible for A's injury, so this reduces the credi-
        bility of his testimony. For the same reasons, the foreman's (F)
        credibility is threatened – however he is able to produce a

maintenance schedule which corroborates his claim that the machine was always maintained satisfactorily, so this point seems well proven.

(A) has much to lose (or gain) so the credibility of his claim that he followed all the safety procedures is not high, because of his vested interest. (C) is a workmate of (A), so his credibility is reduced since he is probably biased in favour of his workmate.

We assume that the health and safety inspector (I) does not know any of those involved, or at least has no relationships with them which would bias him for or against anyone (otherwise he should not be giving his professional judgement). Thus he is independent and has no vested interest in arriving at one judgement rather than another. We also assume he has the relevant training and expertise to judge this issue (otherwise why is he involved?). Furthermore, he must be able to justify his judgement professionally so his reputation is at risk too. On these assumptions, (I) is a highly credible witness and his judgement suggests that the company which designed the saw and its guard is ultimately responsible for the accident.

Interestingly, (C) claims to have told (F) that the saw guard 'was poorly designed and did not function well'. If (C) had the relevant expertise (was familiar with the problems of operating circular saws) and if (F) knew this, it would suggest that (F) failed to act on reliable advice and that would make (F) to blame.

7.11.5 Left to you.

7.11.6 Here is a possible answer – based on particular assumptions:

I assume from the context that this is set in London. The policeman (P) probably has much to lose if he is found to have harmed Fran Lee (F) with a baton blow, so this greatly reduces his credibility. The 'well-known lawyer and human rights activist' (A) was probably sympathetic to the AFA but we do not know his views about the police, so it is hard to estimate if there was any bias regarding them. He will obviously know the law and how it works and his professional reputation is at risk if he says something which turns out to be false, so this lends credibility to his testimony. I shall assume the TV news crew were from a reputable news company (BBC or ITV say) and this lends credibility to their evidence. Furthermore, if there is any possibility of rescuing some of their film, this could provide evidence concerning the accuracy of what they say, so this puts their reputation at risk, which again increases their credibility. No doubt the R33 leaders would deny blame because they have much to lose if they are found to be partly to blame. Equally the R33 member who boasts that he threw the brick refuses to be identified and therefore is not very credible. I shall assume the Dutch tourist could see much of what was happening; presumably she has no vested interest or bias and was merely an impartial observer so all that lends credibility to her testimony. No doubt the hospital spokesperson is independent and speaks with the relevant expertise behind her, but her testimony does not help us decide who struck 'at least one severe blow' to Fran Lee's head. On balance and given the assumptions I have made, several credible witnesses, (F), (N) and (D) corroborate one another and their evidence suggests fairly strongly that (P) – and perhaps other police – were responsible for the head injuries to Fran Lee.

Chapter 8

8.1.1   The inference is simply the move from the first two sentences, taken as side-by-side reasoning, to 'a suitable job for anyone without 'A'-levels is that of driving instructor'.

8.1.2   The inference is the move from everything before 'so', taken as joint reasoning, to 'the world's climate must be getting warmer'.

8.1.3   The inference is the move from the first two sentences, taken as side-by-side reasoning, to 'it is clear that a fundamental change is taking place as employers, content with a higher ratio of temporary staff to permanent staff, alter the structure of their work force'.

8.1.4   This contains two inferences, the first is the move from, 'The outstanding success of Ted's company, which was launched against the advice, and without the support, of bankers, business consultants and financiers' to 'one person's vision can prove all the experts in the world wrong'. The second is the move from 'one person's vision can prove all the experts in the world wrong' to 'Anyone thinking of setting up a business should trust their own judgement, and not be influenced by the advice of others.'

8.1.5   The inference is the move from everything else (probably best construed as joint reasoning) to 'The police force should ban their officers from driving at high speed in pursuit of young joyriders who steal cars'.

8.1.6 This contains two inferences. the first is from 'when prisoners under sentence of death are given the choice between life in prison and execution, 99 per cent of them choose life imprisonment' to 'they fear death more than they fear life imprisonment'. The second is from 'they fear death more than they fear life imprisonment' and 'one is most deterred by what one most fears' taken jointly to 'the threat of the death penalty is more likely to deter most potential murderers than is the threat of life imprisonment'.

8.2 Discussed in the text immediately following the question.

8.3.1 Clearly a poor inference by our test.

8.3.2 As it stands a weak inference by our test. If we add the assumption that 'there is no other possible explanation' it becomes a good inference by our test.

8.3.3 A weak inference by our test.

8.3.4 Not sure what to say about the first inference. Perhaps Ted was just lucky (so his success was not due to his 'vision') – but still he was successful, so provided we do not put too much stress on the reference to 'vision' (but construe that as a reference to vision, luck and hard work) this is good inference by our test. The second inference is poor by our test; what worked for Ted probably will not for most people.

8.3.5 Not so easy to judge by our test; depends on whether there are any alternatives; see discussion in section 9.5, **Example 2**.

8.3.6 Left to you.

8.4.1 Deductively valid. If Tom really hates **everyone** Mary loves, then if she loves him he **must** hate himself. Of course, if it means Tom hates everyone Mary loves other than himself, then it is not deductively valid.

8.4.2 If 'in that case he couldn't have shot the master' means 'if the butler was in the pantry he couldn't have shot the master' then the argument is deductively valid; if the reasons are true the conclusion must be.

8.4.3 Clearly not deductively valid. However, with the added assumption 'there is no other possible explanation', which means in effect 'if the sea level is rising, the world's climate must be getting warmer' it is deductively valid.

8.5.1   Deductively valid.
8.5.2   Deductively valid.
8.5.3   Not deductively valid.
8.5.4   Deductively valid.

8.6   Perhaps Daley and Thompson were both able to give details about the murder which no one could know except the murderer and the police. Perhaps the prosecution was able to show that Daley and Thompson could not have discussed their own evidence with each other so it was given independently and thus corroborated what the other said (see chapter 7 on corroboration). Perhaps they were able to convince the jury that they had no 'motive' other than to tell the truth in this case because they had nothing to gain or lose by giving or not giving their evidence against Stone. These – and perhaps other facts you thought of – could surely convince a jury that the case was established 'beyond a reasonable doubt'.

8.7.1   Left to you.
8.7.2   Left to you.

8.8.1   You probably do not know whether the figures are correct and so cannot comment on the acceptability of the reasons, but the inference is clearly weak; there could be all sorts of social factors causing all sorts of differences, so the reasons could be true and the conclusion quite unwarranted.
8.8.2   Left to you.

8.9.1   Dawkins begins by considering the following inference: 'although there is no positive evidence for the existence of a God, nor is there evidence against His existence. **So** it is best to keep an open mind and be agnostic.' This has seemed a very reasonable inference to many people, but Dawkins argues that there are many similar inferences which no one accepts; for example, 'although there is no positive evidence for there being fairies at the bottom of the garden, nor is there evidence against their existence, **so** it is best to keep an open mind and be agnostic'. He contends that since the second (fairies) inference impresses almost no one, the first shouldn't either. Although it is clear that neither inference is deductively valid, the question is whether they nonetheless have some force. Though almost no one suggests that the 'fairies inference' has any weight, some people think the one about God's existence is very strong – because the consequence of being mistaken (and wrongly believing God does not exist) might be so serious (perhaps even involving eternal damnation!) (For closely related inferences, see Pascal's Wager, Questions appendix, passage 56.)

8.9.2 Argument indicator words make the structure of this argument very clear. Ayer's basic reason is that 'all claims about the nature of God are meaningless'. From this he infers that the sentence 'God exists' is meaningless. From this and the belief that 'only meaningful claims can be meaningfully denied' he infers that the sentence 'God does not exist' must be meaningless too. He then infers from the fact that the agnostic thinks 'Does God exist?' is a meaningful question, that the agnostic must think 'God exists' and 'God does not exist' are meaningful sentences. Thus, he infers, his view conflicts both with atheism and agnosticism.

These are all hard inferences to fault; if it is true that 'all claims about the nature of God are meaningless' it is hard to see how his other conclusions could be false. Thus, if you dispute Ayer's conclusions you have to challenge his basic reason. Philosophers and theologians have been doing this for a long time!

Chapter 9

9.1 Discussed in the text immediately following the question.

9.2.1 This appears to assume that only the benefits to **animals** from toxicity testing will count towards the benefits argument. The benefits argument also counts the benefits to humans in weighing the case for toxicity testing, so the author is mistaken in inferring from 'the benefit to animals cannot be established' to 'the benefits argument fails'.

9.2.2 This assumes that at least some parents will be able to prevent their children from committing crimes. Presumably many children who commit crimes have bad relations with their parent(s), thus their parents may have great difficulty in influencing them, so this may show the inference to 'the Criminal Justice Act . . . should have the effect of reversing this trend' to be flawed.

9.2.3 On the face of it, this inference commits a classic fallacy, since it has the pattern 'if A then B and B is true so A is true' which is a common mistake. However, in this case, it is surely reasonable to attribute the assumption, 'there is no other plausible explanation for the pile of ashes and rubble' and this is very likely to be true, so adding this assumption shows the inference to be a good one (by any reasonable standard) and not a fallacy at all. (For a more extensive discussion of the significance of this example see Everitt and Fisher, 1995, p.171.)

9.2.4   It is not enough to add the assumption 'if Jones has worked hard he will pass the exam'; this makes the argument deductively valid, but any questions about the original inference will now have to be asked of the assumption. For the inference to succeed the speaker must be assuming that Jones is clever enough, that he has been well taught, that the exam is no more difficult than usual, that Jones will not collapse with exam nerves, and the like (since these are all ways in which the inference could misfire). So if all or most of these assumptions are true the inference is a good one, but if some are false it is weak.

9.2.5   The inference 'Mars has long been too dry and cold for life to flourish on its surface' seems to be based on the assumption that 'life requires warmth and water'. Since (I think) this is true of every form of life we know, this seems a reasonable inference. Some people may wish to insist that other forms of life are 'possible' and they will think this is a weak inference.

9.2.6   In the first paragraph the Noodle is surely assuming that if our ancestors did not think of some 'measure' it can not be a good one (or at least that policies and practices which have been in place for some time are generally better than new ones)! Identifying this underlying assumption shows how weak his inference is. Perhaps the measure he is discussing is a poor measure, perhaps it is not; but the inference from the fact that it is *new* to the conclusion that it is *poor* is hopeless. Apart from anything else, circumstances change over time and the measure has to be weighed on its merits. (However, note that it is surprisingly common for older people to say to younger people, 'It was good enough for us, so it should be good enough for you'!)

In the fourth paragraph the Noodle is assuming that if the measure is supported, then further and less reasonable measures will be proposed and these will have to be accepted. This is often called the 'thin-end-of-the-wedge' argument or the 'slippery slope' argument. The Noodle would almost certainly have argued that women should not be given the vote because they would then demand even more – and these additional demands would have to be accepted! Again the inference is hopeless and the measure has to be weighed on its merits. Again this is a very common pattern of inference which has little merit!

9.3   Left to you.

9.4.1   Left to you.
9.4.2   Discussed in the text immediately following the question.

9.5   Discussed in section 11.2.2.

9.6.1   Here are some 'other relevant considerations' which students have suggested: (i) Perhaps the extinction of species is simply a 'natural' process and we should not interfere with it. (ii) If we accept the argument, many species might quickly disappear. For example, pandas and tigers are threatened with extinction because of the loss of habitat and some species of whales are threatened because of over hunting. Surely we simply do not want to lose these species and perhaps thousands or even millions of others? (iii) We might like to eliminate some species, like mosquitoes, which are responsible for spreading disease. (iv) Losing some species might produce great changes in ecosystems (for example losing whales might have a big impact on oceans) – and some such losses might harm us (other such losses might benefit us). (v) Genetic material might be lost forever and we do not yet know how significant that loss might be. (vi) It usually costs money and resources to keep species in existence (because, for example, habitats have to be preserved and guarded) so we may face some hard choices about the use of scarce resources. (vii) The loss of some species might particularly impoverish human life. Surely we have much to gain from a species-rich environment, including being able to extract useful genetic materials and simply being able to wonder at its variety and beauty! (viii) It would be wonderful if there were still some dinosaurs around – in somewhere like Jurassic Park!

Perhaps you thought of other considerations too and you might feel you need to do some research about some of these before being able to resolve this question to your own satisfaction.

9.6.2   Here are some 'other relevant considerations':
(i) It must surely be possible nowadays to make containers which, like aircraft 'black boxes', are almost indestructible in

the event of a crash, thus reducing the risk to paintings being transported by air. (ii) It must also be possible to construct such containers so that they can properly regulate the atmosphere in which the painting is transported. (iii) Paintings are often 'at risk' in their home galleries – from excessive humidity, poor security (some famous paintings have been attacked by vandals), over-zealous cleaning and even from flooding. (iv) Home galleries are often too impoverished to maintain paintings in the best possible atmosphere and security. (v) Many people attend these big art exhibitions – which brings in a great deal of money – so this money could help impoverished 'home' galleries protect and look after the paintings. (vi) Many people get enormous pleasure from these big art exhibitions and they increase interest in such paintings throughout the world and this is good for the paintings.

Again, perhaps you thought of other considerations too.

9.6.3   Left to you.

9.7.1   Largely left to you, but if you skim the piece looking for argument indicator words, you will quickly find the following, and these will help you locate quite a few of Dawkins' arguments:

So it is best to keep an open mind and be agnostic [about the existence of God].

. . . **because** the same could be said of Father Christmas and tooth fairies.

. . . **so** shouldn't we be agnostic with respect to fairies?

. . . **the reason is** that most people have a residue of feeling that Darwinian evolution isn't quite big enough to explain everything about life.

. . . **because** any God worthy of the name must have been a being of colossal intelligence, a supermind, an entity of enormous sophistication and complexity.

. . . **because** it raises a bigger mystery than it solves.

. . . **for** it simply postulates the difficult to explain.

. . . **we can safely conclude** that He [God] is very, very improbable indeed.

Applying other techniques, like the 'therefore' test, will then help you understand the rest of Dawkins' arguments (which he mostly displays very clearly). Doing these things and applying the other lessons we have practised should help you to write a response which genuinely focuses on the issues.

9.7.2   This is entirely for you to answer.

Chapter 10

10.1–10.2   Left to you.

10.3   It is clear that this example about the death of Napoleon exhibits the right structure, it considers two alternatives and provides evidence which tells **against** the cancer option and provides quite a lot of evidence **for** the arsenic poisoning option. Whether this is a good and persuasive argument depends on whether there are other possibilities which should have been considered and other evidence which should have been taken into account or looked for. For example, perhaps we need to check whether there are other ways the arsenic could have got into Napoleon's hair (say through a hair dressing that was commonly used then?). Or is there any other evidence about his behaviour before his death which might suggest other possible causes of death? For most of us the argument will be convincing enough if we have good reason to believe that the experts are right about what his symptoms signify and no other experts have had good evidence for other possible causes of his death. Of course, someone who researches Napoleon's death for a PhD thesis, will need to investigate the evidence and what other experts have said very carefully, but most of us have to rely on experts in a situation like this. Incidentally, this explanation fits well with something else I know, namely that horsemen used to give their horses small doses of arsenic before they entered a show to make their coats shine!

10.4.1   Perhaps there was colossal volcanic activity on Earth at that time which threw enormous quantities of dust and poisonous fumes into the air. Perhaps some disease swept the dinosaurs away. You may be able to think of other possible explanations.

10.4.2   Evidence of colossal volcanic activity could be shown by huge lava flows of the correct date over a huge part of the Earth (as is the case in India). I do not know enough about how disease might be revealed as the cause; perhaps experts could say what to look for in fossils.

10.4.3   Presumably, there are no dinosaur fossils later than 65 million years old? What is said fits well with everything else I know and believe, so the reasoning seems quite strong. You may know more and have a different view.

10.4.4 Left to you.

10.4.5 Maybe some dinosaurs could have survived on these plants; we need to know how extensive the plants were and whether at least some species of dinosaurs ate them to know whether this evidence conflicts with the explanation we have been offered for the death of the dinosaurs.

10.4.6 This seems to render the meteor explanation less likely (unless we can find evidence of other colossal meteors arriving at the right times). Perhaps we need to look for different explanations for different extinctions.

10.4.7 Left to you.

10.5. It is reasonably easy to mark this passage up so that you can see what is going on:

An underwater survey of the Witch Ground, in the North Sea off Aberdeen, has discovered C1[a trawler which was probably sunk by a sudden burst of methane gas escaping from a vent in the sea floor – known as the Witch's Hole]. R1<When methane – or natural gas – bubbles through the sea in big enough volumes, it lowers the density of the water around it to a point at which objects, including ships will no longer float>. R2<'Any ship caught above [such a blow-out] would sink as if it were in a lift shaft'>, said Alan Judd, a marine geologist from the University of Sunderland who led the Witch Ground survey expedition. R3<In this case the trawler had sunk 'flat' with its hull sitting horizontally on the sea bed exactly over the Witch's Hole vent>. R4<This was consistent with the vessel being sunk by a methane blow-out>; R5< if it had been holed[AH] she would have sunk with the holed end lowest>. Even sailors who jumped overboard wearing life-jackets would sink like stones. R6<The Witch Ground and the Witch's Hole in particular, have long been known among fishermen as treacherous waters>. R7<Methane blow-outs are thought to have destroyed about 40 oil platforms around the world; the Witch Ground is just 22 miles from the Forties oil field>.

Does the report consider other reasonable possibilities? Could there simply have been a great storm? Could a submarine have caught in the trawler's nets and dragged it down (as happened in another famous case)? What evidence would show for or against these possibilities? A storm would probably have allowed the trawler time to send a Mayday message and might have allowed the men time to put on safety clothing or launch a safety raft; a methane blow-out might be too sudden to allow any of these? We should look for evidence on these? On the submarine theory, the nets would have to be out; were they? Presumably there is no evidence of the trawler being holed? If the area is known to be treacherous presumably this is because other ships have been lost there so shouldn't we expect to find other ships nearby similarly unholed, sitting 'flat' on the bottom, etc., if this explanation is to be completely convincing?

10.6   Marking this up is easy so we leave that to you. This piece provides three pieces of evidence and two other reasons against believing that 'consumption of cholesterol affects the level of blood cholesterol(Ch)'. Assuming the evidence is from reliable sources (and the MRC is reputable) they tell against Ch. Assuming the other reasons are true too, they also raise questions about Ch. If what this says is true it is interesting and persuasive to me. Back to eating butter!

10.7   The piece explains why the number of 'twin births' has increased and why the increase is entirely due to increased numbers of 'fraternal twins'. It then argues that these will continue to increase 'because more women will seek fertility treatments' but will stabilise – with most births still being single births. Given the figures, it seems a plausible argument.

10.8   Discussed in the text immediately following the question.

10.9–10.10   Left to you.

Chapter 11

11.1   Left to you.

11.2.1 Hans has complained that your test was unfair. That gives you a problem. Three options are (i) re-mark the paper then discuss the result with Hans, (ii) refer the test paper to a colleague for scrutiny and Hans's paper for re-marking, (iii) do nothing.

11.2.2 Left to you.

11.2.3 Here are some options: (i) threaten the Japanese Government with the use of the bomb, (ii) try to negotiate peace, (iii) demonstrate the power of the bomb to the Japanese on an uninhabited area, (iv) don't use the bomb but continue the war with conventional arms, (v) drop the bomb on military targets, (vi) drop the bomb on cities, (vii) abandon the war.

11.3.1 (i) If you re-mark the paper and discuss the result with Hans, you may change your mark or confirm it; if you discuss it with Hans he may be persuaded of the correctness of your final mark or not; if he is not he may appeal; other students may be affected by the reasonableness of what you do.

(ii) If you do nothing you will be saved some work; Hans may appeal and other students may be disaffected.

11.3.2 Left to you.

11.3.3 (iii) if you demonstrate the power of the bomb to the Japanese on an uninhabited area this will avoid killing thousands of innocent civilians (which will happen if dropped on cities); may persuade them to surrender (but they have fought fiercely despite huge losses so maybe it won't); will limit your scope for further attacks (because you have only two of these bombs); may cost you further American soldiers lives as the conventional war drags on (and this may cost you votes in the next election).

(iv) if you don't use the bomb but continue the war with conventional arms, this will certainly cost you far more American service men's lives (the Japanese fight very fiercely and don't yield easily); it will be costly in conventional arms too; the war will probably drag on for much longer than it would if you use the bomb; all this may cost you votes in the next election.

11.4　Left to you.

11.5.1 The obvious moral principle here is that you should not break promises. Most people act on this principle much of the time (otherwise trust would soon break down), but it might depend on the case.

11.5.2 This is a moral dilemma; on the one hand, most people believe that you should not break promises but, on the other, also most people believe you should save friends from harm if you can. It will depend on the seriousness of the case.

11.5.3 Left to you.

11.6　Discussed in the text immediately following the question.

11.7   Left to you.

11.8.1   Here is a possible brief response: 'We could leave things as they are, try to educate people or ban killing animals for sport. The first option causes a lot of suffering to animals, gives pleasure to those who engage in these sports and disgusts many other people. If it is abhorrent to most people in the UK the third option would spare their feelings, but some people would lose their hobbies and even livelihoods and they would feel very aggrieved. It is important to be tolerant of others and let people live their lives as they choose but cruelty to animals should not be tolerated. Trying to educate people against this activity is a slow process; many animals would suffer in the process and such a policy might not succeed in eliminating this activity.'

11.8.2   Left to you.

11.8.3   Left to you.

11.8.4   Here is a possible brief response: 'We could leave things as they are, try to educate people or compel parents to have their children vaccinated. Because more and more parents are worried about the risks from vaccination, the first course carries a substantial risk of polio outbreaks, with resulting injury to children, perhaps even death. Perhaps education could succeed in persuading more parents to have their children vaccinated, but many are increasingly suspicious of Government claims about health. Compulsion would generate passionate hostility from some parents, is contrary to our traditions and would probably produce martyrs. We need reliable research on the risks of all options.

11.9.1   You have been made an offer so you have to decide. There are two options; you take the bet or you don't (maybe you could try to negotiate try too!). What are the likely consequences? If you win, you get £1,000; if you lose you lose £100, so you have a 50–50 chance of winning ten times what you risk losing. If you value the possibility of winning £1,000 more than you hate the idea of losing £100 it is rational to accept the bet, but the outcome might be that you lose £100. That's life! (cf. Sutherland, 1992, p. 5f).

11.9.2   It is **very** likely that the coin will land heads at least once, so the chance of losing any money is tiny and the chance of gaining quite a lot is very considerable!

11.10   Left to you.

11.11.1 Left to you.

11.11.2 Here is a possible answer which covers some of the points which could be made: Spending £7.5 million pounds to return one captive killer whale to the ocean does seem an extraordinary waste of money, especially when you consider the other things for which the money could have been used. However, I shall argue that it was right to do this and that there are other lessons we should learn from this phenomenon.

In the first place, since this money was raised for a very specific purpose, namely to return Keiko to the wild, it had to be spent doing precisely that – at least. You cannot campaign to raise money for a cause and then use the money for some quite different cause. In general, people want to know their money goes in support of the cause for which they gave it. Doing otherwise might well be illegal, but even if it is not, it would rightly generate fierce opposition from those who donated money. Furthermore, if money which had been donated for some good cause were used for other purposes, this would undermine people's readiness to give money in other cases.

For all these reasons, Keiko had to be returned to the wild – though any money left over could have been used for related causes, in keeping with the donors' concerns. Notice that the money did not just return Keiko to the Atlantic; it also gave further publicity to a cause which donors cared about – treating animals well in general and perhaps saving whales in particular. It was a symbolic act and it is hard to quantify the effects of such acts.

So, there really were no alternatives. But having said that, what lessons can be learned from this phenomenon? The whole experience suggests to me that other good causes need their own *Free Willy* type films in order to move people. Consider the case of saving the sight of thousands of people in the developing world by funding simple operations; surely it would be possible to make a film which would highlight the plight of such people and thus move others to want to help? Then a campaign to raise funds to restore the sight of such people might be similarly successful. Perhaps it would have to be a sentimental film, but the problem is to move those who can afford it to help those in need.

Of course, there are many possible objections to my proposal; it might be easier to raise money for animals than for people; perhaps *Free Willy* was a very special film; perhaps people will give money for a particular whale (or person) and not so readily for whales (or people) in general; perhaps there is only limited scope for this kind of campaign to work; and so on. But, having said that, it will be clear from all the reasons I have given that I reject the author's conclusion in the *Free Willy* piece and recommend that other good causes try to get studios to make moving, perhaps sentimental, films which they could then use to support their own campaigns.

Of course there are many other possible responses to this piece.

11.11.3 Left to you.

11.11.4 Here is a possible answer which covers some of the points which could be made:

The problem here is to decide whether to accept money for a good cause (in this case to fund a university chair of international relations) when the money comes from a tobacco company. If we do so, the company may get good publicity out of its donation, the university may appear to condone the sale of tobacco and campaigns to reduce smoking may feel weakened. It is hard to know how likely these effects are, but perhaps the university could both accept the money and state its opposition to smoking. That would be a matter for negotiation with the company. If the university does not accept the money, perhaps the chair of international relations will not be appointed, but again we need to know how likely that is.

The implication of this piece is that the campaigners object to accepting money from a source which 'is responsible for much illness and many deaths worldwide'. But the author challenges that argument by saying that cars are probably just as responsible for illness and death (from accidents and pollution) and that armaments companies make 'dangerous products', but in neither case do we refuse to associate with such companies. With these and other examples he seems to want to say there is no way to draw a line here. However, the cases he mentions differ from cigarettes in key respects. Cars bring many benefits and are not addictive; furthermore, we simply do not yet know how to manage without them and we are trying to reduce the harm they do. Armaments companies are necessary too, given the way the world is, and we try to regulate them closely to reduce the harm their products do, especially to innocent civilians. As to butter, it is not addictive and people are free to eat it or avoid it as they wish. No one thinks skis and parachutes are like cigarettes and these examples show how the author has lost sight of the issue!

The author also argues that what tobacco companies do is entirely legal and their donation could benefit thousands of people. Being legal does not make it right but it is important to distinguish between this and money obtained illegally (say through drug trafficking) and it is true that many could benefit from the donation.

The author's fourth argument, that there is no difference between accepting a donation from the tobacco company and accepting money raised through taxes (including those on cigarettes) is disingenuous. Companies give money because they expect favourable publicity and direct gain from their donation; money raised in taxes cannot be traced to any particular source.

Though I think the author's arguments for accepting donations from tobacco companies are mostly poor, I would argue that we should accept the money, for the good that could be done with it, provided this does not prevent us from continuing to campaign against an activity which causes much ill health and death. In the *Preface* to his play *Major Barbara*, George Bernard Shaw puts a similar argument for getting the 'cannon founder's' money into the hands of Major Barbara, the Salvation Army officer.

11.11.5 Left to you.

Glossary

Critical thinking uses ordinary English. Virtually all the language which is used in this book can be found quite easily in a good English dictionary. That is deliberate. Critical thinking simply requires us to use ideas and distinctions which are already available to most sixth form students who understand ordinary English. There is no need for jargon and although a few semi-technical terms (like *ad hominem*, *hypothetical*, *converse*, etc.) can be helpful, most of the language we need in order to engage in even high-level critical thinking is ordinary language. However, it **is** necessary to be clear headed about the use of this language, hence the need for this Glossary. The Glossary explains the meanings of terms and phrases as an aid to keeping students' thinking properly focused, but there is no intention that the usage explained here should differ from (clear-headed) ordinary usage.

Analogy: Sometimes it is helpful to think about one matter by recognising that it is like another, more familiar one. For example people sometimes explain what the movement of molecules in a gas is like by saying that they move like a large number of snooker balls bouncing off one another (but in three dimensions rather than just two). If someone reasons 'by analogy', they say 'A is very like B in a number of respects so A is (probably) like B in another respect which interests us'; for example, in chapter 1 I say that critical thinking is like basket ball in that it comprises various skills, so you can (probably) improve your critical thinking ability in the same way that coaches teach basket ball.

Argument: In the context of critical thinking, the term 'argument' refers to a set of claims, some of which are presented as reasons for accepting some further claim – the conclusion. The reasons are presented with the aim of persuading the hearer or reader to accept the conclusion. Many clear examples are provided in the text above; in each of these some basic claims are put forward as reasons which support further claims – the conclusions. Reasons may be factual claims, value judgements, definitions or interpretations (for example, see Question 6.3) and there is a similar variety among conclusions. Arguments can vary enormously in their structure and content, but they always contain a set of claims which are presented as reasons for accepting some further claim – a conclusion and they are always intended to persuade their audience.

There is an everyday sense of 'argument' which means roughly 'quarrel' but this is a quite different usage.

Argument indicators: These are the words we commonly use to show that reasons are being presented in support of a conclusion; they are words like *therefore* ..., *so* ..., *thus* ..., *hence* ..., *consequently* ..., *which proves that* ..., *I conclude that* ..., *it follows that* ...(where the dots are the conclusion) and *because* ..., *since* ..., *the reasons are* ..., *the evidence is* ... (where the dots indicate reasons (see examples ...). Of course, there are many other phrases in English which play a similar role (cf. section 2.3).

Assumption: We commonly call a belief an assumption when it is clearly accepted or 'taken for granted' by a speaker or writer but is *not stated or made explicit* by them; for example, someone engaging in a discussion about miracles may fail to mention that he believes in the existence of an omnipotent Christian God, but this may be obvious from other things he says. This is the most important usage of assumption in our context (see section 4.1).

Note also that in ordinary usage we sometimes call an *explicit* claim made by a speaker or writer an assumption, either (i) because we wish to note that the speaker or writer *has given no reasons for accepting it* or (ii) because *we wish to challenge the claim*. Thus, if someone was arguing the case for believing in miracles and clearly and explicitly based their case on the claim that there is an omnipotent Christian God, one might say (i) 'but this is only an assumption; why should I accept it?' or (ii) 'but this is only an assumption; I don't believe it at all'.

Belief: This term is used in an entirely everyday sense; it refers broadly to the claims/sentences that an individual person holds to be true or right. There are many different kind of beliefs, including scientific claims ('the Earth goes around the Sun'), religious beliefs ('God created man in His own image'), moral principles ('it is wrong to break promises'), prudential beliefs ('it is better to buy a house than to rent in the UK') – and many others. If an individual A believes a claim P, P may be true or false, scientific, religious, moral, mystical or whatever; it may be harmless or pernicious, plausible or not, and much more – it may even be meaningless or vacuous. Many arguments throughout the text express the beliefs of their authors.

Conclusion: If reasons are presented for accepting some other belief, C, then C is called a conclusion (of that argument). Thus the conclusion of example 2 in section 4.1 is 'all the unemployed could solve their unemployment problem by great ingenuity in searching for a job or by willingness to work for less'. If reasons are given for one conclusion, which is then used as a reason for a further conclusion and so on – in a chain of reasoning – the last is called the **main conclusion** and the earlier ones in the chain are sometimes called **intermediate conclusions**. Thus, in the first example in section 3.5, the main conclusion is 'we should prohibit the use of techniques which enable people to choose the sex of their children' and 'if people can choose the sex of their child, it is likely that there will eventually be more males than females in the population' is an intermediate conclusion.

Notice that a conclusion does not necessarily come at the end of a piece of reasoning. It may be stated at the beginning, then argued for (there are many examples in the text). The conclusion of a piece of reasoning might be a factual claim ('so he must be the murderer'), a recommendation ('so you ought to buy this car'), an interpretation ('so Iago should be seen as a treacherous villain') a decision ('so I shall take the job') etc.

Consistent/Inconsistent: Two claims are consistent provided they could both be true or correct at the same time. They are inconsistent if they CANNOT both be true or correct at the same time. Thus, 'Mt Everest is 29,000 feet high' is consistent with 'Mt Everest is in Nepal' but is inconsistent with 'Mt Everest is 15,000 metres high.' The Ten Commandments are consistent with each other but not with 'Do whatever you want to do regardless of others.' People are consistent provided the things they say could be true or correct together; they are inconsistent if this is not the case. Sometimes inconsistency is fairly obvious, as in the Mt Everest example above, but sometimes it is more deeply buried in what people say and believe. Here is a less obvious example of inconsistency, 'People strive only to obtain praise. When certain behaviour brings approval, a baby will try to continue in that way. But, what if your baby's behaviour disappoints you? The less attention you give this behaviour the better; children love drama and may repeat their misbehaviour just to witness your explosion.'

Contradiction: Strictly speaking someone contradicts themselves if they say or believe 'A is true' and 'A is false' at the same time, for example, 'Mt Everest is 29,000 ft high' and 'Mt Everest is **not** 29,000 ft high.' Sometimes contradictions are very evident in what a person says or believes (as in the Everest example) but often they are deeply buried. If someone contradicts themselves they are clearly **inconsistent** (since their claims cannot both be true) but inconsistent claims could both be false, so inconsistency does not necessary imply a contradiction. However, these two terms are commonly used to mean much the same (see the *Oxford English Dictionary*).

Converse: The term converse is usually used to refer to the 'opposite' (in a certain sense) of an **hypothetical**. The converse of any hypothetical 'If A then B' is simply the hypothetical 'If B then A'. Thus the converse of 'If fire is burning then oxygen is present' is 'If oxygen is present; then fire is burning.' Notice that in this example although the initial hypothetical is true, its converse is not. Sometimes the converse of a hypothetical is true and sometimes not.

Counter-example: General claims may be challenged by finding counter-examples. Suppose someone claims that 'all politicians are dishonest'; if we can find one or more politicians who are honest then these are counter-examples to the general claim and it is shown to be mistaken. Whether counter-examples greatly weaken a general claim depends on the case; in this case, the proponent of the original claim might just say 'OK, *nearly* all politicians are dishonest' and this may serve his purpose just as well. To challenge this further claim would require quite a few more counter-examples. In another example, consider the general principle that 'it is always wrong to break a promise'; if you can then describe a situation in which it seems right to break a promise this will be a counter-example to the general principle. For example, if breaking your promise will save the lives of many innocent people in a war situation, this might well be the right thing to do and this would be a counter-example to the general principle.

Disposition: If you say that someone has a 'sunny disposition' you mean that they are inclined to be cheerful; confronted with situations which might worry or displease other people, such a person is more likely to react cheerfully. So dispositions are behaviour patterns; they are a propensity to behave in a particular way; a kind of habit. In our context this idea matters because we do not want students just to be good at doing critical thinking tasks when they are set, but we hope that they will become *disposed* to use the techniques explained and practised here.

Entails: In contexts where a case is being argued or discussed, this term is often used to mean something like 'is a logically inescapable consequence'. For example, a company's Finance Director might say of his company's finances, 'The planned investment programme will entail heavy borrowing' meaning, 'We don't have sufficient cash to finance this investment ourselves and the only way to finance it will be by heavy borrowing.' In everyday contexts, 'entails' is often used more loosely – so that there is a substantial overlap between the common usage of 'entails' and 'implies' (see **Imply/Implication**).

Fallacy: The central usage of this term is to refer to a pattern of reasoning which is mistaken and which people commonly use. For example it is surprisingly common for people to argue 'B came after A so A caused B' (as in, 'I got my cold after Mary so I must have caught it from her'). Another such pattern is what is called the 'ad hominem fallacy', where you argue against what someone says not by addressing their claims but by attacking them (as in 'We should not listen to the complaints of prisoners because they are convicted criminals'). It can be quite difficult to recognise when a piece of reasoning is genuinely a fallacy. The term *fallacy* is also more loosely used to refer to any error in reasoning.

Hypothesis: This is a claim which is put forward 'for consideration' or to be investigated, rather than being presented as true. For example, scientists investigating the death of the dinosaurs put forward the 'hypothesis' that an enormous meteor crashed into the Earth at about the time the dinosaurs became extinct. Subsequent investigation has confirmed this hypothesis to a large extent – there is strong evidence that such a meteor landed in the Gulf of Mexico – so the hypothesis has moved from being an hypothesis to being widely believed to be true (though whether it caused the extinction of the dinosaurs is more open to question).

Hypothetical: This is a sentence which has the general form 'if A then B' where A and B are sentences. For example, 'If you work hard at this course then you will get a good grade' is a hypothetical; so is the sentence 'if people can choose the sex of their child, it is likely that there will eventually be more males than females in the population'. There are many equivalent ways of expressing hypotheticals in English, for example, 'suppose we continue to damage the ozone layer; in that case there will be far more cases of skin cancer', or 'unless we stop damaging the ozone layer, there will be far more cases of skin cancer'; there are many others too (see section 3.6).

Imply/Implication: There is an everyday sense of these words which means roughly 'suggests' or 'leads me to believe', as when the detective says, 'the evidence implies that Smith was present at the murder'.

However, the word 'imply' is often used more strictly to mean 'if . . . then . . .' For example, if someone says, 'the presence of fire implies that there must be oxygen present', they could equally well say, 'if there is fire then oxygen must be present'. In general, to say that 'A implies B' is to say something like 'if A then B', either strictly as in the oxygen example or more loosely as in the detective example. To say that 'A entails B' is usually to say 'A implies B' in this strict usage of 'implies' (see **Entails**).

Inference: In everyday usage, when people speak of an inference they sometimes mean a 'guess' based on the information they have, or the conclusion they have reached – again based on other things they believe. For example, after reviewing the evidence a detective might say, 'The inference is that we should question Jones again about this case.' In our context, the usage is derived from logic, where it means the 'step' from reasons to conclusion, the 'move' from one to the other. Thus, if someone argues, 'Some people have solved their own unemployment problem by great ingenuity in searching for a job or by willingness to work for less so all the unemployed could do this', the inference is the move from 'some people have . . .' to 'all the unemployed could do this'. Though the reason presented in this argument has often been true, the inference to the argument's conclusion is much more questionable. Other instructive examples are given in several chapters, especially chapters 8 and 9.

Knowledge: In its everyday usage this term is used in several ways. One usage refers to knowing some fact (as in 'John knows that chemotherapy will make his hair fall out' or 'John knows that the Earth is 93 million miles from the Sun'); another refers to knowing *how* to do something (as in 'John knows *how* to ride a bicycle'); another refers to *being acquainted* with an object, place or person (as in 'John knows New York').

If someone claims to know the fact, for example, that 'The Earth is 93 million miles from the Sun', then this is something they take to be true. If they are not sure about its truth they will tend not to say they 'know' it, but will probably say they 'suspect it is true' or it is their 'opinion' or some such alternative to 'know'.'

Of course, people *claim* to know things which are in fact *false* and in that case the rest of us would say they do not really *know* it. For a person to *know*, for example, that AIDS is caused by a virus, they would have to accept this, they would have to have good reason to accept it and it would have to be *true*.

Metacognition: This simply means 'thinking about your thinking'.

For example, if you reflect on the thinking you went through in arriving at some decision, you are engaged in metacognition – in thinking about your own thinking. Sometimes you just work out the solution to some problem without thinking about how you are doing it or how you should do it; then you are just thinking, without engaging in metacognition. If you are not very skilled at, say, decision making, many people believe that the way to improve it is through thinking about how you usually do it and then trying to correct the weaknesses by thinking self consciously about how you make the next decision.

Necessary and sufficient conditions: To say that 'A is a necessary condition for B' is to say that 'if A is not the case, B will not be the case either'. Thus, if a teacher says 'a good musical ear is a necessary condition for learning to play the violin', this is the same as saying 'if you do not have a good musical ear, you will not be able to learn to play the violin'.

To say that 'A is a sufficient condition for B' is to say that, 'if A is the case, then B will be the case also'. Thus, if a lawyer says, 'being born in the UK of British parents is a sufficient condition for obtaining a British passport' this is the same as saying, 'if you are born in Britain of British parents you can have a British passport'. Clearly, although a good musical ear is necessary for learning to play the violin, it is not sufficient (you will need lots of practice too). Equally clearly, although being born in the UK of British parents is sufficient to get a British passport, it is not necessary, since other people can qualify for British passports too.

Reasons: Arguing a case consists in giving reasons for a conclusion. The reasons are presented as supporting the conclusion and are intended to persuade an audience to accept the conclusion. Thus, in the first example in section 3.5, 'most prospective parents want sons' is given as a reason for believing that 'if people can choose the sex of their child, it is likely that there will eventually be more males than females in the population' – which in turn is one of the reasons for the main conclusion. If someone offers reasons for a conclusion they present themselves as both believing the reasons and believing that they support the conclusion.

Sufficient conditions: (see **Necessary and sufficient conditions**).

Supposition (and **Suppositional reasoning**): A supposition is a sentence which begins with the word 'suppose' or some synonym. For example, someone who is thinking about current experiments on genetically modified crops might say, 'Suppose these experiments do risk dangerous contamination of other crops . . .?' Such a sentence does not commit the speaker to the view that these experiments do carry a dangerous risk; he or she is simply speculating about what would be the case **IF** this were so. Reasoning from such starting points is often called 'what if' reasoning, or hypothetical reasoning or suppositional reasoning. This kind of reasoning is very common in theoretical contexts. The police have to use it a good deal too, for example asking 'What if Smith really was in Amsterdam at the time of the murder . . .?' For a famous example see the Questions appendix, passage 51.

Truth: This term is used in an ordinary, everyday sense. Physical scientists aim to establish truths about the world, like Newton's laws of motion. Biologists try to establish truths about living things, like which genes determine which human characteristics. Psychologists aim to establish truths about the human mind, for example whether it works in some important respects like a computer. When these questions are answered with sufficient evidence then we tend to speak of the truth of the matter. Before we are sure, we tend to speak of hypotheses, opinions, beliefs, conjectures, guesses, etc. Truths are often called facts. It is disputed whether the term 'true' should be applied to moral, political, religious and other beliefs.

Valid/Invalid: 'Valid' is often used as a very general term of approval, as in 'The Headmaster's policy on truancy is perfectly valid' but it also has a very specific meaning in the context of argument appraisal where it is short for 'deductively valid'. Consider the argument 'If Smith's fingerprints are on the gun then he is the murderer. His fingerprints are clearly detectable on the gun. So he must be the murderer'; in this argument, IF the two reasons are true, then the conclusion MUST be true; it is IMPOSSIBLE for the reasons to be true and the conclusion false. Such an argument is called 'deductively valid' or 'valid' for short. Validity in this sense is a matter of the *relationship* between the reasons and their conclusion. In this usage, reasons and conclusion may be true or false (but not valid) and arguments as a whole are valid or not (but not true or false). An argument is said to be **invalid** if it is not valid (cf. chapter 8).

Bibliography

Dewey, J. (1909) *How We Think*. D.C. Heath and Co.

Ennis, R.H. (1996) *Critical Thinking*. Prentice Hall. (A good critical thinking text.)

Everitt, N. and Fisher, A. (1995) *Modern Epistemology: A New Introduction*. New York: McGraw-Hill.

Fisher, A. (1988) *The Logic of Real Arguments*. Cambridge: Cambridge University Press. (A way of handling complex reasoning.)

Fisher, A. and Scriven, M. (1997) *Critical Thinking: Its Definition and Assessment*. Edgepress and Centre for Research in Critical Thinking, University of East Anglia.

Fisher, A. and Thomson, A. (1993) *Testing Reasoning Ability*. Centre for Research in Critical Thinking, University of East Anglia.

Glaser, E. (1941) *An Experiment in the Development of Critical Thinking*. Advanced School of Education at Teacher's College, Columbia University.

MacCormick, N. (1978) *Legal Reasoning and Legal Theory*. Oxford: Oxford University Press.

McPeck, J.E. (1981) *Critical Thinking and Education*. Oxford: Martin Roberston.

Morton, A. (1988) 'Making arguments explicit: the theoretical interest of practical difficulties', in A. Fisher (ed.), *Critical Thinking: Proceedings of the First British Conference on Informal Logic and Critical Thinking*, University of East Anglia.

Norris, S. and Ennis, R. (1989) *Evaluating Critical Thinking*. Pacific Grove, CA: Critical Thinking Press and Software.

Passmore, J. (1967) 'On teaching to be critical', in R.S. Peters (ed.), *The Concept of Education*. London: Routledge & Kegan Paul, pp.192–211.

Paul, R., Fisher, A. and Nosich, G. (1993) *Workshop on Critical Thinking Strategies*. Foundation for Critical Thinking, Sonoma State University, CA.

Phipson, S.L. & Elliott, D.W. (1980) *Manual of the Law of Evidence*, 11th edition. London: Sweet & Maxwell.

Scriven, M. (1976) *Reasoning*. New York: McGraw-Hill. (A classic text on how to improve reasoning skills.)

Sutherland, S. (1992) *Irrationality: The Enemy Within*. London: Penguin Books.

Swartz, R.J. and Parks, S. (1993) *Infusing Critical and Creative Thinking into the Curriculum*. Pacific Grove, CA: Critical Thinking Press. (Very good account of how to teach transferable and critical thinking skills.)

Swartz, R. and Parks, S. (1994) *Infusing the Teaching of Critical and Creative Thinking into Elementary Instruction*. Critical Thinking Press and Software.

Swartz, R.J. and Perkins, D.N. (1989) *Teaching Thinking: Issues and Approaches*. Pacific Grove, CA: Midwest Publications.

Index

acceptability
  definitions 84
  value judgements 84
acceptability of claims 84–8
  certainty of claim 84
  fit with other beliefs 86–7
  influence of context of claim 85
  when expertise/research required
    for decision 85–6
  widely known or believed 86
  see also credibility
acceptability of reasons 79–92
  see also credibility
affirming the antecedent 115
ambiguity 75
analogy, meaning of term 235
analysis of arguments 56–8
arguing a case 15
argument indicators 23–4, 31
  meaning of term 236
argumentation 11
arguments
  analysis 56–8
  compared with causal
    explanations 147
  conditions for success 111, 122
  deductively valid 111–12,
    113–17, 122
    and patterns of argument
      114–17
  evaluation 43, 56–8
  how to express clearly 29–30
  meaning of term 235–6

'more likely than not on balance
  of evidence' 112, 118–21
other relevant
  considerations/arguments 56,
  57–8
presentation of well-argued case
  131–6
'proved beyond reasonable
  doubt' 112, 117–18
reasons for failure 110–11
versus explanations 42–4, 46
see also inferences; reasons
assumptions 19, 20–1, 47–50, 59
  belief as 47
  explicit claim as 47–8
  implicit 48–50
  meaning of term 236

'because' 24, 39, 42–3
belief 47
  meaning of term 236
brainstorming 130–1, 157

causal explanations 43, 82, 138–53
  compared with arguments 147
  example 140–1
  language of 147–9
  language used 27
  pattern of reasoning 138–40
  questions for skilful explanations
    142–7
  weaknesses in our thinking
    about causes 141–2

chain of reasoning 31, 35–6
circumstantial evidence 101–2
civil courts, 'more likely than not on balance of evidence' 112, 118–21
claims
  acceptability, *see* acceptability of claims
  justifying by reference to credibility considerations 102–3
  kinds of 82–4
  nature of 90
clarification 61–77
  according to audience 64–5
  language used 27
  problems requiring clarification in reasoning 74–6
  sources 65–9
    definition/explanation from authority in field (reporting specialised usage) 66–7
    dictionary definition (reporting normal usage) 65–6
    stipulating a meaning 67–9
  vague terms 63
  ways of clarifying terms and ideas 69–73
    amount of detail required by audience 74
    drawing contrasts 72–3
    explaining history of expression 73
    giving necessary and sufficient conditions 69–71
    giving synonymous expression (or paraphrase) 69
    use of examples (and non-examples) 63, 71–2
communications 11
competencies required 7–8
conclusion indicators 22–3, 24
conclusions 18–19, 56, 57
  drawing more than one 45
  jumping to 141
  meaning of term 237

consequences 43
consistent/inconsistent, meaning of term 237
context 50–5, 59
  historical 53
contradiction, meaning of term 237–8
converse, meaning of term 238
corroboration 90, 91, 93, 104–5
counter-example, meaning of term 238
credibility 52, 87–91
  see also acceptability of claims; acceptability of reasons
credibility, judging 88–91, 93–106
  circumstances/context of claim 99–100
  corroboration 93, 104–5
  justifications in support of claim 100–3
    direct justification/evidence versus circumstantial evidence 101–2
    justifying claim by reference to credibility considerations 102–3
    primary versus secondary sources 101
  nature of claim 93
  person/source to be judged
    expertise/training 93, 94–5
    observation skills 95–7
    reputation 93, 97–8
    vested interest 93, 98–9
  questions about nature of claim which influence credibility 103–4
  thinking map 105
criminal courts, 'proved beyond reasonable doubt' 112, 117–18
critico-creative thinking 13, 58, 129

decision theory 156
decision making 154–69
  common flaws 155–6
  decision procedures and making right decision 165–8

model 156–63
   consideration of alternative
      courses of action 157–8
   consideration of consequences
      of alternatives 159–60
   consideration of how
      likely/unlikely and
      valuable/undesirable
      consequences are 160–1
   moral and ethical
      commitments 161–2
   weighing up best alternative in
      light of consequences 162–3
   why decision is necessary
      156–7
   thinking map 163–4
deductively valid arguments
   111–12, 113–17, 122
   and patterns of argument
      114–17
deductively valid reasoning 111,
   122
definitions, acceptability 84
definitions (as claims) 82, 83
definitions of critical thinking 2–7
   John Dewey and reflective
      thinking 2–3
   Robert Ennis 4
   Edward Glaser 3–4
   Richard Paul 4–5
   Michael Scriven 10–11
denying the consequent 116
Dewey, J. 2–3, 8
dictionaries 65–6
direct evidence 101–2
disjunctions 40–1
disposition 3, 12
   meaning of term 238

Ennis, R. 4
entails, meaning of term 238–9
evaluation 11
   claim, language used 27
   explanation 43
   support offered, language used
      27
evaluation of arguments 43, 56–8

evaluation of inferences 107–37
   assumptions, 'if reasons are true
      the conclusion is' 128
   consideration of other relevant
      considerations 129–31
   implicit assumptions 124–8
   judging inferences skilfully –
      thinking map 137
   standards for
      deductive validity 111–12,
         113–17
      'more likely than not on
         balance of evidence' 112,
         118–21
      'proved beyond reasonable
         doubt' 112, 117–18
evaluation of reasoning 79, 80–2
evidence 83
   direct justification/evidence
      versus circumstantial 101–2
expertise 90, 91, 93
explanations
   evaluations 43
   functioning as reason 44
   versus arguments 42–4, 46
explicit claim, as assumption 47–8
expressing a claim, language used
   27

factual claims 82, 83, 84
fallacy, meaning of term 239
fallacy of equivocation 75

giving reason for conclusion,
   language used 27
Glaser, E. 3–4, 7–8
   *Watson–Glaser Critical Thinking
      Appraisal* 3

historical context 53
history of expression, use in
   clarification 73
Hume, D. *Enquiries Concerning
   Human Understanding* 103–4
hunch 84–5
hypothesis, meaning of term 239
hypotheticals

meaning of term 239
not breaking-up 41, 46

identifying author's meaning 30–1
'if' 41
imagination 146
implications 3
    meaning of term 239–40
implicit assumptions 48–50, 124–8
inductions 120
inferences
    description 108, 122
    evaluating *see* evaluation of
        inferences
    meaning of term 240
    test for good 108–11, 122
    see also arguments
inferred judgement 104
inferring, language used 27
information 11
instruments, accuracy 96
interpretation 11, 27

jumping to a conclusion 141

knowledge, meaning of term 240

LaFeber, W. 34

meaning
    development over time 68
    stipulating 67–9
metacognition 5, 11
    meaning of term 240–1
modus ponens 115
modus tollens 116
'more likely than not on balance of
    evidence' 112, 118–21

nature of claim 90
    and credibility 93
necessary and sufficient
    conditions, meaning of term 241

observation statement 104
observations 11
omission of reasoning words 29

other relevant
    considerations/arguments 56,
    57–8

patterns of reasoning *see* reasoning
    patterns
Paul, R. 4–5
per genus et differentiam 73
presenting an argument 15
Principle of Charity 125
'proved beyond reasonable doubt'
    112, 117–18

reason indicators 23, 24
reasoning
    chain of 31
    deciding when present 15–17
    deductively valid 111, 122
    examples 17–22
    language of 15–32
    structure of 30–1
reasoning patterns 33–46
    chain of reasoning 35–6
    drawing more than one
        conclusion 45
    joint reasons 36–8, 46
    side-by-side reasons 33–5, 37,
        46
reasoning words, omission 29
reasons 3
    acceptability *see* acceptability of
        reasons; credibility
    meaning of term 241
    see also arguments
recommendations 82
    language used 27
reflective thinking 2–3
reputation 90, 91, 93, 97–8
requirements for critical thinking
    14

Scriven, M. 10–11
'since' 24
skills required for critical thinking
    7–8
'so' 24, 30, 35, 37, 39
Socrates 2

sources, primary versus secondary
101
supposition, meaning of term
241–2
synonymous expression, use in
clarification 69

'that's why' 42, 43
'then' 41
'therefore' 22, 24, 30, 35
therefore test 25–7
thinking about your thinking
(metacognition) 4–5
thinking maps 56–9
credibility 105
decision-making 163–4

judging inferences 137
'thus' 23, 30, 35
truth, meaning of term 242

vague terms 63
vagueness of language 70–1
valid/invalid, meaning of term
242
value claims 83–4
value judgements 82
acceptability 84
vested interest 93

*Watson–Glaser Critical Thinking
Appraisal* 3
Wittgenstein, L. 71